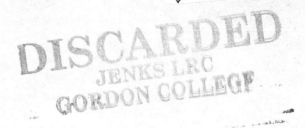
W9-BCL-167

THE
REFERENCE
SHELF

PRESERVING THE WORLD

ECOLOGY

edited by STEVEN ANZOVIN

THE REFERENCE SHELF

Volume 62 Number 1

THE H. W. WILSON COMPANY

New York   1990

THE REFERENCE SHELF

The books in this series contain reprints of articles, excerpts from books, and addresses on current issues and social trends in the United States and other countries. There are six separately bound numbers in each volume, all of which are generally published in the same calendar year. One number is a collection of recent speeches; each of the others is devoted to a single subject and gives background information and discussion from various points of view, concluding with a comprehensive bibliography that contains books and pamphlets and abstracts of additional articles on the subject. Books in the series may be purchased individually or on subscription.

Library of Congress Cataloging-in-Publication Data

Main entry under title:

Preserving the world ecology / edited by Steven Anzovin.
   p. cm. — (The Reference shelf ; v. 62, no. 1)
  Includes bibliographical references.
  Summary: A compilation of essays dealing with world ecological -environmental issues and their political and possible preservational dimensions.
  ISBN 0-8242-0790-4
  1. Ecology. 2. Pollution—Environmental aspects. 3. Man--Influence on nature. [1. Ecology. 2. Environmental protection.] I. Anzovin, Steven. II. Series.
QH541.145.P74 1990
333.7'2—dc20

                  89-77707
                        CIP
                        AC

Cover: Jungle highway in Brazil, showing roadwork clearing and leveling the roadbed of Brazilian highway BR 364 outside Rio Branco, Brazil, in preparation for paving. International environmentalists say the paving of the highway will cause ecological destruction in the Amazon jungle and uproot native Indians.
Photo: AP/Wide World Photos

Printed in the United States of America

CONTENTS

PREFACE

Ecology is the relationship between life and its environment. The science of ecology is a new one, but it has already had a profound effect on how we view our role in nature. The study of ecosystems has shown time and again that we can no longer assume, as our ancestors did, that our effect on the Earth is only local and reversible. People live on every continent and major island, and our numbers are growing beyond the capacity of many areas to sustain. The pollution of our industries can be found in the highest levels of the atmosphere, in the ice of central Antarctica, and at the bottom of the sea, triggering global changes we only dimly understand. Species that we unknowingly destroy in our need for land will never reappear on the Earth.

While some agonize over the damage we are doing, others argue that the only way to maintain and increase our standard of living is to use the resources of the Earth—surely science will solve each environmental problem as it arises. Yet ecologists are among the most pessimistic of all. Almost thirty years ago Rachel Carson predicted a "silent spring" in which there would be no birds to sing, all being poisoned by pesticides. More recently, NASA climatologist James Hansen made headlines by testifying before the Congress of the United States that the Earth is entering an unprecedented warming period, caused by the emission of industrial gases, that would have disastrous consequences for our way of life. A recent popular study of the environment even posits the possible "end of nature."

The evidence of human effects on the global ecology has spurred the rise of a new social-political movement, environmentalism. Since the early 1970s, environmentalists have attempted, with limited success, to bring ecological issues to the forefront of world debate. The United States is among the most advanced in terms of a general awareness of environmental problems, but people in most countries are still too concerned with the basic tasks of sustaining the lives of themselves and their families to have the time to worry about such abstract problems as the ozone layer or the greenhouse effect. Nonetheless, activists have been heartened by the focus on the global environment in recent summits of world leaders. Perhaps we are ready to acknowledge, in the words of the Native American chant, that "the Earth is our mother, we must take care of her."

The range of ecological problems facing the world is broad. This compilation of articles, essays, and speeches treats several important aspects of the subject. The first section of readings surveys many of the ecological issues, from ozone depletion to deforestation to marine pollution to acid rain, that call for concerted international attention. But not all environmental trends are well-understood or clear-cut in their solutions. Section II covers one example—the complex debate over human-induced changes in the Earth's climate. Controversial evidence on the increase in carbon dioxide and other gases in the atmosphere has led to competing theories that the world will become stiflingly hot—or perhaps cold enough to usher in a new Ice Age. With scientists uncertain about the environmental results of human actions, it's no wonder that political leaders are often unable to fashion effective environmental policy. Section III, "The Politics of Ecology," provides a variety of perspectives on the political dimension of environmental issues. The articles in the final section outline some measures environmental activists are taking to halt or slow the destruction of the world ecology; as these articles show, international ecological awareness begins with individual action.

The editor wishes to thank the authors and publishers who kindly granted permission to reprint the material in this collection. Special thanks are due to Diane Podell of the B. Davis Schwartz Memorial Library, C. W. Post Center, Long Island University.

STEVEN ANZOVIN

January 1990

I. A WORLD AT RISK

EDITOR'S INTRODUCTION

The web of life on Earth is sustained by countless nested, interdependent systems—the cycles of sun, moon, atmosphere, ocean, land, planetary interior, and life itself all interact with unimaginable complexity and exquisite balance. The Earth-life system, which scientists call the biosphere, has adjusted itself to changing conditions for the last 3 billion years. Despite upheavals and extinctions, the basis for life has never been seriously threatened. Now, however, the environment faces new challenges that it may easily endure—challenges posed by the ecological willfulness and ignorance of humans. Ecologists and environmentalists have been pointing for years to the evidence of waste around us, but we have been slow to grasp that the Earth is not invulnerable, and that we now have the power to damage her beyond repair.

This first section discusses some of the many environmental problems that beset us today. Vaclav Smil, a professor of geography at the University of Manitoba, and Sandra Postel and Lester R. Brown of the Worldwatch Institute, offer separate assessments of the general state of the Earth at the end of the 1980s. "We are the first," writes Brown, "to be faced with decisions that will determine whether the Earth our children will inherit will be habitable."

One of the greatest ongoing tragedies is the rapid extinction of species caused by human settlement, agriculture, industrialization, and pollution, especially in the tropics. This extinction is likely to match or exceed the mass extinctions of past geologic ages. In the third article in this section, tropical botanist Peter H. Raven cites the alarming statistic that two to three species may be lost every hour, nearly all of them completely unknown to science. The products of civilization, notably throwaway plastic packaging, are taking their toll in the oceans as well, as Michael Weisskopf's article for *Smithsonian* shows. Humans suffer also from pollution. Jon R. Luoma's article for *Audubon* shows how acid rain, a problem most often discussed in terms of dead lakes and dead fish, affects human lungs with insidious effect.

7

OUR CHANGING ENVIRONMENT[1]

Seventy-five years ago the age of the explorer was coming to a close. Although another generation was to pass before the last isolated tribes of New Guinea were contacted by outsiders, successful journeys to the poles—Robert Peary's Arctic trek in 1909 and Roald Amundsen's Antarctic expedition in 1911—removed the designation of terra incognita from the two most inaccessible places on Earth. Four centuries of European voyaging had accumulated a mass of descriptive information about the lands, rivers, oceans and living organisms of the planet, and most of this knowledge had been admirably systematized in such great feats of early science as Carolus Linnaeus's classification of biota, Alexander von Humboldt's sweeping writings and the maps of the British Admiralty.

But our understanding of how the environment actually works was still primitive. To list just a few key examples: flourishing biochemistry was laying the foundations for understanding the complexities of grand biospheric cycles; Charles Darwin's theories were turning attention to the interplays between organisms and their surroundings; and physiologists were offering coherent insights about the nutritional needs of plants, animals and men.

But the blanks dominated: the absence of sensitive, reproducible analytical methods precluded reliable monitoring of critical environmental variables; Wilhelm Bjerknes set down the basic equations of atmospheric dynamics in 1904—but climatology remained ploddingly descriptive for several more decades; the need for an inclusive understanding of living systems was in the air—but the fundamental quantitative tenets of ecology were still unknown.

If science was on the verge of great discoveries, so was the everyday treatment of the environment. New attitudes to protect unique natural settings and the first environmental control techniques were emerging after a century of rapid industrial expansion that treated land, water and air as valueless public property:

[1]Article by Vaclav Smil, professor of geography at the University of Manitoba. *Current History*. 88:9+. Ja '89. Copyright © 1989 by Current History, Inc. All rights reserved. Reprinted by permission.

the final decades of the nineteenth century saw the establishment of the first large natural reserves and parks, and the new century brought primary treatment of urban waste water and the invention of electrostatic cleaning of ash-laden flue gases.

The two world wars and the intervening generation of economic turmoil were not conducive to gains in environmental protection, but science made some fundamental advances. In 1925, Alfred Lotka published the first extended work that established biology on a quantitative foundation. In 1929, Vladimir Ivanovich Vernadskii ushered in the study of the environment on an integrated, global basis with his pioneering book on the biosphere. In 1935, Arthur Tansley defined the term ecosystem, one of the key terms of modern science. And in 1942, Raymond Lindeman, following Evelyn Hutchinson's earlier ideas, published the first quantifications of energy flows in an observed ecosystem.

Meanwhile, the environment of industrialized countries continued to deteriorate. Three pre-1914 classes of innovations commercialized between the world wars accounted for most of this decline. The thermal generation of electricity, accompanied by emissions of fly ash, sulfur and nitrogen oxides and by a huge demand for cooling water and the consequent warming of streams, moved from isolated city systems to large-scale integrated regional and national networks.

The automobile industry shifted from workshop manufacturing to mass production, which made cars affordable for millions of people. The emissions of unburned hydrocarbons, nitrogen oxides and carbon monoxide spread over urban areas and into the countryside, which was increasingly buried under asphalt and concrete roads. And the synthesis of plastics grew into a large, highly energy-intensive industry generating a variety of toxic pollutants previously never present in the biosphere, introducing huge numbers of nondecaying wastes into the environment.

Post-1945 developments amplified these trends. New environmental risks were introduced as the rich world entered the period of its most impressive economic growth, terminated only by the 1973-1974 quintupling of oil prices. In just 25 years, the consumption of primary commercial energy nearly tripled, electricity generation grew about eightfold, car ownership increased sixfold and production of most kinds of synthetic materials grew more than tenfold.

New environmental burdens were introduced to farmlands and other ecosystems as the rapidly expanding use of nitrogenous fertilizers (derived from synthetic ammonia first produced in 1913) and the growing applications of the just-discovered pesticides (DDT was first used on a large scale in 1944) left nitrates in groundwater and streams and led often to dangerously high insecticide and herbicide residues in plant and animal tissues.

Environmental pollution, previously a matter of regional impact, started to affect more extensive areas around major cities and conurbations and downwind from concentrations of power plants as well as the waters of large lakes, long stretches of streams and coastlines, and many estuaries and bays. More sensitive analytical techniques were recording pollutants in the air, waters and biota thousands of kilometers from their sources.

Only a few remedies were introduced during the 1950's, most notably in combating air pollution. London's heavy air pollution, culminating in 4,000 premature deaths during the city's worst smog episode in December, 1952, led to the adoption of Britain's Clean Air Act, the foundation of the first comprehensive effort to clean a country's air. Throughout the rich world, electrostatic precipitators able to remove more than 98 percent of all fly ash were becoming a standard part of large combustion sources, and black particulate matter started to disappear from many cities and visibility improved; this trend was further aided by the introduction of natural gas in home heating.

Environmental Awareness

The big attitudinal shift came in the 1960's. Rachel Carson's influential warning about the destructive consequences of pesticide residues in the environment was often described as the beginning of new environmental awareness, but the impulses came from many quarters. Accumulating evidence of spreading air pollution was especially important in influencing public opinion: objectionable particulates were removed from the urban air, but invisible pollution began to affect areas far from the most prolific sources of combustion.

Europeans were the first to note this phenomenon. International monitoring networks established in 1948 and Swedish observations started in the early 1960's pointed to worrisome changes in the composition of the continent's precipitation. In

1967, Svante Odén described for the first time the dangers of acid deposition caused by the long-range transport of acid air pollutants followed by degradative changes in lakes and soils in sensitive receptor areas.

The decade of the 1960's also brought many exaggerated claims. In the United States, perhaps the most famous scare was Barry Commoner's warning, first presented in 1968 and amplified in many later writings, about the serious imbalance of the country's nitrogen cycle. Commoner feared that the rapid introduction of inorganic nitrogen carried such health risks that limits on fertilization rates, economically devastating for many farmers, might soon be needed to avert further deterioration. Synthetic nitrogen in agroecosystems is a problem but a much more manageable one than was suggested by Commoner's misinterpretation of the existing evidence, which was clearly refuted by Samuel Aldrich.

But there was no shortage of other targets. Once the interest in environmental degradation began, the Western media (ever watchful for bad news) and scientists (whose work is so often governed by fashionable topics) kept attention alive with a barrage of new worries. Soon the environmental concerns were adopted by such disparate groups as the leftist student protesters, who discovered yet another reason to tear down the ancien régime, and large oil companies, which discovered that fish thrive around the legs of offshore drilling platforms and advertised accordingly, with two-page glossy spreads.

The summer of 1970 marked the first attempt at a systematic evaluation of global environmental problems: the Study of Critical Environmental Problems sponsored by the Massachusetts Institute of Technology. The items were not ranked, but the order of their appearance in the summary indicated the relative importance perceived at that time. First came the emissions of carbon dioxide from fossil fuel combustion, then particulate matter in the atmosphere, cirrus clouds from jet aircraft, the effects of supersonic planes on stratospheric chemistry, the thermal pollution of waters and the impact of pesticides. Mercury and other toxic heavy metals, oil on the ocean and the nutrient enrichment of coastal waters closed the list.

Just a month later, President Richard Nixon sent Congress the first report of the President's Council on Environmental Quality, noting that this was the first time in history that a nation had taken comprehensive stock of the quality of its surroundings. Soon afterward his administration established the Environmental Protection Agency by pulling together segments of five departments and agencies; and the environment entered big politics. The same thing happened on the international level, where attention was focused on the first-ever United Nations–organized Conference on Human Environment in Stockholm in 1972. Swedes talked about acid rain, Brazilians insisted on their right to cut down all their tropical forests in their dash to development and the Maoist Chinese claimed to have no environmental problems at all.

The actions taken by OPEC (the Organization of Petroleum Exporting Countries) in 1973–1974, the global economic downturn, and misplaced but deeply felt worries about ruinous shortages of energy turned public attention away from the environment temporarily, but new studies, new revelations and new sensational reporting kept environmental awareness high. Notable 1970's concerns included the effects of nitrous oxide from intensifying fertilization on stratospheric ozone, the carcinogenic potential of nitrates in water and vegetables, and both the short-term effects of routine low-level releases of radionuclides from operating nuclear power plants and the long-term consequences of high-level radioactive waste that had to be stored for millennia.

And with the economic plight of poor nations worsened by the higher prices of imported oil came the "discovery" of the continuing dependence of all rural and some urban Asian, African and Latin American populations on traditional biomass energies—wood, charcoal, crop residues, dried dung—and the realization of how environmentally ruinous such reliance can be in societies where recent advances in primary medical care have pushed the natural increase of population to rates as high as 4 percent a year.

Massive deforestation and the ensuing desertification in dry subtropical countries and heavy soil erosion and intensified flooding in rainy environments have other causes as well: inappropriate methods of farming, predatory commercial logging, and often government-sponsored conversion of forests to pastures producing beef for export.

To this must be added the effects of largely uncontrolled urban and industrial wastes, including the release of toxic substances that would not be tolerated in rich countries, appalling housing and transportation conditions in urban areas, the misuse of agricultural chemicals and the continuing rapid losses of arable land to house large population increases and to accommodate new industries. Not surprisingly, when an ambitious American report to the President surveyed the state of the environment in 1980 it devoted much of its attention to the immense environmental burdens of the poor world.

In human terms this degradation and pollution present an especially taxing challenge to China, the world's most populous country. When Chairman Deng Xiaoping's "learning from the facts" axiom replaced Chairman Mao Zedong's "better red than expert," the flood of stunning admissions and previously unavailable hard data provided a depressing comprehensive account of China's environmental mismanagement, whose single most shocking fact may be the loss of one-third of China's farmland within a single generation in a nation that must feed a little more than one-fifth of the world's population from one-fifteenth of the world's arable land.

And the environmental problems of the poor world were even more prominent in another global stocktaking, in 1982, at the Conference on Environmental Research and Priorities organized by the Royal Swedish Academy of Sciences in Rättvik. The meeting's list of ten research priorities for the 1980's was headed by the depletion of tropical forests and the reduction of biological diversity, while the list of management priorities included first of all hazardous chemicals, the depletion of tropical forests and desertification due to overgrazing.

The most recent environmental mishaps and worries have echoed and intensified several recurring concerns. Such accidents as the cyanide poisoning in Bhopal in 1984 and the news about the daunting efforts to clean up thousands of waste sites make hazardous toxic wastes a matter of lasting apprehension, and the Chernobyl disaster in 1986 strengthened the popular fear of nuclear power. At first, an almost unbelievable discovery of a seasonal ozone hole above Antarctica revived the worries about the rapid and intense human-induced change in the atmosphere, a concern further intensified by a new wave of writings and reports on the imminent warming of the atmosphere because of the accumulation of "greenhouse" gases.

The Environmental Challenge

What then is the state of our environment, and what are our prospects? Simple questions may go to the heart of the matter—but simple answers would be highly misleading. Of course, this has not prevented many observers from providing precisely such simple answers during the last 20 years. On the one hand, the environmental catastrophists (a Western intellectual species descended from Robert Malthus) offer vivid descriptions of existing dangers and predict even greater imminent horrors. For some of these doomsayers the question has been not "how shall we live, but indeed if we are going to live at all for very much longer."

On the other hand, the techno-optimists (utopians?) argue that human inventiveness and management skills will soon take care of all environmental ills; they portray a less polluted and ecologically more stable future with less precarious life for a more populated world.

Julian Simon and Herman Kahn have been the most notorious wholesalers of this coming nirvana, seriously weakening their message of hope as an antidote to catastrophic moaning by advocating incredibly naive interpretations of existing realities and future possibilities.

These verbal forays from the mentally antipodal, well-fortified camps of true believers change nothing. Allegiance to one of these groups may confer a feeling of intellectual superiority and righteousness, but a sensible appraisal of the state of the global environment must eschew sloganeering simplifications. There are many environments, many scales, many threats, and many solutions.

Atmosphere, land, waters, and biota form an exquisitely interconnected co-evolutionary system, but the term "global" obviously has another meaning besides its use in the currently fashionable appraisals of climatic changes affecting the whole biosphere. Such changes are seen as inherently more dangerous than local or regional degradations. But "global" can also simply describe the extent of myriad of local occurrences; in this sense soil erosion, rather than climatic changes, must rank as the world's leading global environmental worry.

Climatic change will create losers—but there will also be winners, with milder winters, or higher precipitation, or longer growing seasons. Soil erosion leaves no winners—and the rates of loss are as bad in one-fifth of America's farmlands as they are in the fields of South China or West Africa. But soil erosion is a rather unexciting topic; to an outsider it represents an invisible creep of gradual losses. As such, it cannot garner headlines equal to the sensationalized stories of climatic change, which see every warmer summer as the beginning of the slide toward an uninhabitable planet.

Looking at the global environment from what might be labeled the receiving end is also instructive, because it involves an often overlooked bottom line: people live longer everywhere. Western life expectancies are uniformly over 70 years; the Chinese have pushed their life expectancy to 70; Indians to nearly 60. The cumulative effects of lifetime exposure to a huge array of air and water pollutants, to pesticide residues in food, to higher absorbed radiation and to greater urban noise have not been deleterious enough to stop a steady rise in life expectancy.

This does not mean that overall degradation is at a tolerably low level because there are areas and population groups at much higher risk than can be indicated by national averages. Many shrill claims that the planet has been turned into an intolerable cesspool with carcinogens lurking everywhere have no foundation in the most important measure of personal environment: the length of one's sojourn on Earth.

Undoubtedly, an important reason for this good news is that in many instances the technical fix has worked wonders, bringing today's pollution levels to fractions of their historic highs or means. Electrostatic precipitators have already been mentioned; state-of-the-art devices can remove 99.99 percent of all particulate matter from power plant and industrial stacks. To those who remember the grime of cities energized by coal without particulate controls, the transformation has been impressive.

Mobile air pollution sources can be tackled almost as effectively. Before the introduction of automotive emission controls in 1968, American cars averaged 6.6 grams of unburned hydrocarbons per kilometer (g/km); today they emit less than 0.26 g/km, a 96 percent reduction. Typical uncontrolled nitrogen oxide emissions were 2.56 g/km; today's standard with catalytic converters is 0.62 g/km (a 76 percent reduction), and Nissan's exhaust gas recirculation and fast-burn technique achieve less than 0.13 g/km, a 95 percent decrease.

Specific technical fixes are now available to control hundreds of pollutants, but the most effective general approach has been energy conservation. The post-1973 increase in energy prices finally broke the historic pattern of high energy consumption growth rates in the rich countries. During the first ten years of the new energy era, the Big Seven economies (the United States, Japan, West Germany, France, the United Kingdom, Italy and Canada) boosted their combined gross national product (GNP) by 20 percent (in constant dollars)—while their 1982 primary energy consumption was virtually identical with the 1973 total. This trend is still continuing; the countless opportunities for more efficient energy conversions are far from exhausted.

A typical North American Snowbelt bungalow may still need about 250 million Btu's of fuels and electricity for every square meter (m^2) of living area each year, but superinsulated houses, costing marginally more than the old structures, can be heated with less than 75 million Btu's. In 1988, the North American car fleet averaged about 28 miles per gallon—but there are comfortable family sedans that average well over 40 miles per gallon. New paper made from virgin pulp costs twice as much energy as the recycled product—but North America's recycling rate is only half the Japanese rate.

No actions have such positive environmental effects in rich countries as continued vigorous energy conservation efforts ranging from high-tech innovations to mundane material recycling. And the studies of the poor world's energetics show that, while those countries must increase their per capita energy consumption, much of that rise can also come from eliminating conversion inefficiencies that are in general much more harmful and whose effects are environmentally more ruinous than the inefficiencies in the rich nations. For example, China uses at least three times as much energy for each unit of GNP as Japan, and because its pollution controls are weaker it generates at least five times more emissions for each unit of consumed energy.

Two of the world's current high-profile environmental worries can be greatly ameliorated by energy conservation: rising atmospheric carbon dioxide and acid deposition. Effective management of acid deposition is in sight, with a combination of controls on the emissions of stationary and mobile sources of sulfur and nitrogen oxides. These moves, yet to come in a United States–Canadian agreement, are already under way in Europe, where sulfurous emissions will be cut by half before the mid-1990's. But these reductions may not bring an end to the disturbing phenomenon of *Waldsterben*. This slow death of forests, especially coniferous forests, has multiple causes: other major factors implicated besides acid deposition include extreme weather, pests, ozone and heavy metals.

Energy conservation may reduce carbon dioxide emissions, but there is no practical way to control the generation of the gas, and even very low growth rates of fossil fuel consumption will eventually translate into the doubling of pre-industrial concentrations, which stood between 250 and 300 parts per million (ppm). Since the start of regular monitoring in 1958, CO_2 levels have risen from 315 to 344 ppm; 600 ppm, the level commonly labeled the doubling of CO_2, will most likely be surpassed before the end of the next century.

The most accurate available models of global climate indicate that the doubling of CO_2 would raise the average tropospheric temperature between 2 and 4 degrees centigrade (C); the effect would be negligible in the tropics and most pronounced in the polar latitudes. This would lead inevitably to global climatic changes: shifts in precipitation patterns, altered boundaries of major vegetation systems, more chances of hazardous summer weather, and a mild rise of ocean level (biblical flooding simply cannot arise with such a temperature increase in a matter of a few centuries).

The Earth has seen many pronounced climatic changes, but this change would be the first time the transformation would be anthropogenic, and its rate would be unusually rapid. Clearly, there is a cause for concern—but certainly not for panic. Higher CO_2 levels and warmer weather would also have beneficial effects, above all increased efficiency of photosynthesis and higher water use efficiency in plants. These two effects could increase yields of principal crops by up to 40 percent, and might allow the cultivation of lands that now received too little precipitation.

CO_2 is only one of the "greenhouse" gases—nitrous oxide and methane are the other most important contributors—whose practical controls are elusive (for example, more fertilization means more N_2O, more paddy fields and more domestic animals means more CH_4). Some warming appears inevitable (although it may be considerably less than the still crude computer models indicate) but it should be regarded as an evolutionary challenge calling for effective adaptation—not as a regrettable or even a catastrophic change. With most of the world's food production concentrated between 30° and 50° N, would we prefer another round of advancing glaciers?

The other class of environmental challenges that is not amenable to technical solutions is the preservation of genetic diversity: the protection of tropical ecosystems is a particularly important part of this effort. Many recent writings have offered a highly pessimistic account of this prospect, with virtually all the world's forests destroyed within two or three generations. Their demise would mean the disappearance of up to 1 million plant and heterotroph species (the current total is not known but it is possibly between 2 million and 3 million), a rate of loss unparalleled during the long history of the biosphere. Clearly, such a development might be a threat to the very survival of civilization.

A combination of the local realization of the indispensability of forest conservation (slowly but clearly taking place in many tropical nations), substantial forest-targeted foreign aid (why should everyone not pay for the preservation of uniquely rich ecosystems?) and the eventual decline of population growth in tropical countries (a trend already discernible in Brazil, Colombia, Indonesia and Thailand) may well preserve a large chunk of the tropical species' diversity. A practical action plan shows this to be a realistic possibility.

And while current losses are certainly undesirable and highly degrading at the local level, historic perspective indicates that the fear of the loss of invaluable germ plasm may have been exaggerated: with the exception of cassava, all the principal cultivated food plants have originated either in the subtropics or in temperate regions. Moreover, in the not too distant future a technical fix can also become important here. The advances of genetic engineering, already staggering in its first generation, must be taken into account when contemplating man's future ability to develop new pesticidal, drug or food species. The understanding of cellular biochemistry and genetic coding can be as potent a source of such novelties as random discoveries in tropical rain forests.

Recent changes ranging from impressive declines of energy consumption rates to successful diffusion of conservation tillage methods, and recent international actions aiming at major reductions of sulfurous pollution in Europe and the gradual global elimination of chlorinated fluorocarbons (1988 Montreal Accord) prove that human beings can counteract degradative trends, that humans can behave in adaptive ways, preserving the inestimable and irreplaceable natural goods (topsoils saved by conservation tillage) and services (the ozone-protecting function of the stratosphere maintained by the elimination of halocarbons).

But even these successes would be overwhelmed by continuously rising populations. There is no doubt that the most important indicator of the global environmental outlook in the next 75 years will be the rate of population growth. Debates about the carrying capacity of the Earth are worthless unless one specifies exactly the energetic foundations, material flows and quality-of-life indicators to be enjoyed (or endured) by given billions of people. At the current count of 5 billion human beings and with the current division of riches (roughly one-fifth very rich, another fifth tolerably well off, the rest in different gradations of poverty) we are already committed to a wide range of practices that have widespread environmental impact and whose drastic modification would change the image of our world.

Notwithstanding the illusory exhortations of soft-path proponents (those who rely on decentralized renewable, small-scale energy sources), trying to do without fossil fuels would cut the industrial world's standard of living by at least 75 percent, and it would virtually eliminate the poor world's chances for any relatively fast economic gains; the inevitable transition to renewable energy sources (or to nuclear energy) will take many generations to accomplish, and our heavy dependence on fossil fuels will continue certainly past the year 2050, most likely well into the 22d century.

Trying to do without synthetic nitrogenous fertilizers would force a reduction of the global population by at least 1.5 billion: there is simply not enough organic nitrogen to be recycled into crops to feed 5 billion people. Eventually, this practice may be supplanted by genetically engineered nitrogen fixation in all kinds of plants (today only leguminous species can do the trick) but, once again, generations of dependence on synthetic ammonia lie ahead.

Without stabilization of the global population sometime during the next century, the intensifying resource needs and growing waste metabolism of·industrial civilization (with the success of technical fixes overwhelmed by the sheer increase of total output) will rapidly diminish any hope for maintaining a biosphere both supporting a decent life for its inhabitants and preserving a habitable milieu for future generations.

In the long run, the rise of environmental consciousness will have effects comparable to the consequences of the last three great Western transformations—the Renaissance, the Reformation and the Industrial Revolution. A legacy of centuries of predatory attitudes and an adversarial ethos cannot be discarded in a matter of years; yet a new way of understanding is making its way slowly, and often in roundabout ways characteristic of civilization's advance.

No single species has ever transformed the biosphere as much as human beings have since the beginning of this century—and much of this transformation has led to degradation, a trend that cannot continue with impunity. But during the past four generations humans have also learned more than all humans learned in all the preceding millennia about the complexity of the biosphere, about its amazing resilience, about the ways of using and managing the ecosystems in sustainable ways.

Nimble adaptability has been the hallmark of our species. This quality has carried us through enormous environmental upheavals and it has brought longer and richer lives to an ever-increasing number of people. In the coming years, our deepening understanding of the biosphere must be translated into effective action to preserve the integrity of the Earth's environment. The record may not look reassuring, but unprecedented challenges bring extraordinary responses. Apprehension may be in order—but our hope lies in not underestimating our adaptive capabilities. One must always hope that the Linnaean designation of our species—*sapiens*—is correct.

LIFE, THE GREAT CHEMISTRY EXPERIMENT[2]

All humankind has a stake in the life-and-death game of agriculture. The rules of the game are governed by the growth patterns of crops and fairly predictable regimens of warmth and rain. For centuries, farmers have marched to their fertile fields, played the game with great skill, and most often won.

Changes in longstanding rules to which farmers have carefully adapted threaten not only their livelihoods but, ultimately, food security for the earth's hungry populations. We see hints of these effects during severe droughts, most dramatically in Africa in recent years and, to a lesser degree, in the southeastern United States last summer. Further shifts in agricultural conditions worldwide could generate unprecedented pressures on global food supplies.

Within the next fifty years, the earth's climate may change more than it has since agriculture began some 10,000 years ago. Human activities have caused a buildup in the atmosphere of chemical compounds that are known as "greenhouse gases." These gases let the sun's radiation pass through, but trap the longer-wavelength radiation emitted from the earth, which otherwise would escape into space. The anticipated result is a global warming and a worldwide shift in temperature and rainfall patterns. Crops in key food-producing regions will become vulnerable to heat waves, drought, and the loss of water for irrigation.

Scientists have long suspected that carbon dioxide (CO_2) plays a central role in regulating the earth's temperature. Since 1860, the combustion of fossil fuels (coal, oil, and natural gas), in power plants, home furnaces, factories, and automobiles, has released some 185 billion tons of carbon into the atmosphere. In addition, the clearing and burning of forests for cropland and pasture has contributed more than 100 billion tons. Since the early 1800s, the level of CO_2 has increased about 30 percent, and is still rising.

Recently, scientists have found new gases among the greenhouse gang of culprits. Methane and nitrous oxide (laughing gas)

[2]Article by senior researcher Sandra Postel and president Lester R. Brown of the Worldwatch Institute. Reprinted with permission from *Natural History*, April 1987. Copyright the American Museum of Natural History, 1987.

have also been increasing in the atmosphere as emissions from human activities have added to those from natural sources. And a family of synthetic chlorine compounds, used in such diverse consumer products as aerosol sprays, refrigerators, and air conditioners, could be second only to carbon dioxide in contributing to the greenhouse effect. Many scientists believe that, collectively, the climate-altering potentials of greenhouse gases other than CO_2 are now about as important as that of CO_2 alone.

The earth's climate will change gradually as the concentrations of greenhouse gases increase. Indeed, evidence exists that the warming has already begun. But climate modelers typically focus their predictions on what will happen from the equivalent of a doubling of carbon dioxide over preindustrial levels, which, taking into account all the greenhouse gases, could occur as early as the year 2030.

Most models agree that temperatures will rise everywhere, though by greater amounts in the temperate and polar regions than in the tropics. Since a warmer atmosphere can hold more moisture, average precipitation worldwide is expected to increase by 7 to 11 percent. In many regions, however, this additional rainfall would be offset by higher rates of evaporation, causing soil moisture—the natural water supply for crops—to decrease.

Recent model results indicate that large grain-producing regions of North America, the Soviet Union, and possibly, China could dry out during summertime. More than half of the world's cereal exports come from North America, and the United States alone accounts for more than two-thirds of total exports of corn. A drier average growing season, along with more frequent and severe heat waves and droughts, could lead to substantial crop losses in these major breadbaskets.

As a rule of thumb, for example, corn yields in the United States drop 10 percent for each day the crop is under severe stress during its silking and tasseling stage. Five days of severe temperature or moisture stress during this critical period would cut yields in half. With the anticipated climate change, such stressful conditions probably would occur frequently in the U.S. cornbelt.

While some regions suffer, prospects for expanding production could improve in others. Warmer and wetter conditions might increase rice production in India and much of Southeast Asia. The picture remains unclear for Africa. But reconstructions of the so-called Altithermal period some 4,500 to 8,000 years ago, when summertime temperatures were higher than at present, suggest that northern and eastern Africa could get more rainfall. If so, average flows of the Niger, Senegal, Volta, and Blue Nile rivers would increase, permitting an expansion of irrigation.

In northern latitudes, higher temperatures and milder winters might open vast tracts of land to cultivation. Agricultural production in Canada, northern Europe, and the Soviet Union might expand northward.

Unfortunately, shifting crop production to areas benefiting from climate change would not only be costly but would also have to overcome some serious constraints. Thin, nutrient-poor soils cover much of northern Minnesota, Wisconsin, and Michigan, so a northward shift of the U.S. cornbelt in response to higher temperatures would result in a substantial drop in yield. Poor soils would also inhibit successful northward agricultural migrations in Canada, Scandinavia, and the Soviet Union. Centuries would be needed for more productive soils to form. While the present desert regions of North Africa were savannas suited for grazing during the Altithermal period, these lands also would require a long time to regain their former fertility.

Low-lying agricultural areas face the added threat of a substantial rise in sea level. Since water expands when heated, oceans will rise with the increase in global temperature. Warmer temperatures will also melt mountain glaciers and parts of polar ice sheets, transferring water from the land to the sea. By the middle of the next century, sea levels could rise as much as three feet, increasing risks of flooding in agricultural lowlands—where much of the world's rice is grown. Of particular concern are the heavily populated, fertile delta regions of the Ganges River in Bangladesh, the Indus in Pakistan, and the Chang Jiang (Yangtze) in China.

The productivity of major food crops will respond not only to changes in climate but directly to the higher concentration of CO_2 in the atmosphere. Carbon dioxide is a basic ingredient for photosynthesis, the process by which green plants transform solar energy into the chemical energy of carbohydrates. Experiments suggest that as long as water, nutrients, and other factors are not limited, every 1 percent rise in the CO_2 concentration may increase photosynthesis by 0.5 percent.

Adapting to climatic change will exact heavy costs from governments and farmers. The expensive irrigation systems supplying water to the 670 million acres of irrigated cropland worldwide were built for present climatic regimes. These irrigated lands account for only 18 percent of total cropland, yet they yield a third of the global harvest. Irrigated agriculture thus plays a disproportionately large role in meeting the world's food needs. Shifts in rainfall patterns could make existing irrigation systems—including reservoirs, canals, pumps, and wells—unnecessary in some regions, insufficient in others. Moreover, seasonal reductions in water supplies because of climatic change could seriously constrain irrigated agriculture, especially where competition for scarce water is already increasing.

A look at one key food-producing region—the western United States—highlights how costly climatic change could be. Some climate models suggest that much of this area could experience a reduction in rainfall, along with the rise in temperature, which would diminish the water supply. Assuming a 10 percent decrease in precipitation and a 3.5°F increase in temperature, supplies in each of seven western river basins would be reduced some 40 to 76 percent. Such reductions would create severe imbalances in regional water budgets. With no climatic change, only in the Lower Colorado region would water consumption exceed supply by the end of the century. With the assumed climatic change, however, consumption in the year 2000 would exceed the renewable supply in four regions, with local shortages probably occurring in the other three river basins.

Since agriculture is by far the biggest consumer of water, balancing regional water budgets would likely require that irrigation cease on a substantial share of cropland. This is happening now in portions of the Lower Colorado, where consumption already exceeds the renewable supply. Correcting the large imbalances resulting from such an altered climate could require that as many as 11.4 million acres be taken out of irrigation in these seven western U.S. regions—roughly one-third of the area currently irrigated.

A reduction of that magnitude would have high costs, measured either by the capital investments in obsolete dams, canals, and irrigation systems or by the replacement value of that irrigation infrastructure. Investment needs for expanding irrigation vary widely, but assuming expenses of $600 to $2,000 per acre, replacement costs could range from $7 billion to $23 billion in the United States alone. Worldwide, maintaining food security under the altered climate could require new irrigation systems with a global price tag of $200 billion.

The need for new drainage systems, flood control structures, cropping patterns, and crop varieties would greatly magnify the costs of adapting to a changed climate. According to some ballpark estimates, the annual cost of a greenhouse gas–induced warming of 4.5°F could amount to 3 percent of the world's gross economic output. Much of this expense would result from the loss of capital assets in agriculture. Poorer countries would have the most difficulty adapting, and as food production typically generates a relatively large share of their incomes, their people would suffer most.

Moreover, as climate expert William W. Kellogg points out, the need to adapt to climatic change will arise "against a backdrop of increased world population, increased demand for energy, and depletion in many places of soil, forests, and other natural resources." The disruptions created by a changing climate may thus bring new pockets of famine, losses of income, and the need for huge capital investments, which many countries will find difficult to afford.

Some change in the world's climate is already inevitable. Yet since carbon dioxide is the key variable in the climate equation, the magnitude of climatic change—and the pace at which it unfolds—will depend greatly on society's future use of coal, oil, and natural gas. Especially with the recent drop in oil prices, restraining carbon emissions will require investments in energy efficiency and alternative energy sources beyond what the market alone would induce. It will also demand a virtual cap on carbon emissions from industrial countries to allow for needed growth in energy use in the Third World.

Preserving forests and planting trees can also help minimize the threat of climatic change. The clearing and burning of tropical forests adds perhaps 20 percent to the amount of carbon released to the atmosphere each year from the burning of fossil fuels. Trees also remove carbon dioxide from the air during photosynthesis. Increasing global forest cover would thus help stabilize atmospheric CO_2 levels.

Averting a major change in climate is possible, but requires immediate action. No nation has yet taken steps explicitly geared toward limiting emissions of CO_2. Cooperation among governments is essential, since carbon emissions anywhere contribute to climatic change everywhere. But meaningful reductions could begin with concerted national measures by the world's three largest users of coal—China, the Soviet Union, and the United States.

More and more sick, dying, and dead trees are the most visible evidence of human-induced changes in the earth's chemistry. During the last several years, forest damage linked to air pollution and acid rain has spread rapidly throughout central and northern Europe.

In the autumn of 1983, West German officials galvanized both scientists and the citizenry with a startling finding: 34 percent of the nation's trees were yellowing, losing needles or leaves, or showing other signs of injury. The cause? Preliminary evidence pointed to air pollutants and acid rain. A more thorough survey in 1984 confirmed that tree disease was spreading. Foresters found that trees covering half of the nation's 18.2 million acres of woodlands were damaged, including two-thirds of the fabled Black Forest in the southwestern state of Baden Württemberg.

Spurred by West Germany's alarming discovery, other European nations assessed the health of their own forests. A sobering picture emerged.

Trees covering nearly 48 million acres in Europe—an area the size of Austria and East Germany combined (14 percent of Europe's total forested area)—now show signs of injury linked to air pollution or acid rain. The key symptoms for the conifers, the hardest hit, parallel those found in West Germany: yellowing of needles, casting off of older needles, and damage to the fine roots through which trees take up nutrients. In eight countries—Austria, Czechoslovakia, Finland, Luxembourg, the Netherlands, Poland, Switzerland, and West Germany—one-quarter to half the forested area is damaged.

National estimates often mask serious damage in specific regions. Total damage in Sweden is placed at about 4 percent, but an estimated 20 percent of the forested area in the south is affected. In 1984, foresters in France surveyed portions of the French Jura and Alsace-Lorraine, adjacent to West Germany's Black Forest, and found that more than a third of the trees were injured, at least 10 percent of them severely. In some heavily polluted regions of Eastern Europe, numerous trees are now in the last stages of decline. In Poland, for example, dead and dying trees cover 1 million acres, and trees with lesser damage occupy an additional 4.6 million acres.

The alpine regions of Austria, France, Italy, Switzerland, and West Germany exhibit the worst damage. Swiss officials worry about the increased risk of landslides and avalanches as dying trees are removed from forested hillsides. Already some villagers have been told to evacuate.

North Americans must travel to mountaintops in the eastern United States to see the kind of massive tree disease and death spreading throughout Europe. In the high-elevation forests, most red spruce trees are undergoing serious dieback—a progressive thinning from the outer tree crown inward. More subtle signs of ill health come from the discovery that pine trees in a broad region of the Southeast grew 20 to 30 percent less between 1972 and 1982 than between 1961 and 1972. In a November 1985 report, U.S. Forest Service analysts stated that the net annual growth of softwood timber in the Southeast "has peaked and turned downward after a long upward trend."

Although less well documented, declines in growth appear to have occurred throughout the Appalachians, extending north into New England. In written testimony presented to the U.S. Senate in February 1984, soil scientist Arthur H. Johnson noted that similar growth reductions preceded the "alarming incidences" of forest damage in Europe.

Hundreds of scientists in the affected countries continue to search for the cause of this unprecedented forest decline. Collectively, they offer a bewildering array of hypotheses, attesting to the difficulty of unraveling a mystery within a complex natural system. Most agree, however, that air pollutants—probably combined with natural factors, such as insects, cold, or drought—are a principal cause. Explanations focus on acid rain, sulfur dioxide, nitrogen compounds, heavy metals, and ozone, which singly or in combination cause damage through the foliage and forest soils.

Changes in soils may be irreversible for the near future. A severely damaged forest in Eastern Europe shows the kinds of soil alterations that can take place. Large portions of the Erzgebirge, a mountain range northwest of Prague, Czechoslovakia, are now a wasteland. Near the industrial city of Most, where power plants burn high-sulfur coal, sulfur dioxide concentrations average much higher than in most other industrial areas, and thirteen times higher than in a seemingly undamaged rural forest about 100 miles to the southeast. Peak concentrations register several times higher than the average. The numerous dead and dying trees in this industrial region may thus be succumbing to the classic smoke injury known to occur near large sources of uncontrolled pollution.

Chemical measurements of runoff water from the Erzgebirge suggest that acidification has profoundly altered the soil's ability to support a forest. Czech geochemist Tomas Paces found that losses of the nutrients magnesium and calcium from the damaged forest were several times greater than from the undamaged rural forest. Runoff of aluminum, which normally remains bound up in soil minerals, was thirty-two times greater from the damaged forest. With the loss of calcium and other elements that can buffer incoming acidity, aluminum mobilizes to serve as the buffering agent. In soluble forms, this metal can be toxic to trees. Finally, outputs of nitrate exceeded those from the undamaged forest by a factor of twenty. Paces believes this reflects the damaged forest's inability to properly recycle nitrogen—a loss of basic ecosystem function.

Forests in the industrial regions of Eastern Europe have received extremely heavy pollutant loads during the last few decades. Few forests outside these regions have been drastically damaged. But the possibility of more widespread destruction from chemical stress may increase with time. Ecologist C. S. Holling of the University of British Columbia points out that natural systems may absorb stress for long periods so that change occurs very slowly. Eventually, however, systems may reach a stress point, and as "a jump event becomes increasingly likely and ultimately inevitable," forest ecosystems could collapse.

Substantial economic losses have already resulted from the existing level of pollution stress on forests. The Czechoslovakian Academy of Sciences estimates the cost of acid pollution at $1.5 billion annually, with forest damage accounting for much of the total. In West Germany, researchers at the Technical University of Berlin forecast that German forest industries will suffer direct losses averaging $1 billion annually through the year 2060. Healthy forests, in addition to supplying timber, protect the quality of streams and groundwater supplies, control soil erosion, and provide recreation. Adding in projected losses of these functions, the Berlin researchers estimate that the total cost of forest damage in West Germany over the next several decades will average $2.4 billion per year.

In Switzerland, forest damage threatens the tourist industry that underpins the economy of some Alpine cantons. In North America, sugar maple harvesters lament a drop in maple syrup production and visible deterioration of the sugar maple trees. With weather conditions or other natural factors unable to explain the sugar maple decline, acid rain and air pollution have emerged as probable causes.

In the United States, field and laboratory experiments, combined with the findings of reduced tree growth, strongly suggest that ozone is reducing the productivity of some commercial forest species. Ozone results when certain nitrogen and hydrocarbon pollutants, emitted largely by automobiles, mix in the presence of sunlight. In many rural areas of Europe and North America, summer ozone concentrations now measure two to three times higher than natural background levels.

Researchers at Cornell University subjected four tree species—white pine, hybrid poplar, sugar maple, and red oak—to a range of ozone concentrations typically found in the United States. In all four species, net photosynthesis, a measure of a tree's growth, decreased proportionately with increases in ozone. So even with no outward sign of damage, trees covering large regions are very likely losing vigor and growing slower. Growth reductions of even 1 to 2 percent per year amount to a large loss of timber over a tree's lifetime.

Chronic stress from a variety of chemical pollutants now places a substantial share of the industrial world's forests at risk. In just one year, forest damage in West Germany jumped from 34 percent to 50 percent. The damage increased only slightly during 1985 and 1986, perhaps because of weather conditions beneficial to the trees. Forest damage in all of Europe is now 14 percent, and growing. No one knows how many of the injured trees will eventually die or if and when forest damage will rapidly worsen. Whether the unexplained decline in growth of eastern United States forests portends a similar decline also remains unknown.

With many uncertainties and a variety of pollutants under suspicion, any effective action to protect forests has proved difficult. Most efforts so far have focused on single pollutants or technologies to control pollutants from specific sources. Some twenty-one nations are now committed to reducing their sulfur dioxide emissions by at least 30 percent within a decade. Austria, Sweden, and Switzerland recently enacted pollution control standards for automobiles roughly equal to those in the United States. New cars will likely employ catalytic converters to curb the nitrogen and hydrocarbon compounds that contribute to the formation of acid rain and ozone.

The oil price increases of the seventies were a largely unheralded boon for the environment. Higher prices led consumers and industries to use energy more efficiently, which in turn lowered the output of carbon, sulfur, and other fossil fuel pollutants. Without West Germany's 8 percent decline in total energy consumption between 1979 and 1984, air pollution damage to the nation's forests probably would be worse.

Despite improvements made during the last decade, enormous potential remains for increaisng energy efficiency in the world economy. The existing world automobile fleet, for example, travels an average of eighteen miles per gallon of fuel. Test vehicles now under study can achieve three to five times greater fuel economy, reducing pollutant emissions commensurately. Setting progressively stricter standards could help achieve this technical potential far faster than will market incentives alone.

Similarly, great gains could be made by setting efficiency standards for common household electrical appliances. U.S. legislation that seems likely to become law in 1987 would require major appliances to be 15 to 25 percent more energy efficient by 1990 than they were in 1985. This measure alone would eliminate the need to build 20 to 25 large power plants, thereby restraining emissions of carbon dioxide, sulfur dioxide, and nitrogen oxides.

Forest health is inescapably linked to energy use. Any strategy that offers hope of saving the industrial world's forests must include rapid introduction of pollution control, concerted boosts in energy efficiency, and shifts from fossil fuels to less-polluting energy sources. Meanwhile, with each passing year of continued pollution stress, the cost of lost forest productivity mounts, as does the risk of forest decline and death.

The first case of environmental cancer turned up more than two centuries ago. In 1775, epidemiologist Percival Pott found high rates of scrotal cancer among British chimney sweeps and related the cause to their unusually high exposure to soot, a by-product of combustion.

Since then, the health hazards of environmental pollutants have spread widely to the general population. The same fossil fuel pollutants that damage forests also harm people. In the United States alone, they may cause as many as 50,000 premature deaths each year, mostly through effects on the respiratory system.

Metals, including lead, cadmium, and mercury, have become a growing cause for concern. Released into the atmosphere through the combustion of fossil fuels, incineration, and other high-temperature processes, metals return to earth in concentrations 100 to 10,000 times greater than natural levels. If introduced into the body in large enough quantities, they can cause varying toxic effects, including cancer and damage to the liver, kidneys, and central nervous system.

More recently, the proliferation of synthetic chemicals applied to croplands, dispersed into the air, and disposed as waste on land has added new dimensions to environmental health risks. Some 70,000 chemicals are at present in everyday use, with between 500 and 1,000 new ones added to the list each year. Estimates of the share of cancer deaths they cause vary, but the most widely accepted range from 1 percent to as much as 10 percent. Because of the long lag time—often twenty to forty years—between exposure to a cancer-causing chemical and the appearance of the disease, the number of cancers induced by synthetic substances could increase markedly over the coming decades.

One family of synthetic chemicals, the chlorofluorocarbons (CFCs), pose some of the most far-reaching health risks because of their capacity to alter the chemistry of the atmosphere. In the early seventies, four decades after CFC production began, scientists began warning that these compounds could destroy the life-protecting layer of ozone in the upper atmosphere.

Ozone, a chemical that forms irritating urban smog in the lower atmosphere, performs a vital function in the upper atmosphere. It absorbs ultraviolet radiation from the sun, which if allowed to reach the earth would have many harmful effects, such as inducing skin cancer and damaging crops. Once aloft, the CFCs migrate to the upper atmosphere where the sun's intense rays break them down, releasing atoms of chlorine. This chlorine in turn drives a series of reactions that destroy ozone. Largely as a result of worldwide CFC emissions, stratospheric concentrations of chlorine are now more than twice natural levels.

Virtually all CFCs produced are eventually released to the atmosphere, so trends in production largely determine future effects on the ozone layer. Production of CFC-11 and CFC-12, the most worrisome members of the CFC family, rose steadily from the early thirties to the early seventies as demand grew for their use in aerosol sprays, air conditioners, refrigerators, and insulating foam products. Production dropped for several years after the United States and several other industrial countries banned or restricted aerosol uses of CFCs. Yet since 1982, worldwide production has again turned upward.

A recent assessment by the U.S. Environmental Protection Agency, though preliminary, warns that if current trends continue, an additional 40 million cases of skin cancer—800,000 of them leading to death—could strike U.S. residents over the next eighty-eight years. Increased exposure to ultraviolet radiation would also likely impair human immune systems, making people more vulnerable to disease. More people would develop cataracts. Because greater amounts of radiation could increase the formation of smog, respiratory problems and other pollution-related health effects could also increase.

Concern about the pace and predictability of ozone depletion has heightened recently with the discovery of a "hole" in the ozone layer over Antarctica. There, ozone levels drop by about 40 percent each September and October, shortly after sunlight reappears following the continent's cold, dark winter. This finding took scientists by surprise, and they cannot yet explain why it occurs. Whether it portends a more-rapid-than-expected depletion of the ozone layer globally is a looming and urgent question.

International negotiations regarding CFCs are in progress but so far have not produced concrete results. A cost-effective first step would be a worldwide ban on using CFCs in aerosol products, which account for roughly one-third of annual CFC production globally. Such a ban actually proved beneficial to the U.S. economy, with available substitutes saving consumers an estimated $165 million in 1983 alone.

But even stronger action is needed to reduce the risks of ozone depletion. U.S. negotiators have proposed freezing global CFC emissions over the near-term, and then gradually phasing them out. This proposal would not only protect human health, but could ultimately preserve the habitability of the earth.

Our longstanding struggle to improve the human condition may founder as we enter uncharted territory. Our efforts to feed and enrich the lives of all humans have brought about global chemical changes, some of which may be irreversible. A frustrating paradox is emerging. The same efforts we employ to improve living standards are themselves beginning to threaten the health of the global economy. Everyday activities such as driving automobiles, producing food, and generating electricity are adversely affecting the earth's capacity to support continuously expanding human numbers.

A human population of 5 billion, expanding at 82 million per year, has combined with the dramatic power of industrial technologies to expand the scope of human-induced environmental change. We have inadvertently set in motion ecological experiments that involve the whole earth, and as yet we do not have the means to monitor the results.

A sustainable society satisfies its needs without diminishing the prospects of the next generation. By many measures, contemporary society fails to meet this criterion. Questions of ecological sustainability are arising on every continent. The scale of human activities has begun to threaten the habitability of the earth itself. Nothing short of fundamental adjustments in population and energy policies will stave off the host of costly changes now unfolding.

The ozone depletion and pollution-induced forest damage described in the preceding pages are relatively recent discoveries. Yet the activities believed to have brought about these threats—the release of chlorofluorocarbons and fossil fuel pollutants—have been under way for decades. Taken by surprise, industrial societies may trap themselves into costly tasks of planetary maintenance—perhaps seeding clouds in attempts to trigger rainfall where it has diminished with climatic change or seeking means of protection from increased exposure to ultraviolet radiation or liming vast areas of land sterilized by acidification. While perhaps giving brief local relief, these efforts will be like applying bandaids to a profoundly sick patient.

Because environmental systems can reach thresholds beyond which change occurs rapidly and unpredictably, we need early warning systems that would alert society in time to avert disaster.

Despite impressive progress, the scientific groundwork has yet to be laid for monitoring the earth's life-support systems. Meanwhile, the pace of change quickens.

We have crossed many of nature's thresholds in a short period of time. No one knows how the affected natural systems will respond, much less how changes in natural systems will in turn affect economic and political systems. We can be reasonably certain that deforestation will disrupt hydrologic cycles and that ozone depletion will induce more skin cancer. But beyond these first-order effects, scientists can provide little detail.

Any system pushed out of equilibrium behaves in unpredictable ways. Small external pressures may be sufficient to cause dramatic changes. Stresses may become self-reinforcing, rapidly increasing the system's instability.

The environmental problems of the chemical age stretch beyond the authority of existing political and social institutions. Matters of the global environment now warrant the kind of high-level attention that the global economy receives. World leaders historically have cooperated to preserve economic stability, even to the point of completely overhauling the international monetary system at the 1944 conference in Bretton Woods. They periodically hold summit meetings on international economic problems. Policymakers carefully track economic indicators to determine when adjustments—national or international—are required. Similar efforts are needed for the global environment, including the delineation and tracking of environmental indicators, along with mechanisms for making prompt adjustments when the environment is threatened.

Technological and demographic changes are leading us into the twenty-first century with political institutions inherited from the nineteenth. The need to comprehend our responsibility in time to exercise it successfully presses upon us. The values that guide the management of technology in modern societies have not been clearly articulated, and the need for cooperation is not yet widely recognized in a world where diplomacy remains tied to anachronistic definitions of national sovereignty. That we know so little about the consequences of our activities is humbling. That we have brought so much responsibility upon ourselves is sobering.

A sustainable future calls upon us to simultaneously arrest the carbon dioxide buildup, protect the ozone layer, restore forests, stop population growth, boost energy efficiency, and develop renewable energy sources. No generation has ever faced such a complex set of issues requiring immediate attention. Preceding generations have always been concerned about the future, but we are the first to be faced with decisions that will determine whether the earth our children will inherit will be habitable.

DISAPPEARING SPECIES: A GLOBAL TRAGEDY[3]

An alarming number of the plants, animals, and microorganisms on earth will become extinct during our lifetime. As much as 15% of the world's organisms—a rate amounting to an average of two to three species *per hour*—may become extinct over the next 30 years. Because we know so little of the living things that inhabit the tropics, where most species occur, the great majority of those that do become extinct will never have been seen by any scientist, named, or studied.

At least two-thirds of the world's estimated 4 to 5 million species occur only in the tropics, with fewer than a sixth of them classified or known in any way. The tropical forests in which they occur, once covering an area about equal to that of the United States, have now been slashed back to half of their former extent, with the rest being destroyed at the rate of more than 2% per year and expected to be gone or at least severely damaged within no more than a few decades.

This process of destruction is accelerating rapidly. The tropical forests certainly will never recover from this onslaught—nor will the forests' estimated 3 million resident species of plants, animals, and microorganisms, nearly all of which exist only in these forests.

Loss of Species

The significance of this rapid disappearance of the world's species is summarized in the Conservation Foundation *Letter*:

[3]Article by Peter H. Raven, director of the Missouri Botanical Garden and president of the Organization for Tropical Studies. *The Futurist*. 8+. O. '85. Copyright © 1985 by the World Future Society. All rights reserved. Reprinted by permission.

The consequences of the current rapid loss of species diversity are potentially very serious. The sustainability of our basic food crops depends upon periodic crossbreeding with closely related wild plants; already a quarter or more of our prescription medicines are derived from chemical compounds discovered in nature; recent progress in genetic engineering offers the prospect of still further advances valuable to medicine, agriculture, and industry.

Preventing unnecessary extinction of species is thus not just a matter of aesthetic or ethical interest, but of vital social and economic concern.

Many tropical organisms have very narrow geographical ranges, have highly specific ecological requirements, seek out unusual foods, conceal themselves in unique situations, or mate only at highly specific times in particular places. As an illustration of this high degree of specificity, 440 species of South American land birds—about 25% of the total species present—have ranges of less than 20,000 square miles, compared with only eight species of birds—2% of the total—with similarly restricted ranges in the United States and Canada.

Because they often have such narrow distributions, tropical organisms are unusually vulnerable to extinction through disturbance of their habitats.

Nearly 20% of the world's organisms are found in the forests of Latin America outside of the Amazon basin, and another 20% are found in the forests of Asia and Africa outside of the Congo basin—at least 750,000 species each. *All* of the forests in which these organisms occur will have been destroyed by early in the next century, while those in the Congo and Amazon basins themselves will last a little longer. What would be a reasonable estimate of the loss of species that will accompany such destruction?

The loss of half the species in these forests over the next 30 years would amount to at least three-quarters of a million species, most of which we know nothing about. This amounts to more than 50 species a day—fewer in the immediate future, more in the early part of the next century. And the accelerating rate of extinctions will continue due to the subsequent destruction of the remaining large forest blocks.

The Case of the Hawaiian Islands

An example of the process of extinction is provided by the birds and plants of the Hawaiian Islands. When the Europeans first landed in Hawaii about 200 years ago, at least 43 species of land birds occurred there. Subsequently, 15 of these have become extinct, 19 are classified as threatened or endangered, and only nine—about 21% of the total—have relatively flourishing populations.

Smithsonian Institution researcher Storrs Olson has demonstrated that the overall picture is actually much worse, however. Olson has discovered 45 additional species of land birds as fossils. These birds were all present in Hawaii when the Polynesians landed there some 1,500 years ago. In other words, less than a third of the birds that were in Hawaii at that time have survived to the present, and only about 1 in 10 of the original birds still exists at a healthy population level. Undoubtedly, additional species of land birds existed in Hawaii 1,500 years ago that have not yet been discovered as fossils, so these estimates are in fact conservative ones.

For plants, the figures are also disturbing. According to estimates provided by Warren L. Wagner of the Bishop Museum in Honolulu, the total number of native flowering plants that existed in Hawaii 200 years ago was about 1,250 species. About 10% of them have already become extinct, and another 40% are threatened or endangered—many of them at the brink of extinction. Therefore, no more than half of the total Hawaiian plants that existed 200 years ago remain at reasonably viable population levels.

Madagascar: Paradise Lost?

The situation in Hawaii is by no means unique. Throughout the West Indies, a large number of land vertebrates have become extinct once their areas were colonized by humans. Another example is provided by the island of Madagascar. Lying about 200 miles off the east coast of Africa, Madagascar is about twice the size of Arizona.

This large island is inhabited by approximately 12,000 species of plants, some 7,000 of which are found nowhere else. Madagascar is also the only place where lemurs—one of the major groups of primates—survive. There are 19 living species of lemurs and at least 14 additional ones that have become extinct since human populations first reached Madagascar. In addition, two species of giant tortoises, up to a dozen species of large flightless elephant birds, and a hippopotamus have become extinct during the past 1,500 years.

Despite these extinctions, Madagascar might still be home to a total of at least 200,000 kinds of plants, animals, and microorganisms, well over half of which are found nowhere else.

Shockingly, however, less than 10% of the land surface of Madagascar is still covered with natural vegetation. This remnant is home for one of the richest and most unusual assemblages of organisms found on earth—probably between 4% and 5% of the world total. Many, if not most, of these species will almost certainly become extinct during the next several decades, as people cut into and destroy the remaining small forest remnants.

Puerto Rico

Some foresters have made the claim that there has been only a limited amount of extinction in Puerto Rico, despite the extensive deforestation that occurred in the highlands there early in this century. But the lowlands of Puerto Rico, rich in endemic species, were completely deforested more than two centuries ago, and no one knows how many species were lost there, says José Vivaldi, head of the Scientific Research Area of the Puerto Rican Department of Natural Resources.

Smithsonian researcher Storrs Olson points out that there has been extensive loss of species in all groups of vertebrates within the time that people have occupied Puerto Rico. There is no scientific reason to imagine that the pattern of extinction in Puerto Rico has differed from that observed elsewhere in the tropics.

The pattern of development of Puerto Rico during this period has differed from that of other tropical areas in at least two significant ways. First, when the highland forests were largely cleared in the first part of this century, nearly 100 square miles of undisturbed forest were preserved in three separate reserves, which later provided a source for restocking the rest of the area.

Second, during the past 30 years, many Puerto Ricans have left the highlands and gone to the cities to look for work, letting these only partly destroyed forests recover. Despite all these unusual factors, Vivaldi estimates that at least a fifth of the plant life on the island may be in immediate danger of extinction.

The Extinction Threat in Brazil

The beautiful Atlantic forest region of eastern Brazil is home to 20 species and subspecies of monkeys, more than 10% of the world total. Two-thirds of these species are entirely confined to this region. These include the golden lion tamarin, of which fewer than 200 still exist in the wild, and the muriqui, the largest, most ape-like, and most endangered of all New World monkeys.

These forests likewise are the only habitat for over half of their plant species, such as *Harleyodendron*, a tree legume discovered for the first time less than a decade ago and of possible economic importance, like most legumes. Unfortunately, less than 1% of these forests—almost untouched 150 years ago—remain, now only as scattered fragments.

At least three-quarters of the species of monkeys in this region are in immediate danger of extinction—an extreme example of the threat posed to primates worldwide. The remaining forests are being cleared, and the demands of São Paulo, the world's largest city, are accelerating the process. Similar examples may be drawn from areas such as coastal Ecuador, Central America, tropical Asia, and the West Indies, where the situation is equally grave.

The Pattern of Loss

The constant loss of species on islands arises in part from the necessarily small populations that can exist on islands. Consider Barro Colorado Island, an island of about six square miles that was formed between 1911 and 1914 by the damming of the Río Chagres to form the Panama Canal. Set aside as a reserve in 1923, Barro Colorado Island was home at that time to 208 species of breeding birds. Over the next 60 years, at least 45 of these birds became extinct.

At least six more species have become extinct subsequently, and total losses now amount to a quarter of the original number in less than 65 years, with maximum habitat protection provided during this entire period of time. And this substantial extinction has occurred despite the fact that Barro Colorado Island is separated from source areas on the mainland by a distance of approximately 650 feet—just over the length of two football fields.

Similarly, the fragmentation of mainland habitats into small patches, a process happening throughout the tropics, has an important effect in accelerating the extinction of the species that may survive temporarily within those patches. In these small populations, inbreeding becomes an important factor, just as it is in zoos, and incursions by humans inevitably become more serious and extensive as the size of the patches decreases.

The lesson for us is clear: Just as species become extinct more rapidly on islands, where their populations are small, than they do elsewhere, so they become extinct more rapidly in isolated patches of forest—and for similar reasons. As more and more of the potential source areas are destroyed, the process accelerates.

The survival of species in isolated patches of tropical forest in being studied experimentally by a group of U.S. and Brazilian scientists. Ranchers who are clearing land near Manaus, in Amazonian Brazil, for cattle production have agreed to leave a series of forest patches, ranging in size from a few acres to a few thousand acres, with comparable areas of uncut forest being studied by similar methods. The results of the study will obviously be valuable in understanding the process of extinction that is so characteristic of the tropics worldwide.

A New Age of Extinction?

About 90% of the world's less-developed countries lie wholly or partly in the tropics. By the year 2020, the population of the mainly tropical, less-developed countries will swell to more than 64% of the world's total. More than one-fourth of the people living in these countries today are malnourished, and they are dealing with the natural resources of their countries largely without regard for their sustainability, since there are no options available for them.

A human population with these characteristics will certainly exterminate a major proportion of the living species of plants, animals, and microorganisms on earth before it begins to approach stability. To ignore or attempt to minimize the importance of events of this magnitude is to court disaster.

In fact, the extinction projected within our lifetimes and those of our children may be about as extensive as that which occurred at the end of the Cretaceous Period, 65 million years ago, when about 20% to 30% of the total number of species may have disappeared permanently. The dinosaurs died out then, along with many other kinds of organisms, and there has been no comparable event since.

With the loss of these organisms, we shall be gving up not only the opportunity to study and enjoy them, but also the chance to utilize them to better the human condition, both in the tropics and elsewhere. The entire basis of our civilization rests on a few hundred species out of the millions that might have been selected, and we have hardly begun to explore the properties of the remainder.

The process of extinction cannot be reversed or completely halted. Its effects can, however, be moderated by finding the most appropriate methods of utilizing the potentially sustainable resources of tropical countries for human benefit. This will take the pressure off of the natural vegetation of these countries, where sound conservation can succeed only if it is closely linked with ecologically sound development.

PLASTIC REAPS A GRIM HARVEST IN THE OCEANS OF THE WORLD[4]

It is dawn on the Gulf of Mexico, nature's rush hour. Sunbathers and pleasure boaters, sleeping off the arid heat of July, haven't yet descended on the shore. All along the water's edge, seabirds strut and dive for fish, while ghost crabs and ground squirrels scurry for food. But this morning there's a human intrusion. A large, bearded man slowly drives a tan pickup truck down the beach, his right hand gripping the steering wheel, his left continuously punching a portable computer to record what the tide brought in.

As Tony Amos jabs computer keys programmed for the most common discoveries, he rattles off the items in the staccato tone of an inventory clerk:

"Plastic bottle, plastic bottle, plastic bag, Styrofoam, plastic glove, plastic lids, foam packaging, plastic rope, plastic produce sack, Karo syrup jug, six-pack ring, another glove, Styrofoam cup, cup, plastic bag, plastic fishing line, plastic bleach bottle, plastic egg carton, piece of plastic net, 50-pound plastic bag of sea salt, Bic lighter.

"More synthetic gloves—this is going to be a world-record glove day. . . . Here's an interesting plastic bottle, mineral water made in France. There's a Mexican bleach, a green bottle. You see a lot of them. . . . Oh God, more gloves. . . . "

Finally he brakes and gets out to inspect a specimen for which there is a special computer key designated "dead." A three-foot-long redfish, its scales shimmering in the sun, has washed ashore. The fish is ringed tightly by a black plastic gasket, which has caused a deep gash and eroded the gills. Apparently, months earlier, the fish had darted into the gasket, which had lodged behind its gill cover. As the fish grew, the plastic ring became a noose, damaging the gills and thus eventually cutting off the animal's supply of oxygen.

Amos has come to expect such casualties. An oceanographer at the University of Texas Marine Science Institute who has combed the same seven and a half miles of beach every other day for ten years, he is one of a growing number of scientists who are documenting plastic pollution of the ocean and its perils for the creatures that live there.

The thousands of plastic objects that Amos logs in during every sweep of Mustang Island's beach represent a tiny fraction of the debris floating a few miles off the Texas shore. And the problem extends far beyond the Gulf. Throughout the world, important water bodies—especially the oceans—have become virtual wastebins for the tons of plastic products dumped daily by commercial fishermen, military vessels, merchant ships, passenger liners, pleasure boats, offshore oil and gas drilling operations, the plastics industry and sewage treatment plants.

No one knows how much plastic pollutes the seas. In 1975, the National Academy of Sciences estimated that seven million tons of garbage are dumped into the world's oceans every year. There was no overall breakdown for plastics, but the academy itemized trash from several specific sources. Measured in terms of weight, less than 1 percent of that litter was categorized as plastic. But some experts believe such findings greatly understate the problem because plastic is so much lighter than other debris. The production of plastics has more than doubled since 1975. Plastic soft drink bottles, for instance, were not introduced until the late '70s. This dramatic increase is reflected in more recent studies of marine debris. A 1985 report estimated that merchant ships dump 450,000 plastic containers each day into international waters.

Another measure of the problem is the vast amount of plastic that is washed ashore. Mustang Island and other tourist beaches along the Gulf of Mexico, a body of water that shelters a busy international port and hosts extensive offshore oil activities, look like cluttered landfills. One three-hour-long cleanup of 157 miles of Texas shoreline in September 1987 reaped 31,773 plastic bags, 30,295 plastic bottles, 15,631 plastic six-pack rings, 28,540 plastic lids, 1,914 disposable diapers, 1,040 tampon applicators and 7,460 plastic milk jugs.

It is one of the sad ironies of modern times that the synthetic developed by Man to outlast and outperform products made from natural materials is ravaging nature in the process. Since the exigencies of World War II spurred large-scale production of plastic as a substitute for scarce resources, it has become the favored American material—more durable than wood and rubber, lighter than metals, safer than glass and less expensive than leather. It is present in virtually every product line from Army helmets to artificial hearts to Styrofoam cups.

Today, the plastics industry occupies a major place in the U.S. economy, employing more than one million workers in almost every state and in 1985 producing $138 billion in finished goods. The 1.2 trillion cubic inches of plastic manufactured in that year was nearly double the combined output of steel, aluminum and copper.

As with all revolutions, however, there is a "trade-off," as Ronald Bruner, of the Society of the Plastics Industry, describes it. The very durability of the synthetic has created a massive disposal problem, especially in the marine environment where seagoers traditionally unload their domestic wastes and gear. Bruner contends that it is not plastics themselves that are the problem, but rather the way people dispose of them. Regardless of where the blame lies, the problem has caught up with us. Whereas other materials degrade relatively quickly or sink to the bottom, plastic persists. Buoyant, it floats on the surface and can be easily mistaken for food. Often transparent, it nets or entwines animals that cannot see it. It is the most common type of sea litter today.

Like Individual Mines Floating Around

A number of scientists believe that plastic is the most far-reaching, man-made threat facing many marine species, annually killing or maiming tens of thousands of seabirds, seals, sea lions and sea otters, and hundreds of whales, dolphins, porpoises and sea turtles. "You can go to an oil spill or a toxic chemical spill and see animals struggling to survive," says David Laist, senior policy and program analyst for the U.S. Marine Mammal Commission. "But those dangers are concentrated in one place. With plastic pollution, it's a different situation. Plastics are like individual mines floating around the ocean just waiting for victims."

Until only recently, no laws have specifically prohibited ocean disposal and dumping of plastics. As a result, vessels worldwide have made the ocean their home—and their dumping grounds, disposing of wastes with a wantonness that never would be permitted on land. Joe Cox, of the American Institute of Merchant Shipping, explained the rationale for dumping: "You go weeks without seeing any other people and you begin to think there's an awful lot of water out there. Taking it down to the baseline of human behavior, it's just easier to do it."

Plastic's devastating effect on an entire population of marine animals was first observed in the late 1970s. The victims were the northern fur seals of the Pribilof Islands, which are located in the Bering Sea west of Alaska. Scientists from the National Marine Mammal Laboratory (NMML—a division of the National Marine Fisheries Service) found that, beginning in 1976, the seal population was declining at a rate of 4 to 6 percent annually. They concluded that plastic entanglement was killing up to 40,000 seals a year.

Naturally curious, the seals were playing with fragments of plastic netting or packing straps floating in the water, often catching their necks in the webbing, according to Charles Fowler, an NMML biologist who visits the islands every summer during mating season. The debris can constrict a seal's movements, preventing normal feeding. Unable to extricate itself, the animal eventually drowns, starves to death, or dies of exhaustion or infection from deep wounds caused by the tightening of the material around its back and neck. Many seal pups grow into the plastic collars, which tighten as their necks thicken. In time, says Fowler, the plastic severs the seal's arteries or strangles it.

Fowler says that often more than one seal can become entangled in the same piece of netting. He once came upon a mother and pup whose necks were ringed this way. "Every time the mother moved," the biologist recalls, "she dragged the pup along with her. It was a pathetic sight."

Some of the fur seals are also dying in the large plastic nets used by foreign fishing boats in the North Pacific. Draped like curtains for miles across the ocean, these nets become death traps for many unintended victims, including birds. Unable to see the translucent material, they dive for fish trapped in the nets, get caught and then drown.

Whales are also among the victims. They sometimes lunge for schools of fish and surface with netting caught in their mouths or wrapped around their heads and tails. A whale dragging hundreds of feet of net may be unable to eat. The extra weight impedes the whale's movement and can exhaust it. Beached whales have been found on both the East and West coasts, their bodies emaciated and entangled in plastic net. In the fall of 1982, a humpback whale tangled in 50 to 100 feet of net washed up on a Cape Cod beach. It was starving and so thin that its ribs were showing. "In a couple of hours, the animal was so weak it simply died," said Phil Clapham, cetacean research director at the Center for Coastal Studies in Provincetown. "At that point, it had been digesting its stomach."

Mounting Rescue Efforts for Whales

In the past four years, Clapham's center has received reports of entanglement of about 20 humpbacks, an endangered species with not more than 8,000 survivors in the North Atlantic. Twelve were dangerously ensnared; two eventually died. The center mounts rescue efforts to save entangled whales. One success story involves a 25-ton female humpback, which staffers called Ibis because a line under her tail suggested the long, curved bill of that elegant bird. A playful, friendly whale that swam near boats in the early 1980s, she was a favorite of scientists and whale watchers along the New England coast.

In the summer of 1984, Ibis got tangled in 300 feet of net. She was briefly seen in October and then not spotted again. Experts at the center feared she had drowned. But on Thanksgiving Day Ibis, very thin, tired and still badly entangled, appeared just outside Provincetown Harbor. Crews in small, inflatable boats approached her and managed to hook a rope onto the tangled net. The rope was attacked to buoyant floats, which were designed to thwart Ibis' attempts to dive.

After trying to submerge a few times, Ibis gave up. She simply lay on the water's surface, allowing the rescuers to pull the net out of her mouth and off her tail. Freed in two hours, she recovered and two weeks later set forth for her winter migration. A healthy whale returned the following May, and by June 1986, Ibis was swimming with a calf. "A lot of champagne was flowing among the whale scientists on the East Coast," recalls Clapham.

Such happy endings are rare for the victims of plastic entanglement. Along Florida's coasts, brown pelicans diving for fish sometimes go for fishermen's bait and get hooked. Sport fishermen will usually cut the line, thinking the pelican will then be free. But the line is a killer. Sometimes the synthetic wraps so tightly around the bird's feet and wings that these limbs atrophy. More often, the lines snag branches of the squat, gnarled mangrove trees clustered on the islands where the birds traditionally roost.

"Then the birds just hang there until they're skeletons," says Ralph Heath, who runs a seabird rescue mission near St. Petersburg. "They don't last long once they're suspended from the tree limbs. They can't bite the line loose. They can't shake it loose. So, they keep thrashing until they die."

From a distance, the mangrove islands along Florida's west coast dazzle in the sun, ornamented by large pelicans perched on boughs. But inside the tropical grove, skeletons of seabirds dangle from plastic strands, feathers broken in the furious struggle for survival, splintered wings fallen to the swampy island floor. Since Heath founded his Suncoast Seabird Sanctuary in 1972 (*Smithsonian*, August 1974), he has witnessed hundreds of such hanging deaths. He has rescued thousands of other entangled birds, freeing them from tree limbs or cutting off lines and hooks.

Cruising Boca Ciega Bay in a 24-foot motorboat, Heath anchors near a mangrove island owned by the sanctuary. He is looking for injured birds. An assistant hurls Spanish sardines into the water, luring dozens of pelicans from the rookery. Heath spots a bird with a bloody wing and scoops it up with a net. A piece of fishing line is wound around its flank, deeply etching its humerus and cutting into tissue. Heath carefully disentangles the bird and returns it to the water. "If it wraps any tighter, it acts like a tourniquet and cuts off circulation," he explains. During the next 20 minutes he nets and disentangles five more birds. "Once that happens, it's all over."

Heath has found pelican chicks dead in their nests, strangled by hundreds of feet of fishing line that had probably been dragged there by their parents. He has seen pelicans garroted by plastic six-pack rings—including one with a fish stuck in its throat, held there firmly by the plastic yoke.

In small shapes and sizes, plastic resembles the food supply of some marine creatures. But it is dangerous to consume. Seabirds, mistaking spherical resin pellets (the raw material used to manufacture plastic products) for fish eggs and other natural food, suffer intestinal blockage and ulceration. Whales are also victims of plastic ingestion. On New Year's Day 1984, an infant pigmy sperm whale beached itself alongside its dying mother on Galveston Island in the Gulf of Mexico. Named Lafitte after a French pirate who had once landed there, the calf was taken to an aquarium and nursed. Lafitte seemed to be healthy, eating some squid and diving playfully in the holding tank. Suddenly he stopped eating and on January 11, he died. Dr. Raymond Tarpley, a Texas A & M University veterinarian, participated in the necropsy. The conclusion: Lafitte had died of severe infection of the abdominal cavity lining. In the animal's stomach he found, among other items, a 30-gallon plastic garbage-can liner, a plastic bread wrapper and a corn-chip bag.

Most worrisome is the danger of plastic to indiscriminate eaters such as ocean turtles, especially hatchlings that spend their early lives at sea surviving off surface organisms. To a turtle, says zoologist George Balazs of the National Marine Fisheries Service in Honolulu, a transparent plastic bag or particle can look like a jellyfish, plankton or the larval stage of a crab. Once in the turtle's intestines, he adds, the indigestible material can block fecal matter, prevent assimilation of nutrients and make the turtle too buoyant to dive for food. It is gruesome—but true—that dead turtles with plastic bags and fishing line extending from both ends have been found in the Gulf of Mexico, in the Hawaiian Islands and along the East coast. "When turtles eat that much plastic," says Balazs, "you reach a point of no return. Their ability to swim around is severely impaired. Then they're at the mercy of the ocean."

In a way, the marine plastic pollution problem crept up on American lawmakers. While several international conventions and federal laws have included provisions to limit or prohibit marine dumping of chemicals, oil and other substances, none of them has applied directly to the more recently recognized problem of plastic debris. The 1973 International Convention for the Prevention of Pollution from Ships (MARPOL) contained an annex (Annex V) that would prohibit ocean disposal of plastics, limit other garbage disposal and require ports to provide facilities for receiving trash from incoming ships. But that annex needed separate ratification and it languished, lacking the requisite number of signatory nations to become international law (at least 15 nations representing half of the world's gross commercial shipping tonnage). The holdouts included the United States.

A key turning point occurred in 1984 when a conference on marine debris was held in Honolulu under the auspices of the National Marine Fisheries Service (a division of NOAA, the National Oceanic and Atmospheric Administration). That meeting brought into focus the scope of the problem and led to the founding of NOAA's Marine Entanglement Research Program. It also mobilized governmental agencies and environmental groups to push for ratification of Annex V.

In the wake of that conference, Congress was urged by the U.S. Coast Guard, the Marine Mammal Commission, NOAA and numerous environmental groups to ratify the annex. Finally, in the last week of 1987, the United States completed its ratification process, pushing the percentage of tonnage represented by signatory nations over the level necessary for Annex V to become effective.

Parties to the law now have one year to put their domestic programs in place. Thus, beginning on December 31, 1988, it will be illegal for ships registered in signatory nations, and all other ships within the waters of those countries that prohibit dumping, to discard plastics into the ocean.

"I think that it is a remarkable thing that it happened," says Kathy O'Hara, who is a marine biologist and plastics specialist for the Center for Environmental Education. "It was an incredible public-awareness event. A lot of the environmental community's energy was focused for the last two years on U.S. ratification. It definitely will make a difference."

But O'Hara and other environmentalists also point out that although the annex will help, it will by no means solve the problem. It only deals with ocean disposal, for one thing, ignoring pollution from such land sources as sewage treatment plants and plastics manufacturers. In addition, nations not party to the annex don't have to adhere to its conditions unless their ships are in the waters of party nations.

Moreover, it will be difficult to get compliance. Consider, for instance, the disposal choices facing a captain bringing his ship into U.S. waters from a foreign port. An already existing American law requires that any garbage on this ship that has been in contact with food must be incinerated or sterilized before port disposal. (This law's purpose is to prevent the spread of pests or infectious diseases.) Facing incineration fees as high as $450 per truckload, however, fewer than 3 percent of ships now bring their trash into American ports, often choosing instead to throw it overboard at sea. Much of this trash is plastic. Although Annex V will severely restrict this option, the temptation to cheat is obvious. The U.S. Coast Guard, which will enforce Annex V for the United States, is currently developing regulations for its implementation.

There is the additional problem of military vessels, which are exempt from Annex V. American warships alone discharge four tons of plastic every day, says Larry Koss, environmental program manager for the U.S. Navy's shipboard program. While U.S. military vessels are being required by Congress to comply with Annex V within five years, each signatory nation will be handling this question independently. Koss says the Navy is exploring the idea of a special thermal waste processor for plastics that will compact large loads of the synthetic trash into small bricks that can be more easily stored and carried by ships to port.

The plastics industry also is addressing the problem of plastics disposal. One spotlight is turned on degradable plastics; the technology for some types is already in place and research continues for wider and appropriate applications. Several companies now offer degradable resins for sale, and a few manufacturers in the United States, Italy and Canada are making degradable plastic bags. A photodegradable agricultural mulch has been available for several years, and to comply with laws in 11 states, manufacturers have developed six-pack rings that also break down in sunlight.

There has been some progress, too, in the area of recycling. Plastic industry sources say that, in this country, 20 percent of all plastic soft drink bottles are being recycled into items like polyfill stuffing, paintbrushes and industrial strapping. Technology is also available for "commingled" recycling—mixing different types of plastic in the recycling process—and that process is now being used to produce a new building material called plastic lumber.

Ronald Bruner, spokesman for the industry's trade association, says his members feel the "black eye" of stories linking their products to wildlife losses. The environmental concerns are warranted, he says, but they should not overshadow the great benefits of the plastics revolution. "Look at how many human lives plastic saves. Take disposable products like syringes that prevent the spread of disease; in medical procedures, the use of plastic in sutures, prosthetic devices."

Meanwhile, back on Mustang Island, Tony Amos drives his truck along the beach every other morning, documenting the plastic debris that the tide has brought in. "I never know what I'm going to find next," says Amos, the professional trashcomber, who estimates that up to 90 percent of the plastic items he finds are dumped off ships. To prove his point, he boasts a personal collection of plastic containers that could have orginated only on foreign vessels—Korean shampoo, Cuban bleach, Moroccan mineral oil and toilet bowl cleaners from Hong Kong and Czechoslovakia. He agrees that Annex V is a solid step toward addressing the problem, but he points out, as do many others, that further steps must follow. People in his line of work don't tend to get overly optimistic. "I have pictures of girls in bikinis lying among piles of the stuff on the beach," says Amos. "People have almost got used to this. Maybe it'll become acceptable—part of the environment." It's something to think about.

THE HUMAN COST OF ACID RAIN[5]

Take a deep breath, Some ten million times each year you ventilate about a pint of atmosphere deep into trachea, bronchi, bronchial tubes, bronchioles, and moist alveolar membranes for purposes of gas exchange—oxygen diffusing into blood, carbon dioxide diffusing out.

The majority of us don't pay much attention to the mechanics of it, vital of function though it be. But a significant minority must. According to the American Lung Association, breathing problems afflict about one out of every five of us noticeably and many more of us subtly, insidiously, and eventually. The obvious problems can range from an intermittent condition doctors call "twitchy lungs" to the chest tightness and wheezing of asthma, to chronic bronchitis, cystic fibrosis, and emphysema. The less obvious problems include diminished lung function and a slow alteration in lung architecture that can go unfelt and undiagnosed for years but can nevertheless lead to miseries ranging from moderate discomfort to difficulty in exercising or doing heavy work outdoors, to lost workdays, to considerable pain, to early death.

Some leading health experts warn that the same pollutants that cause acid rain can instigate or exacerbate these health problems. They also suggest that respiratory disease would almost certainly be diminished as a side benefit of any congressional action that attempts to protect lakes, streams, forests, fish, and wildlife by sharply reducing the pollutants responsible for acid rain.

Each year in the United States, largely while burning or refining fossil fuels for energy, we dump some 25 million tons of sulfur dioxide, a pollutant gas, into the air. The furnaces of coal-burning utilities and nonferrous-metal smelters are the major sources of this pollution. Sulfur dioxide, at sufficiently high levels, has long been considered a threat to public health—irritating the lungs, stressing the heart, and lowering the body's resistance to respiratory infections.

[5]Article by Jon R. Luoma. Reprinted from *Audubon*, the magazine of the National Audubon Society. 90:16+. Jl '88. Copyright © 1988 by Jon R. Luoma. All rights reserved. Reprinted by permission.

In the eastern half of North America the gas also is the chemical precursor of about two-thirds of the acidity in acid rain—more properly called "acid deposition," since it includes snow, fog, and even microscopic dry acidic particles called acid aerosols. The remainder of human-made acid deposition comes from nitrogen oxides, pollutant by-products of combustion in many types of engines and furnaces. Since many sources of sulfur dioxide spew their pollutants with little emission control, and since highly efficient control technologies are available, most proposed initial solutions to the acid-deposition problem have focused on controlling this gas. Congress is considering bills to reduce emissions by 30 to 40 percent over periods of seven to ten years. Without these controls, sulfur dioxide emissions will increase.

A German scientist, M. Firket, was among the first to link sulfur dioxide and its acid by-products to public health threats. In 1931 Firket published a paper called "The Causes of Accidents Which Occurred in the Meuse Valley During the Fogs of December 1930." The accidents in question were deaths from the first medically chronicled "killer fog." In that month industrial and residential air pollution poured into a Meuse Valley atmosphere socked in by a temperature inversion, a sort of atmospheric lid over a piece of the Earth which prevents warm gases from escaping. Because of the inversion, pollutants could not rise out of the valley and instead accumulated close to the ground. Firket reckoned that sixty residents of the valley died from inhaling sulfur gases and acids during the episode, and several hundred more suffered lung irritation and asthma-like paroxysms. Autopsies on ten of the dead showed severe lung congestion. Firket further calculated that if a fog of that pollutant intensity ever settled over the city of London, there would be 3,179 attributable deaths. No one paid much notice.

Then, in October 1948, the Pennsylvania steel-mill town of Donora suffered a fog that lasted two days, killed eighteen of the small town's residents, and left about 5,900, or 43 percent of the rest, gasping and wheezing. But the worst was yet to come. In December 1952 the Great Fog settled over London, and the intensely polluted air ended the lives of an estimated four thousand residents. Firket's estimates, it seems, had been on the sanguine side. Subsequent incidents in both London and New York City debilitated more victims.

Fear of such disasters helped bring about the Clean Air Act in 1970 and its renewal and revision in 1977. Environmental Protection Agency regulations flowing from the act attempt to limit sulfur dioxide gas levels in the air we breathe—the ambient air. But rather than strictly requiring factories and powerplants to limit their emissions, the early version of the act assumed that a diluted concentration of pollutant gunk was acceptable. Thus, each state was required to jump through an astonishing series of bureaucratic hoops to develop localized "implementation plans" so that pollution could be controlled, but not wastefully over-controlled. Later amendments required stricter emissions caps. But many sources of pollution, including dozens of huge coal-fired powerplants, were grandfathered by the amendments. Although today's scrubbers can remove 95 percent or more of the gas, dozens of huge plants remain scrubberless and can be expected to belch sulfur fumes into the atmosphere for another thirty years or more. And it's perfectly legal.

Sulfur dioxide levels did drop after passage of the Clean Air Act, but emissions are again increasing, and some sixty counties, including much of the urbanized Midwest and East, still violate minimal health standards. According to the American Lung Association, about 115 million Americans continue to be exposed to air pollution levels exceeding federal health standards. Moreover, there are no specific standards for acid aerosols, which are so tiny that they tend to be drawn deep into the lungs. EPA has only begun the laborious process of investigating whether acid aerosol standards should be adopted.

According to lobbyists from the automobile, coal, and coal-burning electric utility industries, the Clean Air Act is fully protecting public health. "The Clean Air Act Is Working" a headline in a recent utility public relations brochure happily reports, as if to suggest that the utilities themselves had drafted the act they once lobbied so vigorously against. But now, such prominent physicians' organizations as the American Lung Association, the American Academy of Pediatrics, and the American Public Health Association have begun to disagree. Current levels of sulfur dioxide and acid aerosols, they say, constitute a threat to public health.

Bailus Walker, a professor of public health at the State University of New York at Albany, former commissioner of public health for the State of Massachusetts, and president of the American Public Health Association, testified last year before Congress: "Acid rain affects more than just fish or trees—it indirectly affects the health of people."

The specific concerns are wide-ranging—from a long-standing worry that unregulated short-term doses of sulfur dioxide are causing asthma attacks to concern that microscopic acidic aerosols might be invading people's lungs. There is also troubling speculation that acid deposition, by leaching toxic metals into drinking water, may be linked to a range of localized maladies, including lead poisoning and Alzheimer's disease.

Despite the level of concern, there are gaps and uncertainties in existing research. To understand air pollution's effects on human health, a researcher can follow three lines of analysis: experiments on humans, experiments on animals, and epidemiological studies. Unfortunately, each method faces unavoidable limits that make it virtually impossible to establish a firm connection between health and pollution—the same sort of limits that have made it possible for the tobacco lobby to decry the overwhelming evidence of their products' potential hazards. But Dr. Thomas Godar, a practicing pulmonary disease specialist at the St. Francis Hospital in Hartford, Connecticut, and president of the American Lung Association, says, "Knowing what we already know, we don't need to have people dropping dead in the streets to appreciate that long-term health effects are occurring and that there's reason to be concerned."

Although long-term, lethal experiments on human subjects might provide the best proof, scientists obviously cannot carry out such experiments. Nor can they expose subjects to sublethal but permanent damage. "Our clinical studies have to be designed so that they show only a minimal risk and only a reversible risk. You just don't conduct experiments that provoke an asthma attack or put a subject in the hospital," says Dr. Mark Utell, a University of Rochester School of Medicine researcher who has conducted several highly regarded studies on human volunteers. In these studies a subject is placed into an airtight chamber or fitted with an inhalation mask and dosed with a measure of artificially polluted air for a few minutes. After the brief fumigation, subjects will huff and puff into monitoring gadgets that measure lung capacity and function. The idea is to look for what will amount to very tiny changes, such as reductions in lung function, from the brief exposure. Critics of the procedure can always argue, however, that any detected disruption of lung function is merely temporary and therefore of no particular consequence.

Although most research scientists lack similar ethical qualms about research on lab animals, studies on guinea pigs and other animals are equally limited. A critic of even the most meticulous animal research can always insist that guinea pigs aren't humans and that their respiratory systems may respond differently.

If this were a simple world, epidemiological investigation would be the best of the three approaches. It would be neat and orderly and would offer a precise statistical scope for looking at pollutant damage to large populations. A researcher could, for example, compile all the data for daily levels of sulfur dioxide collected by monitoring gadgets in, say, Peoria. This information, when it is correlated with chronological data about visits to doctors for respiratory ailments, cases of chronic lung disease, and early deaths, should yield many answers. Do rates of illness or death rise or fall in relation to fluctuations in pollutant levels? How do data from Peoria compare with similar data from Gary, Indiana, or Lubbock, Texas?

But it isn't such a simple world. Those in Gary or Lubbock may have different smoking habits, may come from different educational and economic backgrounds, may have different healthcare levels. They may have greater or lesser degrees of stress at home or on the job, or better diets. One city or another may have more or fewer smokers. There may be genetic differences among ethnic groups. The weather in one city may affect the transport or chemistry of the pollutant mix in the local atmosphere. In the end, sorting out the epidemiological signal amidst all the statistical background noise is a task for a Hercules among number-crunchers.

Yet, despite all the complications, Dr. Philip Landrigan, a pediatric lung specialist and professor of medicine at the Mount Sinai Medical Center in New York, insists that "converging lines of evidence" from all three research arenas now point in the same troubling direction. While none of the lines taken alone may be conclusive, and while there are gaps and contradictions, Landrigan and many of his colleagues agree that the evidence is now too compelling to ignore.

Low-dose laboratory studies on humans have shown that exposures to sulfur dioxide gas can indeed induce gasping and wheezing. In these experiments, those with normal, healthy lungs suffer only at sulfur dioxide levels exceeding those usually found in the air over the United States. However, and most significantly, some studies have shown that some mild asthmatics and others among the one-fifth of us with breathing problems experience chest tightness and wheezing symptoms at about 100 parts per billions of sulfur dioxide administered for five minutes. That's a level found in the real world, where pollution lasts not for five minutes but for hours, days, or forever. Such levels are prevalent in many parts of the industrialized Midwest, where coal burners and refineries proliferate. In 1985 Ashtabula County, Ohio, and Jefferson County, Indiana, for example, *averaged* about four times that level. And sulfur dioxide emissions in Miami, Arizona, downwind from a smelter, averaged 1,500 ppb.

Medical science still knows little about the specific effects of sulfuric acid aerosols. But some short-exposure studies on humans have shown that these tiny particles can diminish both the sense of smell and respiratory function in mildly asthmatic human test subjects. Studies have also shown that tiny acid particles can interfere with the respiratory tract's rate of mucociliary clearance—the body's defense mechanism that rids the lungs of tiny particles and disease organisms.

Because their respiratory plumbing is so underdeveloped, small children, especially those under two years of age, might be as vulnerable as mild asthmatics. No small children have been subjected to this sort of respiratory experiment, and, for ethical reasons, most likely none ever will be. But Dr. Richard Narkewicz, president of the American Academy of Pediatrics, says that since both groups tend to respond similarly, the experiments with mild asthmatics can serve as a model for effects on young children. Obviously, a small child with asthma is even more susceptible.

Studies on animals have used pollutants for longer periods of time and often at higher doses. In one study guinea pigs showed symptoms of airway constriction after exposure for as little as one hour to concentrations of 160 parts per billion of sulfur dioxide gas. Guinea pigs exposed to as little as 40 ppb of sulfuric acid aerosols showed similar signs of bronchial constriction. Not all the guinea pigs responded at that level. Differences in age and, presumably, genetic makeup meant that each animal, like each smoker, became ill at a different dosage. Predictably, the studies showed that as aerosol levels went up, more animals fell ill. Animal studies have shown that chronic exposure to acid aerosol pollutants increases the size and number of mucus secretory cells. In 1983 and 1987 studies with rabbits showed that exposure to 100 to 200 ppb of acid aerosols for only one hour per day, five days per week, can cause cell changes. The significance: Some of those changes occur in human smokers and appear to be early signs of chronic lung disease.

Fran Du Melle, director of government relations for the American Lung Association, notes that the third avenue of investigation, epidemiology, is riddled with problems. "It allows you to look at very large populations. But there are a lot of confounding factors, lots of noise, and you're looking for what amounts to a very small signal. The only way you get an obvious body count is if you peak so high that you've got people lining up in the emergency room gasping for air."

Although many epidemiological studies show higher rates of premature deaths in polluted areas, the pollution lobby can marshal a few that show little or no effect. In total, however, a pattern emerges. Common sense suggests that mere sampling flaws or design errors would skew the results equally above and below the norm. Yet there are no epidemiological studies showing *improvements* in premature death rates because of air pollution. Landrigan, the Mount Sinai professor, insists that the probabilities lean heavily toward the evidence of damage. In fact, the congressional Office of Technology Assessment deemed the epidemiology convincing enough to predict, in 1984, that current sulfate and other small particle levels were causing an estimated 50,000 premature deaths each year in North America. However, EPA, which once relied on epidemiology, has virtually abandoned it under the Reagan Administration.

Despite the complications and limitations, there are now some compelling studies that go further than mixing data into a pot to see what rises to the top. These studies reinforce the notion that sulfur pollutants are damaging public health. A long-term study by Harvard University scientists has compared air pollution and the day-to-day health of a sample of residents in six cities—ranging from the dirty-air Steubenville, Ohio, area to the clean-air Portage, Wisconsin, area—and has shown a strong relationship between total air pollution levels and such symptoms as chronic cough and bronchitis rates among children. Another study of a sample of families in four Utah communities showed increases in cough and phlegm in direct relationship to sulfur dioxide and sulfate levels. More recent studies in Canada, conducted at children's summer camps, have shown a statistically significant, positive correlation between breathing problems and the comings and goings of polluted air masses. Another Canadian study compared lung function among children in Tillsonburg, Ontario, where acid deposition levels are high, and children in Portage la Prairie, Manitoba, where levels are low. Not only did children in the more polluted area show greater rates of chest colds, respiratory allergies, and cough with phlegm, but the average lung function was down about two percent. That latter finding may not seem significant, but recall that it is an *average*. Because of individual variations, some subjects will show no change and others, inevitably, will show more. Notes Dr. Landrigan, "These are real, measurable changes. While they might not seem like much, if you apply them across large populations of millions of people you're going to find greater rates of asthma attacks. Any physician who's dealt with a child having a severe asthma attack wouldn't call that a small change."

For lack of adequate research, the indirect effects of acid deposition are still unknown, including the effect on humans of increased levels of toxic metals liberated from soil or plumbing by acid runoff or drinking water. Some scientists have speculated that more acidic waters can leach lead from the pipes or joints of older water systems. In a recent Ontario study, analysts found that tapwater that had been standing in plumbing contained levels of copper and lead exceeding recommended minimum health standards. Studies in the Adirondacks showed that about 11 percent of residential wells and about 22 percent of cisterns contained lead levels exceeding EPA standards. Lead has been linked to brain damage in children. Some researchers have suggested a link between aluminum and Alzheimer's disease. Aluminum, virtually omnipresent but normally harmlessly bound up in almost all soils, can be leached away by acid runoff. Acid rain has also been shown to liberate mercury in its most toxic form, methyl mercury, which can then accumulate in the fatty tissue of fish and, eventually, in humans who eat the fish.

The weight of evidence seems at least great enough to lend considerable force to arguments for stringent sulfur dioxide controls. The American Lung Association's Du Melle suggests that some impressive economic studies also debunk much of the coal and electric utility lobbies' claims that sulfur dioxide regulations should remain frozen because of the high costs of emissions control. "It's easy for anyone to figure the cost of a doodad on a smokestack," she says. "It's less simple to calculate the toll pollution takes on public health. But some of the studies we've seen indicate that the costs of sulfur dioxide damage to health are far higher than the costs of control." A 1982 study showed that pollution reductions brought about by the Clean Air Act between 1970 and 1978 saved about $14 billion per year in costs associated with early death and another $2 billion annually in costs associated with illness. Another study commissioned by the European Economic Community showed that a 34 percent reduction in sulfur dioxide emissions would increase average life expectancies by about a year and a half and that savings from costs related to death and illness would approach $6 billion. And a 1979 study in the United States suggested that a 60 percent average reduction from 1978 particle and sulfur dioxide gas emission levels could save more than $40 billion yearly in illness and death costs. Costs, in these cases, include such cold factors as projected lost wages and medical bills. It's probably safe to assume that no one has pinned down a dollar value for pain, miserable health, or loss of a loved one.

In response to the physicians, and with echoes of the tobacco lobby, the Consolidation Coal Company of Pittsburgh submitted detailed testimony to the U.S. Senate, carefully picking apart each known study on sulfur dioxide and health for "uncertainties, inconsistencies, and unanswered questions." Landrigan finds efforts to debunk research on the problem to be "something like the old shell game at the carnival. But the other side is to say, who should bear the burden of proof? Considering that there's good evidence that these pollutants are causing permanent damage to vital functions, might it not make more sense to stop this since we have the means to do it? Go ahead and continue the research. If science can exonerate the pollutants, then go ahead and put them back into the air." As he told Congress, "I would argue that under the present circumstances EPA cannot afford to wait, possibly for several more years, for more precise research data on the adverse effects of acid air pollution on the lungs."

Said Godar on behalf of the American Lung Association, "I would point out that the death of a human is a rather severe endpoint when one looks at cause and effect."

II. THE DEBATE OVER GLOBAL WARMING AND CLIMATIC CHANGE

EDITOR'S INTRODUCTION

Historically, the Earth has gone through periods of changing climate. The Mesozoic Era, when dinosaurs were the dominant land animals, was generally warmer and wetter than today, while as recently as 10,000 years ago—an eyeblink in geologic time—much of the landmass of the Northern Hemisphere was covered by glaciers hundreds of feet thick. In principle, say climatologists, similar changes could occur in the future, given the right conditions.

The geologic evidence for climatic change is currently fueling a scientific debate over what is happening to the global climate now, and how human activities are affecting it. Recently developed climate models raise the possibility of a rise in global temperature due to the atmospheric accumulation of carbon dioxide and other gases. Carbon dioxide in the atmosphere acts like the glass roof of a greenhouse, allowing light and energy in from the sun, but reflecting heat back to the Earth. This process, popularly known as the "greenhouse effect," has been at work on Earth since life arose, and is the process that keeps the globe at a benign temperature.

According to many researchers, however, industrial civilization is raising the levels of atmospheric carbon dioxide higher than at any time in the past. This could intensify the greenhouse effect, causing global warming that would disrupt life as we know it. A rise in global temperature of only a few degrees would turn large areas in the middle latitudes into deserts. Coastlines would be redrawn and major cities flooded as the seas rise, fed by melted ice from the warming ice caps. The geopolitical structure of civilization would be drastically refigured. Nor is global warming necessarily a threat for the distant future. The unusual weather in the U.S. in 1988 and 1989 intensified public fears that global warming was already under way.

The first two articles in this section examine evidence for global warming and suggest steps we can take to slow down the process. However, the problem with the global warming scenario is that nobody knows if it is really true, or if other processes might intervene to send the climate on a different course. The complex dynamics of the atmosphere are poorly understood, and may be so chaotic as to make accurate predictions impossible. In an article for *Natural History* magazine, Wallace S. Broecker shows how shifts in ocean currents have led to cold periods in the past, and may have unpredictable consequences in the future. The fourth selection is from a UN report on the climatic effects of nuclear war; an increase in the greenhouse effect would be moot if we usher in a nuclear winter. In the final selection, Peter Shaw notes the element of end-of-the-millennium hysteria in global warming fears. Shaw claims that focusing on a "distant, unprovable catastrophe" distracts us from the real, immediate problems we face.

ENDLESS SUMMER:
LIVING WITH THE GREENHOUSE EFFECT[1]

On June 23 the United States sizzled as thermometers topped 100 degrees in 45 cities from coast to coast: 102 in Sacramento; 103 in Lincoln, Nebraska; 101 in Richmond, Virginia. In the nation's heartland the searing heat was accompanied by a ruinous drought that ravaged crops and prompted talk of a dust bowl to rival that of the 1930s. Heat waves and droughts are nothing new, of course. But on that stifling June day a top atmospheric scientist testifying on Capitol Hill had a disturbing message for his senatorial audience: Get used to it.

This wasn't just a bad year, James Hansen of the NASA Goddard Institute for Space Studies told the Senate committee, or even the start of a bad decade. Rather, he could state with "99 percent confidence" that a recent, persistent rise in global temperature was a climatic signal he and his colleagues had long been

[1]Article by Andrew C. Revkin, senior editor, *Discover* magazine. *Discover*. 9:50+. 0'88. © 1988 Discover Publications.

expecting. Others were still hedging their bets, arguing there was room for doubt. But Hansen was willing to say what no one had dared say before. "The greenhouse effect," he claimed, "has been detected and is changing our climate now."

Until this year, despite dire warnings from climatologists, the greenhouse effect has seemed somehow academic and far off. The idea behind it is simple: gases accumulating in the atmosphere as by-products of human industry and agriculture—carbon dioxide, mostly, but also methane, nitrous oxide, ozone, and chlorofluorocarbons—let in the sun's warming rays but don't let excess heat escape. As a result, mean global temperature has probably been rising for decades. But the rise has been so gradual that it has been masked by the much greater, and ordinary, year-to-year swings in world temperature.

Not anymore, said Hansen. The 1980s have already seen the four hottest years on record, and 1988 is almost certain to be hotter still. Moreover, the seasonal, regional, and atmospheric patterns of rising temperatures—greater warming in winters than summers, greater warming at high latitudes than near the equator, and a cooling in the stratosphere while the lower atmosphere is warmer—jibe with what computer models predict should happen with greenhouse heating. And the warming comes at a time when, by rights, Earth should actually be cooler than normal. The sun's radiance has dropped slightly since the 1970s, and dust thrown up by recent volcanic eruptions, especially that of Mexico's El Chichon in 1982, should be keeping some sunlight from reaching the planet.

Even though most climatologists think Hansen's claims are premature, they agree that warming is on the way. Carbon dioxide levels are 25 percent higher now than they were in 1860, and the atmosphere's burden of greenhouse gases is expected to keep growing. By the middle of the next century the resulting warming could boost global mean temperatures from three to nine degrees Fahrenheit. That doesn't sound like much, but it equals the temperature rise since the end of the last ice age, and the consequences could be devastating. Weather patterns could shift, bringing drought to once fertile areas and heavy rains to fragile deserts that cannot handle them. As runoff from melting glaciers increases and warming seawater expands, sea level could rise as much as six feet, inundating low-lying coastal areas and islands. There would be dramatic disruptions of agriculture, water resources, fisheries, coastal activity, and energy use.

"Average climate will certainly get warmer," says Roger Revelle, an oceanographer and climatologist at the University of California at San Diego. "But what's more serious is how many more hurricanes we'll have, how many more droughts we'll have, how many days above one hundred degrees." By Hansen's reckoning, where Washington now averages one day a year over 100 degrees, it will average 12 such scorchers annually by the middle of the next century.

Comparable climate shifts have happened before, but over tens of centuries, not tens of years. The unprecedented rapid change could accelerate the already high rate of species extinction as plants and animals fail to adapt quickly enough. For the first time in history humans are affecting the ecological balance of not just a region but the entire world, all at once. "We're altering the environment far faster than we can possibly predict the consequences," says Stephen Schneider, a climate modeler at the National Center for Atmospheric Research in Boulder, Colorado. "This is bound to lead to some surprises."

Schneider has been trying to generate interest in the greenhouse effect since the early 1970s, although largely unsuccessfully. Frightening as the greenhouse effect is, the task of curbing it is so daunting that no one has been willing to take the necessary steps as long as there was even a tiny chance that the effect might not be real. Since greenhouse gases are chiefly the result of human industry and agriculture, it is not an exaggeration to say that civilization itself is the ultimate cause of global warming. That doesn't mean nothing can be done; only that delaying the effects of global warming by cutting down on greenhouse-gas emissions will be tremendously difficult, buth technically and politically. Part of the problem is that predicting exactly what will happen to the local climate, region by region, is a task that's still beyond the power of even the most sophisticated computer model.

Some parts of the world could actually benefit from climate change, while others could suffer tremendously. But for the foreseeable future the effects will be uncertain. No nation can *plan* on benefiting, and so, says Schneider, we must all "hedge our global bets," by reducing emissions of greenhouse gases. "The longer we wait to take action," he says, "and the weaker the action, the larger the effect and the more likely that it will be negative." Says meteorologist Howard Ferguson, assistant deputy minister of the Canadian Atmospheric Environment Service, "All the greenhouse scenarios are consistent. These numbers are real. We have to start behaving as if this is going to happen. Those who advocate a program consisting only of additional research are missing the boat."

While the greenhouse effect threatens to make life on Earth miserable, it is also part of the reason life is livable in the first place. For at least the last 100,000 years atmospheric carbon dioxide, naturally generated and consumed by animals and plants, was in rough equilibrium, at a couple of hundred parts per million. Without this minute but critical trace to hold in heat, the globe's mean temperature would be in the forties instead of a comfortable 59 degrees. The amount of carbon dioxide has risen and fallen a bit, coinciding with the spread and retreat of glaciers as ice ages have come and gone. But until the Industrial Revolution, atmospheric carbon dioxide levels never rose above a manageable 280 parts per million.

Then, beginning early in the nineteenth century, the burning on fossil fuels, especially coal, took off. By 1900, carbon dioxide levels in the atmosphere had begun to rise steadily, reaching 340 parts per million last year.

Levels of the other greenhouse gases have also risen. Methane, for example, is generated primarily by bacterial decomposition of organic matter—particularly in such places as landfills, flooded rice paddies, and the guts of cattle and termites—and by the burning of wood. Methane concentration in the atmosphere has grown steadily as Earth's human population has grown, rising one percent a year over the last decade. Levels of chlorofluorocarbons, which are used as refrigerants, as cleaning solvents, and as raw materials for making plastic foam, have climbed 5 percent annually.

The amount of nitrous oxide in the atmosphere has quickly increased as well, with about a third of the total added by human activity— much of that emitted by nitrogen-based fertilizers, and half of *that* from just three nations: China, the Soviet Union, and the United States. This gas is also released by the burning of coal and other fossil fuels, including gasoline. And ozone, which forms a beneficial shield against ultraviolet radiation when high in the stratosphere, is an efficient greenhouse gas when it appears at airliner altitudes—as it increasingly does, since it too is a by-product of fossil fuel burning.

All these gases are far more efficient at absorbing infrared energy (the invisible radiation that ordinarily carries Earth's excess heat into space) than is carbon dioxide. Indeed, atmospheric chemists have estimated that the combined warming effect of these trace gases will soon equal or exceed the effect from carbon dioxide. And even as growth has slowed in the industrialized nations, the Third World is rushing full tilt into development. All told, billions of tons of greenhouse gases enter the atmosphere each year.

The big question is, given the inexorable buildup of these gases—a growth that even the most spirited optimists concede can only be slowed, not stopped—what will the specific effects be? It's hard to say, because the relationship between worldwide climate and local weather is such a complex phenomenon to begin with. The chaotic patterns of jet streams and vortices and ocean currents swirling around the globe and governing the weather still confound meteorologists; in fact, weather more than two weeks in the future is thought by some to be inherently unpredictable.

So far, the best answers have come from computer models that simulate the workings of the atmosphere. Most divide the atmosphere into hundreds of boxes, each of which is represented by mathematical equations for wind, temperature, moisture, incoming radiation, outgoing radiation, and the like. Each mathematical box is linked to its neighbors, so it can respond to changing conditions with appropriate changes of its own. Thus, the model behaves the way the world does—albeit at a very rough scale. A typical model divides the atmosphere vertically into nine layers and horizontally into boxes that are several hundred miles on a side.

Climate modelers can play with "what if" scenarios to see how the world would respond to an arbitrary set of conditions. Several years ago, for example, computer models were used to bolster the theory of nuclear winter, which concluded that smoke and dust lofted into the atmosphere in a nuclear war would block sunlight and dangerously chill the planet. To study the greenhouse effect, climatologists first used models to simulate current conditions, then instantly doubled the amount of carbon dioxide in the atmosphere. The computer was allowed to run until conditions stabilized at a new equilibrium, and a map could be drawn showing changes in temperature, precipitation, and other factors.

But Hansen's latest simulations—the ones he used in his startling congressional testimony—are more sophisticated. In them he added carbon dioxide to the atmosphere stepwise, just as is happening in the real world. The simulations, begun in 1983, took so much computer time that they were not completed and published until this summer.

Even the best climate model, however, has to oversimplify the enormous complexity of the real atmosphere. One problem is the size of the boxes. The model used at the National Center for Atmospheric Research, for example, typically uses boxes 4.5 degrees of latitude by 7 degrees of longitude—about the size of the center's home state of Colorado—and treats them as uniform masses of air. While that's inherently inaccurate—the real Colorado contains such fundamentally different features as the Rocky Mountains and the Great Plains—using smaller boxes would take too much computing power.

Another problem is that modelers must estimate the influence of vegetation, ice and snow, soil moisture, terrain, and especially clouds, which reflect lots of sunlight back into space and also hold in surface heat. "Clouds are an important factor about which little is known," says Schneider. "When I first started looking at this in 1972, we didn't know much about the feedback from clouds. We don't know any more now than we did then"

So it is not surprising that while the more than a dozen major global climate models in use around the world tend to agree on the broadest phenomena, they differ wildly when it comes to regional effects. And, says Robert Cess, a climate modeler at the State University of New York at Stony Brook, "The smaller the scale, the bigger the disagreement."

That makes it extremely hard to get national and local governments to take action. Says Stephen Leatherman, director of the Laboratory for Coastal Research at the University of Maryland, "Unless you can put something down on paper and show the effects on actual locations—even actual buildings—then it's just pie in the sky."

There are, however, some consequences of a warming Earth that will be universal. Perhaps the most obvious is a rise in sea level. "If we went all out to slow the warming trend, we might stall sea level rise at three to six feet," says Robert Buddemeier of Lawrence Livermore National Laboratory, who is studying the impact of sea level rise on coral reefs. "But that's the very best you could hope for." And a six-foot rise, Buddemeier predicts, would be devastating.

It would, for one thing, render almost all low coral islands uninhabitable. "Eventually," Buddemeier says, "a lot of this real estate is going to go underwater." For places like the Marshall Islands in the Pacific, the Maldives off the west coast of India, and some Caribbean nations, this could mean nothing less than national extinction. "You're really looking at a potential refugee problem of unprecedented dimensions," says Buddemeier. "In the past, people have run away from famine or oppression. But they've never been physically displaced from a country because a large part of it has disappeared."

Coastal regions of continents or larger islands will also be in harm's way, particularly towns or cities built on barrier islands and the fertile flat plains that typically surround river deltas. Bangladesh, dominated by the Ganges-Brahmaputra-Meghna Delta, is the classic case, says Buddemeier. "It's massively populated, achingly poor, and something like a sixth of the country is going to go away."

Egypt will be in similar trouble, according to a study by economist James Broadus and several colleagues at Woods Hole Oceanographic Institution. Like the Ganges-Brahmaputra-Meghna, the soft sediments of the Nile Delta are subsiding. Given even an intermediate scenario for sea-level rise by the year 2050, Egypt could lose 15 percent of its arable land, land that currently houses 14 percent of its population and produces 14 percent of its gross domestic product.

One mitigating factor for some coastal nations that are still developing, such as Belize and Indonesia, is that they generally have committed fewer resources to the coastline than their developed counterparts—Australia, for example, or the United States, with such vulnerable cities as Galveston and Miami. "Developed countries have billions invested in a very precarious, no-win situation," Buddemeier says. "The less developed countries will have an easier time adapting."

Indeed, the impact on coastal cities in developed countries may be enormous. The Urban Institute, a nonpartisan think tank, is completing a study for the Environmental Protection Agency on what a three-foot sea level rise would do to Miami. Miami is particularly vulnerable. Not only is it a coastal city, but it is nearly surrounded by water, with the Atlantic to the east, the Everglades to the west, and porous limestone beneath—"one of the most permeable aquifers in the world," says William Hyman, a senior research associate at the institute. "The aquifer in Miami is so porous that you'd actually have to build a dike down one hundred fifty feet beneath the surface to keep water from welling up." In an unusually severe storm nearby Miami Beach would be swept by a wall of water up to 16 feet above the current sea level.

Storms are an even greater danger to Galveston, which Leatherman has studied extensively. Given just a couple of feet in sea-level rise, a moderately bad hurricane, of the type that occurs about once every ten years, would have the destructive impact of the type of storm that occurs once a century. And Galveston is typical of a whole range of resort areas on the eastern and Gulf coasts, such as Atlantic City, New Jersey ("almost the whole New Jersey coast, really," says Leatherman); Ocean City, Maryland; and Myrtle Beach, South Carolina. "The point is, all these cities have been built on low-lying sandy barrier islands, mostly with elevations no higher than ten feet above sea level," Leatherman says. "Just a small rise in sea level will result in a lot of complications."

Even as cities become more vulnerable to moderate storms, the intensity of hurricanes may increase dramatically, says Kerry Emanuel, a meteorologist at MIT. Hurricane intensity is linked to the temperature of the sea surface, Emanuel explains. According to his models, if the sea warms to predicted levels, the most intense hurricanes will be 40 to 50 percent more severe than the most intense hurricanes of the past 50 years.

James Titus, director of the Environmental Protection Agency's Sea Level Rise Project, says communities will have two choices: build walls or get out of the way. For cities such as New York or Boston the answer may well be to build walls. But for most other coastal regions, picking up and moving may work out better. One of the first examples of a regional government making a regulation based on the greenhouse effect took place in Maine last year. The state approved regulations allowing coastal development with the understanding that if sea level rises enough to inundate a property, the property will revert to nature, with the owner footing the bill for dismantling or moving structures.

Another worldwide consequence of global warming is increased precipitation: warmer air will mean more evaporation of ocean water, more clouds, and an overall rise in rain and snow of between 5 and 7 percent. But it won't be evenly distributed. One climate model at Princeton University's Geophysical Fluid Dynamics Laboratory predicts that central India will have doubled precipitation, while the centers of continents at middle latitudes—the midwestern United States, for example—will actually have much drier summers than they have now (this summer's drought could, in other words, be a foretaste). Some arid areas, including southern California and Morocco, will have drier winters; and winters are when such areas get most of their precipitation. Moreover, the effect may be self-perpetuating: drier soil, says Syukuro Manabe, the climatologist who developed the model, leads to even hotter air.

The changes could be political dynamite for nations that already argue over water resources. A prime example is Egypt and Sudan, both of which draw their lifeblood from the north-flowing Nile. Sudan has been trying to divert a bigger share of the river's water; but downstream, Egypt is experiencing one of Africa's fastest population explosions and will need every drop of water it can get. A string of droughts in the Sudan could make the conflict far worse. The same situation occurs in many other parts of the world.

Not all the tensions will be international. Within nations, local effects of global warming will cause internecine fights for increasingly scarce water. In the United States, for example, western states have long argued over who owns what fraction of the water in such rivers as the Colorado. In California 42 percent of the water comes from the Sacramento and San Joaquin river basins, which are fed by runoff from the Sierra Nevada and other mountain ranges. Most of the water falls as snow in the winter, which melts in the spring to feed the rivers, reservoirs, and subterranean aquifers. The state's normal strategy for water management calls for keeping the reservoirs low in winter, to provide protection against floods, and keeping them as high as possible in summer, to ensure an adequate supply for the giant farming operations in the Central Valley (one of the most productive agricultural regions in the world) and for arid southern California.

Peter Gleick of the Pacific Institute for Studies in Development, Environment and Security, in Berkeley, California, has devised a widely praised model that predicts a dramatic disruption of the state's water supply in the event of global warming, even if total precipitation remains unchanged. It focuses on the Sacramento River basin, which alone provides 30 percent of the state's water and almost all the water for agriculture in the Central Valley.

According to the model, higher temperatures will mean that what falls in winter will increasingly be rain, not snow, and that more of it will run off right away. California may get the same amount of total annual runoff, but the water-distribution system won't be able to deal with it. "California will get the worst of all possible worlds—more flooding in the winter, less available water in the summer," Gleick says. "This will reverberate throughout the state." San Francisco Bay will feel a secondary effect. As freshwater supplies shrink in the summer, seawater, which has already infiltrated freshwater aquifers beneath the low-lying Sacramento Delta, will continue its push inland. Rising sea level will just compound the effect.

Food is another crucial resource that will be affected by the global greenhouse. Taken by itself, a rise in atmospheric carbon dioxide might not be so bad. For many crops more carbon dioxide means a rise in the rate of photosynthesis and, therefore, in growth; and with increased carbon dioxide some plants' use of water is more efficient, according to studies done in conventional glass greenhouses. Also, as the planet gets warmer, crops might be cultivated farther north. But as usual, things are not so simple. A temperature rise of only 3.5 degrees in the tropics could reduce rice production by more than 10 percent.

In temperate regions also, the picture is mixed. Cynthia Rosenzweig, a researcher based at Goddard, has been using crop-growth computer models to predict effects of carbon dioxide buildup and climate change on wheat, the most widely cultivated crop in the world. Plugging in temperature changes derived from the Goddard climate model, Rosenzweig tested a world with doubled carbon dioxide levels. Because the Goddard model is bad at predicting precipitation, she did separate runs for normal and dry conditions. She found that in normal years the wheat grew better, thanks to the extra carbon dioxide. But in dry years there was a marked increase in crop failures, because of excessive heat. Given the likelihood that heat waves and droughts are increasing, she says, no one should count on better yields in years to come.

The nations most likely to reap the benefits of warmer climate are Canada and the Soviet Union, much of whose vast land area is too cold for large-scale crop cultivation. There has even been speculation that these countries might go slowly on controlling the greenhouse effect, or even oppose such control; anyone who has spent the winter in Moscow or Saskatoon would be sorely tempted by the prospect of better weather.

But again, atmospheric scientists stress that no nation can count on benefits. "The models suggest that ecological zones will shift northward," says planetary scientist Michael McElroy of Harvard. "The southwestern desert to the Grain Belt; the Grain Belt to Canada. There might be winners and losers if this shift occurs slowly. But suppose it shifts so fast that ecosystems are unable to keep up?" For example, he says, there is a limit to the distance that a forest can propagate in a year. "If it is unable to propagate fast enough, then either we have to come in and plant trees, or else we'll see total devastation and the collapse of the ecosystem."

According to Irving Mintzer, a senior associate with the Energy and Climate Project of the World Resources Institute in Washington, there is another reason to be leery of projections for regional agricultural benefits. Just because climatic conditions conducive to grain cultivation move north, that doesn't mean that other conditions necessary for agricultural superpowerdom will be present. Much of Canada, for example, does not have the optimum type of soil for growing wheat and corn.

Wildlife will suffer, too. In much of the world, wilderness areas are increasingly hemmed in by development, and when climate shifts, these fragile ecosystems won't be able to shift with it. Plants will suddenly be unable to propagate their seeds, and animals will have no place to go. Species in the Arctic, such as caribou, may lose vital migratory routes as ice bridges between islands melt.

In the United States the greatest impact will likely be on coastal wetlands: the salt marshes, swamps, and bayous that are among the world's most diverse and productive natural habitats. James Titus of the Environmental Protection Agency estimates that a five-foot rise in sea level—not even the worst-case scenario—would destroy between 50 and 90 percent of America's wetlands. Under natural conditions marshes would slowly shift inland. But with levees, condominiums, and other man-made structures in the way, they can't. The situation is worst in Louisiana, says Titus, which has 40 percent of U.S. wetlands (excluding those in Alaska); much of the verdant Mississippi River delta may well vanish.

In many parts of the tropics, low forests of mangrove trees thrive in the shallow water along coastlines. Their dense networks of roots and runners are natural island-building systems, trapping sediment and cushioning the damaging effects of tropical storms. But rising sea levels will flood the mangroves; the natural response would be for them to shift with the tide, spreading their roots farther inland. But in places where development has encroached on the shore, the mangrove forests will feel the same squeeze that will threaten marshes.

The only way to eliminate the greenhouse problem completely would be to return the world to its preindustrial state. No one proposes that. But researchers agree that there is plenty that can be done to at least slow down the warming. Energy conservation comes first: using less coal, finding more efficient ways to use cleaner-burning fossil fuels, and taking a new look at nonfossil alternatives, everything from solar and geothermal energy to—yes, even some environmentalists are admitting it—nuclear power.

Getting the world's fractious nations to agree to a program of remedial measures sounds extremely difficult, but Stephen Schneider sees signs that it may not be impossible. Schneider was one of more than 300 delegates from 48 countries who attended the International Conference on the Changing Atmosphere, which took place in Toronto, coincidentally, just a week after Hansen's congressional testimony. It was, says Schneider, the "Woodstock of CO_2" (an obvious reference to the "Woodstock of Physics" meeting held last year, during which news of the high-temperature superconductors exploded into the public consciousness).

The meeting was the first large-scale attempt to bridge the gap between scientists and policymakers on a wide range of atmospheric problems, including not just the greenhouse effect but also acid rain and the depletion of the protective layer of ozone in the stratosphere. Four days of floor debates, panel discussions, and closed-door sessions produced an ambitious manifesto calling for, among other things, the following:

• A 20 percent reduction in carbon dioxide emissions by industrialized nations by the year 2005, using a combination of conservation efforts and reduced consumption of fossil fuels. A 50 percent cut would eventually be needed to stabilize atmospheric carbon dioxide.

• A switch from coal or oil to other fuels. Burning natural gas, for example, produces half as much carbon dioxide per unit of energy as burning coal.

• Much more funding for development of solar power, wind power, geothermal power, and the like, and efforts to develop safe nuclear power.

• Drastic reductions in deforestation, and encouragement of forest replanting and restoration.

• The labeling of products whose manufacture does not harm the environment.

• Nearly complete elimination of the use of chlorofluorocarbons, or CFCs, by the year 2000.

Of all the anti-green house measures, the last should prove easiest to achieve. Although CFCs are extremely persistent, remaining in the upper atmosphere for decades, and although they are 10,000 times more efficient than carbon dioxide at trapping heat, the process of controlling them has been under way for years, for reasons having nothing to do with the greenhouse effect. Since the early 1970s atmospheric scientists have known that CFCs could have destructive effects on ozone. CFCs were banned from spray cans in the United States and Canada in the late 1970s, and the appearance of a "hole" in the ozone layer over Antarctica in the early 1980s created an international consensus that CFCs must go. Last year 53 nations crafted an agreement that will cut CFC production by 50 percent over the next decade; the chemicals may well be banned altogether by the turn of the century.

CFCs are a special case, however. Since they are entirely man-made, and since substitutes are available or under development, control is straightforward. "There are only thirty-eight companies worldwide that produce CFCs," says Pieter Winsemius, former minister of the environment of the Netherlands. "You can put them all in one room; you can talk to them. But you can't do that with the producers of carbon dioxide—all the world's utilities and industries."

Also, there is a lack of basic information on the flow of carbon dioxide and the other greenhouse gases into and out of the atmosphere and biosphere. Just as one example, there is no good estimate of how much carbon dioxide, methane, and nitrous oxide are produced by fires, both man-made and naturally occurring. "We need to better assess global biomass burning as a source of greenhouse gases," says Joel Levine of the NASA Langley Research Center in Hampton, Virginia. "We have to understand what we're actually doing when we burn tropical forests and when we burn agricultural stubble after harvest. We don't know on a global basis what the contribution is."

Remarkably, the conference spurred some specific promises from political leaders rather than just vague platitudes. Standing before a 40-foot-wide photorealist painting of a cloud-studded skyscape, prime ministers Brian Mulroney of Canada and Gro Harlem Brundtland of Norway pledged that their countries will slow fossil fuel use and forgive some Third World debt, allowing developing countries to grow in a sustainable way. Says Schneider, "In the fifteen years that I've been trying to convince people of the seriousness of the greenhouse effect, this is the first time I've seen a broad consensus: First, there is a consensus that action is *not* premature. Second, that solutions have to occur on a global as well as a national scale."

In the end, the greatest obstacle facing those who are trying to slow the output of greenhouse gases is the fundamental and pervasive nature of the human activities that are causing the problem: deforestation, industrialization, energy production. As populations boom, productivity must keep up. And even as the developed nations of the world cut back on fossil fuel use, there will be no justifiable way to prevent the Third World from expanding its use of coal and oil. How can the developed countries expect that China, for example, which has plans to double its coal production in the next 15 years in order to spur development, will be willing or even able to change course?

And then there is poverty, which contributes to the greenhouse effect by encouraging destruction of forests. "Approximately seventy-five percent of the deforestation occurring in the world today is accounted for by landless people in a desperate search for food," says José Lutzenberger, director of the Gaia Foundation, an influential Brazilian environmental group. Commercial logging accounts for just 15 percent of tropical forest loss worldwide. Unfortunately for the atmosphere and the forests themselves, working out an agreement with the tropical timber industry will be far easier than eliminating rural poverty.

Industrialized nations, which created most of the greenhouse problem, should lead the way to finding solutions, says State Department official Richard Benedick, who represented the United States during negotiations for cuts in CFCs and who was a conference attendee. The first priority, he says, should be strong conservation efforts—an area in which the United States lags far behind such countries as Japan. The effect of such measures, Benedick feels, can only be positive and the cost is not great. "Certain things make sense on their own merits," he says. Technology can be transferred to developing countries. In some Third World nations a partial solution can be as simple as modernizing energy production and distribution. Upgrading India's electric-power distribution system, Benedick says, could double the effective energy output of existing coal-fired power plants.

Addressing the conference, Canadian minister of energy Marcel Masse noted that there is cause for optimism. One need look no further than the energy crisis of a decade ago. From 1979 to 1985, thanks primarily to conservation, substantial cuts were made in the use of fossil fuels by industrialized nations. Only since 1986 and the current oil glut, said Masse, has there been a resurgence in oil use and coal burning.

Michael McElroy concluded, "If we choose to take on this challenge, it appears that we can slow the rate of change substantially, giving us time to develop mechanisms so that the cost to society and the damage to ecosystems can be minimized. We could alternatively close our eyes, hope for the best, and pay the cost when the bill comes due."

CLIMATE CHAOS[2]

For the past several years scientists have issued ominous warnings about the future of the earth's climate. Predictions of dramatic global change arising from the continued dumping of industrial by-products into the atmosphere and forest loss of massive scale can no longer be ignored. Compelling scientific evidence now strongly suggests that world climate patterns, previously regarded as reliably stable, could be thrust into a state of turmoil. Emissions of natural and synthetic gases are increasing the heat-trapping capacity of the atmosphere through a phenomenon known as the greenhouse effect.

The projected effects of this worldwide climatic disruption dwarf many of the environmental problems of the past and augur political, economic, and social disruptions on an enormous scale. Global warming could have catastrophic consequences for the habitability and productivity of the whole planet. The accompanying strain and upheaval on the international scene in turn could have serious foreign-policy consequences for all countries.

Broad scientific agreement exists on the underlying theory of climate change, although the nature and magnitude of future effects from greenhouse warming as predicted by computer models remain in debate. Some of these, such as a rise in the sea level, have been established with greater certainty than others. Nonetheless, the range of consequences is sufficiently clear and the magnitude of the resources at stake so enormous that policy action is required sooner rather than later. Once a crisis has been reached, it will be too late to act.

The international political and legal system remains ill-equipped to offer a solution that will assure the integrity of the earth's climate. Although the greenhouse theory of warming has been accepted for about a century, policymakers have only recently become aware of its significance for the global environment. The international community cannot afford to continue to delay elevating the greenhouse effect to the top of the foreign-policy agenda. Arresting the impending climate instability will re-

[2]Article by David A. Wirth, a senior attorney at the Natural Resources Defense Council. Reprinted with permission from *Foreign Policy* 74 (Spring 1989). Copyright 1989 by the Carnegie Endowment for International Peace.

quire a concerted international agenda and reorientation of energy and development priorities in virtually all countries of the world. Heading this agenda for action should be a global multilateral agreement that sets strict, binding standards for national emissions of greenhouse gases.

Human activities since the Industrial Revolution have dramatically altered the composition of the global atmosphere. A number of gases, emitted in small but significant amounts, absorb infrared radiation reflected from the surface of the earth. As the concentrations of these heat-absorbing gases increase, average global temperatures will rise.

Emissions of carbon dioxide (CO_2) are the single largest cause of elevated terrestrial temperatures from the greenhouse effect, accounting for approximately one-half of the problem. Concentrations of CO_2 in the range of 280 parts per million (ppm), together with water vapor in the atmosphere, established the preindustrial equilibrium temperature of the planet. Since the middle of the 19th century atmospheric CO_2 levels have increased by about 25 per cent to approximately 350 ppm and are continuing to rise by approximately .4 per cent per year. Elevated CO_2 concentrations result primarily from the intensified burning of fossil fuels—coal, oil, and natural gas—which liberates the chemical in varying amounts. Coal burning releases the most CO_2, while the combustion of quantities of natural gas and oil needed to produce the same amount of energy results in only about 57 per cent and 83 per cent as much CO_2, respectively.

The world's forests are vast storehouses or "sinks" for carbon. Worldwide loss of forest cover, by releasing this vast stockpile of carbon into the atmosphere as CO_2, aggravates the greenhouse problem. Deforestation in Third World countries is particularly severe, with the destruction of tropical forests in developing countries like Brazil and Indonesia exceeding 27 million acres annually from activities such as burning, logging, and conversion to agricultural and pastureland. Indeed, the release of CO_2 into the atmosphere as a result of deforestation amounts to 2–10 billion tons annually.

Concentrations of a second important greenhouse gas, nitrous oxide (N_2O), have also been rising, probably because of heavier fossil-fuel use, greater agricultural activity, and other ecological disturbances. Average global atmospheric levels of N_2O at the end of 1985 were approximately 300 parts per billion (ppb) and are increasing at an annual rate of .2 per cent. Both CO_2 and N_2O, unlike some conventional pollutants, are very stable compounds. CO_2 remains in the upper atmosphere for decades after its release and N_2O for considerably more than a century. Consequently, without major reductions in emissions of these gases with long atmospheric lifetimes, their concentrations will continue to grow.

A group of volatile chemicals known as chlorofluorocarbons (CFCs) is believed to be currently responsible for 15–20 per cent of the global warming trend. These chemicals, unlike CO_2, are strictly synthetic and are not known in nature. They have a number of uses as refrigerants, propellants, solvents, and thermal insulators. A related class of bromine-containing chemicals called "halons" are found in fire-extinguishing systems. Average global atmospheric concentrations of CFC-11 and CFC-12, two of the most commercially important chlorofluorocarbons, in 1985 were approximately .22 ppb and .38 ppb, respectively. Atmospheric concentrations of CFC-11 and CFC-12 are growing at a rate of more than 7 per cent annually as a result of increased world production in recent years.

Although their concentrations are small relative to that of CO_2, CFCs are up to 10,000 times more potent in absorbing infrared radiation. After release, CFCs and halons reside in the atmosphere for close to a century, or sometimes more, because of their great chemical stability at low altitudes. Consequently, an immediate 85 per cent reduction in emissions of CFC-11 and CFC-12, for example, would be necessary merely to stabilize their atmospheric concentrations. With their long atmospheric lifetimes, CFCs and halons eventually reach the upper atmosphere. There, they are the principal culprits in the worldwide loss of the protective stratospheric ozone layer, which shields life on earth from harmful levels of ultraviolet solar radiation.

Methane, the principal component of natural gas, is another significant climate-modifying chemical. It has an atmospheric residence time of about 11 years. Average global concentrations of methane were approximately 1,700 ppb at the end of 1985 and are increasing by about 1 per cent per year, the highest rate of any naturally occurring greenhouse gas, for reasons that are not now clear. Animal husbandry and rice cultivation have been identified as major sources of increased methane emissions. Coal mining and landfills are also significant sources, with large potential for rapid growth in the future.

Low-level ozone is another greenhouse gas. Although ozone in the stratosphere is beneficial, this highly unstable chemical is the leading component of photochemical smog pollution at the earth's surface.

While greenhouse gases are dispersed relatively quickly throughout the global atmosphere after release, industrial emissions of these heat-absorbing chemicals are highly concentrated in the developed world. In 1985, 23 per cent of total global CO_2 emissions of more than 20.5 billion tons of CO_2 originated in the United States—the single largest emitting country and the highest per capita contributor among industrial countries to the greenhouse problem. The second biggest contribution came from the Soviet Union, with 19 per cent of total CO_2 emissions. Western Europe emitted 15 per cent of the total, Japan 5 per cent, and the People's Republic of China 11 per cent. Other developing countries together accounted for only 20 per cent of total industrial CO_2 emissions.

Emissions of CFCs are even more strongly skewed. In 1980 the United States produced roughly 28 per cent of the global total of approximately 817,300 tons of CFC-11 and CFC-12. Western Europe produced about 30 per cent, industrialized Asian countries 12 per cent, and the East-bloc countries an estimated 14 per cent. The entire developing world accounted for just slightly more than 2 per cent of this amount.

Consequences of Greenhouse Warming

An international scientific consensus now supports the assertion that the accumulation in the atmosphere of CO_2, N_2O, CFCs, methane, and low-level ozone could have sweeping and far-reaching effects on the earth's climate. By as early as the year 2030, the heat-retaining capacity of the atmosphere may have increased by an amount equivalent to doubling preindustrial concentrations of CO_2. By the middle of the next century, average global temperatures may have risen by as much as 3°F–9°F. The absolute magnitude of these temperatures, as well as the rapidity of temperature change, will exceed any previously experienced in human history.

The effects of a greenhouse-driven climate disruption will be characterized with complete certainty only after significant damage has already occurred. However, among the most dramatic effects likely to ensue from greenhouse warming is an unprecedented rise in sea level resulting from thermal expansion of the oceans and melting of glaciers and polar ice. Over the past century the average global sea level has increased less than 6 inches. By contrast, the sea level will have accelerated considerably, producing a total increase of up to 1-7 feet by 2075, depending on the degree of global warming that occurs.

The impact of sea-level rise in the United States is likely to be severe. The anticipated increase in the elevation of the oceans could permanently inundate low-lying coastal plains, accelerate the erosion of shorelines and beaches, increase the salinity of drinking-water aquifers and biologically sensitive estuaries, and increase the susceptibility of coastal properties to storm damage. An increase of 5-7 feet in sea level would submerge 30-80 per cent of America's coastal wetlands, which are crucial to the productivity of commercially important fisheries. Extensive existing coastal development may prevent the widespread formation of new wetlands. Even in undeveloped coastal areas, the rapidity of the predicted sea-level rise will mean that existing wetlands would be lost faster than new ones can be created.

The increase in elevation of the oceans will also seriously affect the approximately 50 per cent of the earth's population that inhabits coastal regions. Entire countries, such as the Maldives, could disappear. A rise in sea level of only 3 feet could flood an area of the Nile Delta that constitutes 12-15 per cent of Egypt's arable land, produces a similar portion of the Egyptian annual gross national product (GNP), and is home to a comparable percentage of the country's 51.4 million people. In Bangladesh, a 3-foot rise would inundate 11.5 per cent of the country's land area, displace 9 per cent of the 112.3 million people in this densely populated country, and threaten 8 per cent of the annual GNP.

The range of uncertainties associated with local climatic changes is substantially larger than for global averages. The dramatic anticipated increases in global temperature are virtually certain to cause a wide variety of modifications in regional climates. In middle latitudes, where the continental United States lies, summertime temperature increases are expected to exceed the global average by 30-50 per cent. Forests, many of them economically productive, could begin to die off as early as the year 2000 if they prove unable to adjust to rapidly shifting climatic zones. Regions of agricultural productivity could shift at the expense of the American Midwest, which currently has some of the most fertile soils in the world. A warming of only 3.6°F could decrease wheat and cereal yields by 3–17 per cent. Computer models predict continental drying in middle latitudes, which means that parched soils, scorching droughts, and massive heat waves, like those that devastated crops in the Midwest in summer 1988, could become commonplace. Water levels in the Great Lakes could drop by a foot, interfering with navigation for ocean-going vessels. Extreme temperatures have been shown to elevate human mortality. Some models also project disruptions in atmospheric and ocean circulation patterns. The impact of these changes is highly unpredictable.

Countries with tropical climates could experience especially severe consequences. Semiarid areas like much of sub-Saharan Africa might suffer from even lower rainfall. Many semiarid areas are already marginal for agriculture, are highly sensitive to changes in climate, and have had severe droughts and famines for the last several decades. Tropical humid climates could become hotter and wetter, with an increase in the frequency and severity of tropical storms. Floods, which between 1968 and 1988 killed more than 80,000 people and affected at least 200 million more, could worsen. Natural disasters such as floods, now unusual, could become increasingly common.

Indeed, climate disruption caused by the greenhouse effect may already be evident. Global temperatures in 1988 were again at or near the record for the period of instrumental data, with temperatures elevated by .7°F relative to the average for the 30-year period beginning in 1950. The five warmest years in this century all occurred during the 1980s. Moreover, the rate of global warming for the past two decades was higher than any in recorded history. Whether the planet is already experiencing greenhouse-driven warming as measured against a background of natural temperature variability is still a subject for debate. However, because there is a lag on the order of decades between emissions of greenhouse gases and their effects, the level of heat-absorbing chemicals already released into the atmosphere has irrevocably committed the world to an additional .9°F–2.7°F increase over the next 50 years even if the atmosphere's composition were stabilized today.

The greenhouse effect, if unchecked, is likely to cause unpredictable disruptions in the balance of power worldwide, exacerbating the risk of war. The projected climate disturbance and its accompanying impacts are sufficiently dramatic in quality, magnitude, and rapidity that policymakers should give the most serious consideration to the security implications of the ongoing failure to anticipate and arrest greenhouse warming. The oil crises of the 1970s were widely perceived as a national security issue because excessive dependence on foreign oil threatened the American economy. Prevention of global climate disruption demands the immediate attention of U.S. leaders for the same reason. But so far, the implications of the greenhouse phenomenon have not played the slightest role in long-term strategic planning by the government.

The odds are strongly stacked against every country in the game of climate roulette. Contrary to some speculation, it is very unlikely that any region of the world will be a net "winner" from climate change. The very concept of "winning" implies the existence of a stable warmer climate, which will not occur unless the warming trend is halted. Even the limited goal of a steady-state warmer climate will require major policy reform. Otherwise, greenhouse-gas concentrations and global temperatures will continue to increase indefinitely, nullifying any short-term benefits.

Even if a stable warmer climate were identified as a policy goal, the rate of climate change resulting from greenhouse gases already in the atmosphere would be faster than ever experienced in human history. This climate alteration would undoubtedly result in decades of destruction resulting from an inability to alter human behavior, such as agricultural techniques, fast enough to take advantage of new weather patterns. The transition to warmer climates is expected to be highly disruptive and accompanied by an increase in the frequency, intensity, duration, and geographic extent of extreme weather events like droughts and storms. Moreover, sea-level rise would be certain to entail net harm the world over. No region or individual country should place the health and well-being of its public and environment at stake in what amounts to a crapshoot.

While all countries are likely to be losers in the global climate gamble, some countries have more at stake than others. The United States has a particularly large investment in the status quo. Its current pre-eminence in world affairs ultimately derives from the strength of the country's economy. The productivity of the country's natural resources, such as the incomparably valuable farmland of the Midwest, was an essential prerequisite to America's elevation as a dominant superpower in the latter half of the 20th century. Impending climate change means that this productivity can no longer be taken for granted. The greenhouse effect threatens the overall health of the American economy and could require a massive diversion of resources to nonproductive adaptive activities.

The United States has one of the most productive agricultural sectors on earth, producing nearly 50 per cent of the world's corn and nearly 60 per cent of its soybeans. The United States is also the world's leading exporter of wheat and corn. By contrast, the USSR is now the planet's largest importer of wheat and its second largest importer of corn. Climate models, however, suggest that this pattern could change dramatically if the Midwest became 10–20 per cent drier and crop yields were reduced. The drought of 1988 demonstrated that falling crop yields are a very real possibility. U.S. Department of Agriculture forecasts for the 1988–89 marketing year project that domestic consumption and exports of U.S. grain and soybeans will exceed production by approximately 4.2 billion bushels. At the same time, Soviet agricultural areas, located considerably farther north, could suffer smaller losses in productivity relative to their American counterparts. The difference between last summer's events and the effects of greenhouse-induced climate change would be that the latter is permanent and worsening, not just an isolated calamity.

Adapting to future climate change is also likely to require significant resources in the United States. Fighting the effects of a rising sea level on the heavily developed coasts of the United States, where about 75 percent of the U.S. population will reside by 1990, will be phenomenally expensive. Maintaining threatened shorelines just on the American East Coast by measures such as diking cities could cost $10–$100 billion for a 3-foot rise. Seven out of the 10 most populous cities in the United States are located either on the coasts or on coastal estuaries that would be severely affected by sea-level rise. By contrast, the USSR, which has relatively less exposed shoreline and considerably less investment in expensive coastal infrastructure, would suffer little damage. Only 1 of the 10 largest Soviet cities—Leningrad—would face significant problems from an elevation in sea level. Moreover, the Soviet Union could benefit greatly from improved navigability in its polar coastal areas as Arctic ice melts.

The effects of greenhouse warming will also be felt in other parts of the world, potentially fueling turbulent regional conflicts that could upset the existing global balance of power. Loss of low-lying territory could create refugee problems of an unprecedented scale. Inundation of just the tiny island country of the Maldives would require the relocation of nearly 200,000 people. Competition over territory and natural resources launched by those displaced by sea-level rise could create or exacerbate regional strife. Pressure from the 10 million individuals in Bangladesh that would be uprooted by a 3-foot sea-level rise could heighten regional tensions. Famine created by greenhouse-driven crop failures could also generate regional clashes that might encourage the major powers to take sides. Such an acceleration in showdowns among the superpowers would destabilize the world political balance in highly unpredictable ways, tempting those countries that already have a tendency toward global adventurism and placing U.S. security interests at risk.

Arresting Climate Change

The worst effects of a greenhouse-induced climate cataclysm can be averted. And the sooner action is taken, the more effective it will be. Conversely, the longer a policy response is delayed, the greater the warming that will have accumulated "in the bank" and the more radical the measures that will be required to prevent further climatic upheaval.

CFCs and halons are by far the easiest component of the greenhouse problem to eliminate. Motivated by concern over the pivotal role these chemicals play in depleting the stratospheric ozone layer, 45 countries and 1 international organization have signed the Montreal Protocol on Substances That Deplete the Ozone Layer, which took effect at the beginning of 1989 after negotiations sponsored by the United Nations Environment Programme. The agreement overcame a serious lapse of concern about this issue by U.S. and European policymakers in the early 1980s and a complete breakdown of negotiations in 1985. Aside from representing a diplomatic milestone for international cooperation on environmental problems, the Montreal Protocol is also an important precedent for a multilateral strategy on the more challenging issue of greenhouse warming.

The Montreal Protocol requires an incremental 50 per cent reduction in the consumption of five ozone-depleting CFCs by the end of this century. Beginning in July 1989 consumption of these substances must be frozen at 1986 levels. A reduction of 20. per cent must be achieved beginning 4 years later and an additional 30 per cent beginning in July 1998. The agreement permits each country to implement these requirements as it chooses through recycling, destruction, or abandonment of unnecessary uses of these chemicals. However, the overall strategy is to stimulate the development of alternatives to existing CFCs by constricting supply. The Montreal Protocol contains groundbreaking trade incentives for broad participation, including a ban on imports of controlled substances from countries that are not party to the accord. Its provisions dealing specifically with developing countries resolve delicate equity issues by allowing Third World countries a 10-year grace period to make required reductions.

Despite the precedential importance of the Montreal Protocol, the agreement is inadequate. Because of loopholes and leakages built into the document, the actual reductions in emissions of substances controlled by the protocol will be only about one-third under even the most optimistic assumptions. Consumption of halons, which are up to 10 times as destructive of ozone as the strongest CFC, is merely leveled off and not reduced. The agreement explicitly specifies that production—as distinct from consumption—of CFCs and halons may actually increase by as much as 10 per cent over the 1986 level.

It is now clear that emissions of CFCs and halons must be virtually eliminated because of the overwhelming risks these chemicals pose to climate and stratospheric ozone. Soon after the Montreal Protocol was signed in September 1987, a seasonal thinning of 50 per cent of the ozone layer over Antarctica—the ozone "hole"—was conclusively connected to CFCs. New and widely accepted scientific evidence documents that average global losses in stratospheric ozone of about 3 per cent—two to three times that previously predicted by computer models—have already occurred. Even if CFCs and halons are phased out within 5–7 years, the long atmospheric lifetimes of these chemicals mean that the environment could take up to a century to recover. Moreover, even if production of these dangerous chemicals were to be eliminated altogether, they would continue to seep out of the existing stock of refrigerators, air conditioners, insulation, and other repositories.

To stabilize global concentrations of CO_2 gas it will be necessary to cut global emissions of CO_2 by at least one-half. Burning fossil fuels releases most of the excess CO_2 in the atmosphere. Because no economical technology for removing CO_2 from waste-gas streams is now available, cutting back releases of CO_2 will require a lower total energy consumption and a shift in energy sources toward low- or non-CO_2-emitting technologies. Greenhouse impacts should be an explicit part of all future decision-making processes in the energy sector. Reductions in fossil-fuel use will also help to ease other environmental problems associated with current patterns of energy use, such as acid rain and local air pollution.

Even with the most optimistic assumptions about economic growth, major reductions in CO_2 emissions from industrialized countries can be achieved with energy conservation, efficiency technologies, and renewable energy sources. For example, the 1,200 kilowatt-hours per year used by a typical frost-free refrigerator can be reduced to only 500 with a state-of-the-art model. Current technology can light an office building with an expenditure of only .55 watts per square foot, as little as one-fifth of today's average. It is now possible to produce motor vehicles—which currently account for more than one-fourth of greenhouse gases released in the United States—that have fuel economies of up to 98 miles per gallon, 2–5 times as efficient as those now on the road.

Efficiency improvements have meant that the amount of energy used in the United States today is about the same as in 1973, despite a 40 per cent increase in GNP during the same period. Application of existing efficiency technologies could reduce U.S. CO_2 emissions by 14–18 per cent by the end of the century. In California alone, a steady improvement in efficiency of 3.4 per cent per year has been achieved over the past 12 years with only mild encouragement from state and local governments through policy measures to encourage conservation and efficiency. Through a strategy involving efficiency improvements, national progress could be much faster.

Nuclear energy has been proposed in some quarters as the preferred solution to the problem of greenhouse warming. Although atomic power is a CO_2-free technology, its other risks currently make it the least attractive alternative to fossil fuels. Nuclear energy carries the inherent danger of weapons proliferation. The current generation of nuclear reactors still entails the unacceptable danger of accidents and suffers from a critical lack of public confidence in an increasingly large number of countries. The problem of disposing of waste that will remain hazardously radioactive for many hundreds of thousands of years has yet to be adequately solved. Of the alternative strategies for reducing CO_2 emissions, nuclear energy is among the most expensive. Moreover, to reduce CO_2 emissions by 50 per cent by the year 2020 solely through the expansion of the nuclear industry would require bringing a new plant on line somewhere in the world at the rate of almost one a day starting in the mid-1990s—clearly a practical impossibility. While the nuclear option may be worthy of consideration as part of the public debate on ultimate solutions to the greenhouse problem, increased reliance on nuclear power at present would be both politically infeasible and irresponsible when major, cheap reductions in CO_2 emissions are available with existing technologies.

Reversing deforestation and creating new forested areas will help to offset current levels of CO_2 emissions. New forests, in absorbing CO_2 from the air during photosynthesis, will contribute to climate stabilization by serving as supplementary reservoirs for carbon. Aggressive policies to conserve existing forests and create new forested areas will yield other significant environmental benefits, including erosion control and the preservation of a rich diversity of species whose genetic potential is only now becoming accessible to humankind.

The fundamentals of the greenhouse phenomenon are now well understood and the need for swift policy responses firmly established. While these responses are being implemented, the development and dissemination of technologies to combat climate disturbance—such as CFC-free, energy-efficient refrigerators and low-methane strains of rice—should be a high priority. Increased basis research to resolve remaining uncertainties concerning the magnitude, rate, and effects of greenhouse warming should also be undertaken.

The Role of Developing Countries

An equitable response to the special needs of developing countries is crucial to removing greenhouse threats to the global climate. On the one hand, developing countries have caused little of the problem and industrialized countries must bear the bulk of the blame. On the other hand, as economic development accelerates, Third World countries may account for the preponderance of greenhouse-gas emissions by the middle of the next century. An international solution that provides incentives for the participation of developing countries while fairly distributing the responsibility for implementing solutions is essential to a successful global strategy for combating greenhouse warming.

The consequences of the greenhouse effect strongly suggest that it is in the self-interest of Third World countries to re-examine expeditiously their energy priorities. Developing countries, with fewer resources to adapt to environmental disturbances, stand to suffer disproportionately from a rapid climate change. For example, the productivity of common rice varieties falls off dramatically at temperatures just a few degrees higher than those currently prevailing in many rice-growing areas.

Tapping the tremendous potential for conservation and improved end-use efficiency in the developing world would contribute to a solution for greenhouse warming while meeting much of the Third World's growing energy needs. This strategy also avoids other serious environmental and social problems, such as land degradation, local air pollution, and population displacement, that accompany the building of fossil-fuel-fired power installations. By the year 2020 it may be possible to achieve a universal standard of living far beyond that necessary to satisfy basic needs with little or no increase in global energy consumption from today's levels. However, many developing countries use energy in a highly inefficient manner. Macroeconomic policies in many developing countries, such as electricity price subsidies, discourage conservation and efficiency improvements. Firms in Brazil, where electricity prices are subsidized, manufacture energy-efficient air conditioners for export but cheap, inefficient models for domestic consumption.

Investments in efficiency gains are extremely attractive from many points of view. They require less capital and less foreign exchange than do comparable amounts of new power supply, contributing to overall economic productivity. Through efficiency and conservation, developing countries could avoid at least $1.4 trillion in power-supply expansion costs between now and the year 2008.

Efficiency investments represent a major opportunity for donors like the United States and the World Bank to assist developing countries in making energy choices that both avoid mistakes made earlier in the developed world and reduce risks to the entire planet from greenhouse warming. Nonetheless, development assistance in th environmentally sensitive energy sector often exacerbates the threat of greenhouse warming by emphasizing conventional sources of energy, such as massive fossil-fuel-fired power plants.

The World Bank, which controls an annual energy lending portfolio averaging $3.5 billion, is one of the principal donors supporting power generation projects in the Third World. Through measures such as pricing reforms and improvements in the operation of existing power plants and distribution systems, the Bank has already made a commitment to encourage conservation and the efficient use of energy. There is, however, considerably more that the Bank can do.

The Bank requires preparation of a "least cost plan" to precede investments in the energy sector. Current methodologies for these studies primarily address strategies for increasing energy supply. Support for demand reduction measures, such as end-use efficiency improvements, which are often economically as well as environmentally superior to investments in supply, have not consistently been considered as alternatives to conventional power generation projects in Bank energy-sector strategies. Expanding the universe of alternatives to include demand reduction options would simultaneously help developing countries reduce the rate of growth in their power-generating capacity and reduce greenhouse-gas emissions without sacrificing the energy needed for economic development. Additional staff trained in strategies for encouraging end-use efficiency improvements would significantly increase the Bank's capabilities in this crucial area.

Forest policy is another area where development assistance can provide benefits to Third World countries while simultaneously cutting emissions of greenhouse gases. While there has been great concern in North America and Western Europe about destruction of tropical forests, donor countries historically have devoted little capital to conservation of this crucial resource and have earmarked even less for the creation of new forest areas. Case studies have documented that projects financed with little regard for the integrity of natural resources by donors such as the World Bank have seriously exacerbated forest loss in key countries such as Brazil and Indonesia. Industrialized countries can also help to reverse tropical deforestation and encourage reforestation through changes in domestic policies. Developed countries provide the primary market for tropical hardwoods, virtually all of which are unsustainably harvested, and firms based in industrialized countries often reap the profits of this trade. Governments of industrialized countries can take a serious look at controlling trade in tropical woods and compensate exporting countries for lost revenues through alternative investments.

The Third World debt crisis presents major opportunities for encouraging better forest management in developing countries. As the market value of such debt has fallen, a number of private banks have sold debt owed to them by Third World governments to private conservation organizations, which have then forgiven the debt in return for specific promises by the governments concerned, such as a commitment to conserve a particular area and to support its maintenance with a stream of payments in local currency. Such "debt for nature" swaps are already in place in Bolivia, Costa Rica, and Ecuador, and more are under negotiation. Governments can adopt policies, such as tax incentives, that encourage creditor banks to sell debt for swaps. Creditor governments can reduce interest or principal on sovereign debt in return for promises of policy reform in this critical sector.

Coordinating policies on the international level to fight greenhouse warming will maximize environmental and foreign-policy benefits. Unilateral reductions in releases of greenhouse gases by large emitters such as the United States and the Soviet Union will go a long way toward arresting global climate disruption. However, a multilateral consensus strategy will further the crucial goals of creating incentives for universal participation and establishing an equitable balancing of responsibility for solving the problem.

Existing international mechanisms are an important part of such a strategy. A reassessment of the Montreal Protocol, a process that is provided for by the document itself, is the most expeditious way to eliminate the contributions CFCs and halons make to the global warming problem. The World Bank's institutional structure also includes mechanisms for member countries to redirect priorities in the critical energy and forest sectors.

The remainder of the greenhouse problem could be handled most effectively through a multilateral treaty, with standards binding under international law that would require each country to take prescribed actions to reduce and halt greenhouse warming. Considerable precedent is now in place for multinational environmental agreements containing strict regulatory standards. In addition to the Montreal Protocol, which is an ancillary agreement to the 1985 Vienna Convention for the Protection of the Ozone Layer, several other international agreements establish requirements for controlling emissions of specific air pollutants. The Protocol on the Reduction of Sulphur Emissions or Their Transboundary Fluxes by at Least 30 Percent and the Protocol Concerning the Control of Emissions of Nitrogen Oxides or Their Transboundary Fluxes—both auxiliary agreements to the 1979 Convention on Long-Range Transboundary Air Pollution—set out precise regulatory limitations on releases of specified chemicals. Principles established in the case law of international tribunals and in the 1972 Stockholm Declaration adopted by the United Nations Conference on the Human Environment also discouraged countries from acting in ways that could harm the environment in another's territory.

A multilateral treaty designed to arrest global climate change should satisfy several basic requirements. First, it must require reductions in releases of greenhouse gases of a magnitude and speed sufficient to stabilize the earth's climate. The most important gas to control is CO_2, for which global reductions of at least 50 per cent are necessary. Participating countries should accomplish these reductions by means of environmentally and economically sound technologies that do not present unacceptable risks to public health or global security. The creation of new forested areas might be encouraged by allowing credits against reductions of CO_2 emissions that would otherwise be required and by provisions establishing or promoting forestry programs. Because the agreement could be expected to cover a large number of emissions sources, it should mandate strict mechanisms for enforcement through reporting of emissions, on-site audits, and internationally controlled remote sensing.

Second, the responsibility for making reductions must be distributed equitably. Among the criteria that could be applied is relative national wealth as measured by per capita GNP. Another test could be per capita emissions of CO_2, with the highest reductions required of those countries with the highest emissions per unit of population. Another possibility would be to require the imposition of a fee for carbon emissions, either as a primary mechanism for achieving reductions or as a supplementary measure. Any of these formulas would require proportionally greater cutbacks by the wealthiest countries and leave the poorest countries with the fewest constraints on CO_2 emissions. All countries would be encouraged to use existing energy supplies more efficiently.

A treaty should also require a commitment from the wealthier countries for increased research into non-CO_2 energy supply technologies and development assistance to help poorer countries meet the requirements imposed on them by the agreement. One mechanism for generating the necessary capital is to require countries to contribute to a fund in proportion to their CO_2 emissions. Restricting access to this fund to those countries that accepted the obligations of the treaty would create incentives for broad participation.

Considering the importance of the resources at risk, it would be nothing short of reckless to continue with business as usual. A failure to respond to the threat of greenhouse warming would amount to an affirmative decision to wager the health and well-being of current and future generations against overwhelming odds.

THE BIGGEST CHILL[3]

We, the inhabitants of planet Earth, are performing a gigantic climate experiment. Begun by our grandparents, its results will be recorded by our grandchildren. The experiment involves the production and release into the atmosphere of gaseous mole-

[3]Article by Wallace S. Broecker. Reprinted with permission from *Natural History*, October 1987. Copyright the American Museum of Natural History, 1987.

cules made up of three or more atoms; the most important of these are carbon dioxide (CO_2), methane (CH_4), and the freons (CF_3Cl and CF_2Cl_2). Unlike the two-atom molecules, oxygen (O_2) and nitrogen (N_2), which make up 99 percent of our atmosphere, these multiatom molecules have the capacity to capture packets of outgoing radiation from the earth. Just as a blanket helps retain our body heat, these gases retain the earth's heat. Hence, the result of our experiment will be to make the surface of our planet warmer.

Unfortunately, our knowledge of the earth's climate system is still not good enough to reliably predict the effects of this heating on wildlife, agriculture, and a host of other matters important to humans. We will only know the results of the buildup of these "greenhouse" gases if our learning rate greatly accelerates.

In the face of such uncertainty, one might ask why the experiment is not declared dangerous to the well-being of the planet and abandoned. The reason is that the generation of greenhouse gases is not an enterprise designed by scientists. Rather, it is an inescapable byproduct of our civilization. Carbon dioxide is produced when coal, oil, and natural gas are burned. When carbon atoms, which make up the bulk of these fuels, combine with oxygen molecules from the atmosphere, an amount of CO_2 weighing roughly three times more than the fuel burned is generated. There is no feasible way to prevent this CO_2 from escaping into the atmosphere. Methane is produced by living organisms. The metabolic systems of steers and the bacteria in the mud of rice paddies are methane producers. Hence, some methane will be added to the atmosphere for each hamburger or bowl of rice we eat. Freons are manufactured by industry as foaming agents, refrigerants, and propellants. Except for the freons, the greenhouse gases are products of activities essential to human survival. If five or so billion people are to be maintained on our planet, we must continue the greenhouse experiment. We are hooked.

Scientists struggle to increase our understanding of how the earth's environmental system operates in the hope that we will be able to predict at least some of the coming consequences. If so, we can develop strategies to cope with the "bad" and take advantage of the "good" results of this experiment.

These inquiries have recently revealed a piece of disquieting information. Geological studies suggest the earth's climate system resists change until pushed beyond some threshold; then it leaps into a new mode of operation. The situation is akin to that of a radio with automatic frequency control. When the dial on such a radio is turned, instead of one station fading out and the next one fading in, the radio remains locked on one station until a threshold is crossed, at which point it suddenly jumps to another station. The implication of this finding for future climates is clear: the effects of the greenhouse gas buildup may come in sudden jumps, rather than gradually. Such jumps would pose great threats to humans and wildlife.

Our suspicion that the earth's climate changes in leaps comes from the evidence recorded in deep-sea sediments and in ice. The most studied of these records is the amount of heavy oxygen found in the preserved shells of microscopic animals on the ocean floor. The heavy form of oxygen in water vapor tends to be lost as atmospheric moisture is transported to the icecaps. The larger the icecap, the more heavy oxygen remains behind in the seawater. Thus, in eras when the icecaps were large, shelled organisms contained more heavy oxygen than they did when the icecaps were small; the shells therefore contain a history of the ice ages.

The oxygen isotope record tells us that over the last million years the polar icecaps have changed in a cyclic fashion, going from the rather small size of the current warm period to the very large size at the maximum of the last glaciation. More important, these fluctuations in ice volume have been shown to be in tune with periodic changes in the earth's orbit around the sun, generated by gravitational interactions among the objects making up our solar system. Because the timing of the oxygen isotope changes (as determined by age measurements on deep-sea sediment cores) matches what would be expected if the changes were driven by the earth's changing orbit, scientists are reasonably certain of the cause-and-effect relationship.

Why do changes in the characteristics of the earth's orbit have anything to do with climate? The answer is that these changes alter the earth's seasons. The relative amounts of each year's sunlight received during the winter months, as opposed to the summer months, changes in accordance with the changing orbit. Exactly how changes in the strength of the seasons drive the expansion and contraction of the earth's polar icecaps remains a matter of debate.

While the oxygen isotope record in the deep-sea sediments provided evidence pointing to the earth's orbital cycles as the pacemaker of glaciation, it also tended to lull scientists into concluding that the earth's climate responds gradually when pushed. This conclusion was drawn despite the realization that the response of polar icecaps to changing climate would have to be so sluggish that a smooth oxygen isotope record would be expected no matter how abrupt the changes in environmental conditions might be. So lulled were we that other clues in paleoclimatic records that pointed to abrupt response were largely disregarded.

The awakening came in the early 1980s when Hans Oeschger and his group at the university in Bern, Switzerland, carried out detailed measurements of the CO_2 content of air trapped in the ice from a deep boring made at a site in southern Greenland. These measurements concentrated on a section of the core on which earlier studies made by the Danish group of Willi Dansgaard had shown repeated leaps in Greenland's air temperature. To everyone's surprise, each of Dansgaard's jumps was accompanied by a 20 percent change in the CO_2 content of the air trapped in bubbles in the ice (and hence in the CO_2 content of air above Greenland at the time the ice formed).

Eyebrows were raised by Oeschger's CO_2 jumps because while the temperature jumps could be written off as a curiosity of Greenland, the CO_2 changes could not. The atmosphere's CO_2 is well mixed with its other gases, hence a measurement in Greenland typifies the entire globe. Furthermore, the changes in CO_2 content found by the Oeschger group occurred in times as short as a few hundred years. To bring about these changes in CO_2 requires some extraordinary change in the earth's chemical cycles, particularly those operating in the ocean. Scientists were therefore forced to the realization that the leaps in Greenland's climate were far-reaching, involving the workings of the ocean as well as those of the atmosphere.

The new look at the ocean triggered by the finding of the Oeschger group brought to the fore the potential importance of a curious tie that exists between the functioning of today's ocean and today's atmosphere. This tie results in a globe-straddling ocean current that keeps northern Europe unusually warm. Paris lies almost a full ten degrees farther north than New York, yet its mean annual temperature is similar to that of New York.

The extra heat received by northern Europe is carried by a conveyor-belt-like ocean current. The part of the conveyor closer to the surface moves to the north; the conveyor's deeper part moves to the south. The important point is that the water of the upper part is warm, while that of the lower part is cold. The temperature change occurs at the northern limit of the belt (in the region around Iceland). Here, during the winter months, water warmed during its passage through the tropical and temperate Atlantic meets air cooled during its passage over frigid Canada. The meeting results in the transfer of heat from the sea to the air. The amount of heat is staggering, measuring about 30 percent of that received by the surface of the North Atlantic from the sun. The result of this transfer is twofold. First, the sting of the cold Canadian air masses is removed before the air hits northern Europe. Second, the waters are cooled and consequently made more dense. The extra density allows the water to sink to the abyss and feeds the lower part of the conveyor. Thus the ocean current acts as a pump, extracting heat from low-latitude air and transferring it to high-latitude air.

The water that sinks to the bottom of the northern Atlantic flows down the full length of the Atlantic, around Africa, through the southern Indian Ocean, and finally up the Pacific Ocean. This deep current carries twenty times more water than the combined world rivers.

There is also an ocean conveyor belt in the North Pacific but it runs the opposite way around. Deep waters move toward the north and upwell to the surface. From there they move toward the equator in the upper ocean. So in today's world, the Atlantic Ocean conveyor belt carries tropical heat for delivery to the atmosphere at high northern latitudes, while the Pacific conveyor belt carries cold surface waters southward, pushing the invading warm waters back toward the equator. Today's major ocean current system thus heats the lands adjacent to the northern Atlantic.

While we don't have the complete answer to why our ocean operates in this fashion, we do have the first principles. The pattern of circulation is governed by the sea's salt. To understand this we must consider the transport of water through the atmosphere. The water that evaporates from the ocean falls eventually as rain or snow. Some of this precipitation reaches the land and some reaches the sea. Some precipitation that falls on land evaporates (mainly from plants) and some runs down the rivers and back to the sea. This cycle must exactly balance: for each molecule that evaporates from the sea, one molecule must return to it either by precipitation on its surface or from the mouth of a river. While this is true for the ocean as a whole, it need not be true for each part of the ocean. In fact, in today's world, an imbalance exists between the Atlantic and the Pacific. The Atlantic loses more water by means of evaporation than it gains by precipitation and continental runoff. The situation is reversed in the Pacific, which receives more water as rain and runoff than it loses by evaporation. While this imbalance is compensated for by a net flow of seawater from the Pacific to the Atlantic, it leaves a mark on the ocean's salt budget. Salt does not evaporate. Thus, the transport of water vapor from the Atlantic to the Pacific enriches the waters of the North Atlantic in salt content. The enrichment in salt must be compensated for by a flow of more salty water from the Atlantic to the Pacific. This is accomplished by the great conveyor belt: the water sinking to the abyss in the northern Atlantic carries excess salt.

The ocean conveyor system maintains higher surface water temperatures in the northern Atlantic than in the northern Pacific. Warmer waters have a higher vapor pressure and lose more water to the air by evaporation. Thus the rate of evaporation from the Atlantic is higher than that from the Pacific. This creates a global "still": water is extracted from the warm Atlantic and transferred through the atmosphere to the cool Pacific.

The phenomenon that maintains this situation is a devilish one; the circulation pattern is self-reinforcing and hence self-stabilizing. The deep current is driven by the extra density supplied to the waters of the northern Atlantic through the enrichment of salt. The enrichment of salt is driven by the heat carried by the water that flows northward in the upper Atlantic. Thus we have a classic chicken and egg situation; excess evaporation causes the deep current and the deep current causes excess evaporation.

The self-stabilization of this great conveyor belt is like the radio automatic frequency control already mentioned. And like that control, the mode of operation of the joint ocean-atmosphere operation will jump if pushed too far. The evidence contained in paleoclimatic records seems to be telling us that the conveyor of today's ocean did not function during the glacial time. Hence it is tempting to conjecture that the turning on and off of the conveyor constitutes an important link between the earth's orbits and our climate. When the belt is in operation, the warmth it delivers prevents ice from accumulating on the lands surrounding the northern Atlantic; when the conveyor is not in operation, these lands are sufficiently cold to permit their glaciation. If this is indeed the case, then the orbitally induced changes in seasonality must somehow alter the extent to which the water evaporating from the Atlantic Ocean escapes removal by the precipitation that falls on continental areas whose drainage is back into the Atlantic. Salt buildup is caused only by that fraction of the water evaporating from the Atlantic that escapes these basins and falls as rain in the Pacific or on continental drainage basins feeding the Pacific.

As we do not yet understand enough about the rules controlling the transport of water vapor through the atmosphere, we cannot say why changes in seasonality cause changes in the transport of water vapor from one ocean basin to another. We can only say that compelling evidence exists in the marine-sediment record for a flipping on and off of the ocean conveyor belt. Since the most vulnerable attribute of the conveyor is water-vapor transport from the Atlantic to the Pacific, some link between this transport and seasonality seems logical.

Evidence for rapid jumps in climate on the land surrounding the northern Atlantic was discovered many decades ago by scientists studying pollen grains preserved in sediments. The record from bogs created during the early phases of the retreat of the icecap that covered Scandinavia and the British Isles during the last glaciation (20,000 to 14,000 years ago) shows a transition from the herbaceous shrubs of the cold period back to the forests of a warmer period. Those early postglacial forests persisted for about 2,000 years and then were suddenly replaced by shrubs akin to those of glacial time. This intense cold snap lasted about 700 years and then just as suddenly came to an end, permitting the forests to return. This brief reversion to cold conditions, which punctuated the period of deglaciation, was named the Younger Dryas (dryas is one of the herbaceous plants that clothed the landscape during the glacial time).

Like other signs pointing to rapid climate change, this rather extraordinary and relatively short-lived return to cold conditions was not given very high billing until Oeschger's group found the rapid CO_2 changes. It then became the focus of attention because detailed records for many localities on the earth's surface were available for the time interval when the earth emerged from its last episode of glaciation. Furthermore, the records from those sites showed that the Younger Dryas had a distinct geographic pattern. It is a prominent feature in records from the floor of the northern Atlantic and the surrounding continental areas (Maritime Canada, Greenland, and northern Europe). But it is not found in records from the continental United States.

This geographic pattern has been shown by computer simulations of the global climate system to be what would be expected if the ocean conveyor belt were to be turned off (and with it the enormous amount of heat delivered to the atmosphere above the northern Atlantic). Air temperatures over the eastern fringe of Canada, over Greenland, and over much of western Europe would plunge about 15°F. By contrast, no significant change in temperature would be seen in the United States. Hence, the geographic pattern of the Younger Dryas event points to the ocean conveyor as the causal villain.

Evidence from ocean-sediment cores taken in the northern Atlantic strengthens this case. Not only do the shells of the surface-dwelling plankton show a dramatic shift back to cold-water species during the Younger Dryas interval but also, as shown by Edward Boyle of MIT, the content of the trace metal cadmium in the shells of bottom-dwelling foraminifera indicates that cold deep waters, akin to those present during glacial times, returned during the Younger Dryas.

So we get the following picture. A full-fledged glaciation dominated our planet from about 20,000 to about 14,000 years ago. This corresponded to a time when the earth's orbital cycles gave rise to reduced seasonality at high latitudes in the Northern Hemisphere. During this time the ocean was "on another station," meaning its conveyor belt was not in operation. Then, as the orbits led to gradual strengthening of seasonality, the conveyor was switched back on. The heat released by the conveyor to the atmosphere over the northern Atlantic caused the great ice sheets to melt. But about 2,000 years later the conveyor came to an abrupt halt, bringing back cold conditions to the lands around the northern Atlantic. Then after a 700-year hiatus, the conveyor belt sprang back into action and has run steadily up to the present. Why the brief stoppage?

To understand what appears to be the answer to this question, we must first appreciate that a staggering 12-million cubic miles of water was bound up in the continental ice sheets of the Northern Hemisphere at the peak of the last glaciation. During the 5,000-year period when this ice melted away, the flow of meltwater must have averaged about half the current discharge of the Northern Hemisphere's combined rivers. Where it went would therefore have an important impact on the ocean's salt cycle.

Geologists studying the deposits left behind during the retreat of the largest of the glacial icecaps, the one that covered Canada from the Rocky Mountains to the Atlantic Ocean, have reconstructed the routes taken by the meltwater released from its southern margin. Their studies reveal that during the initial phases of melting, all routes converged on the Mississippi River and hence all the meltwater flowed into the Gulf of Mexico. However, starting about 11,800 years ago, those routes were captured one after another by eastward-leading channels that progressively opened as the ice front retreated to the north. First, the water entering the basins of what are now Lakes Erie and Ontario was diverted to the sea through the Hudson River valley. Then the water entering the basins of what are present-day Lakes Huron and Michigan was diverted to the Saint Lawrence River valley through a channel in the glacially depressed landscape north of Lake Erie. Finally, the biggest and most important of these diversions occurred when a lobe of ice blocking off the eastern end of what is now Lake Superior melted, allowing water to flow into Lake Huron and from there to the Saint Lawrence. At this point all the water melting from the southern margin of the Laurentide ice sheet was flowing eastward into the Atlantic. Nearly all of this water reached the Atlantic via the Saint Lawrence River. While the diversion of the meltwater from the Mississippi to the Saint Lawrence occurred in several discrete steps over a period of about 800 years, the largest of these diversions was the last, involving the meltwater released from about 60 percent of the southern perimeter of the Laurentide ice sheet. As dated by the radiocarbon method, it occurred about 11,000 years ago. Within the margin of error of such age determinations, this corresponds to the time the Younger Dryas began.

Scientists understand why the sudden diversion of a large meltwater flow from the Mississippi River to the Saint Lawrence would affect the ocean conveyor. As stated above, an essential feature of this system is the densification through cooling of high salt content water in the northern Atlantic. Today, the sinking of this water feeds a globe-encircling deep current. The sudden influx directly into the northern Atlantic of an amount of water equivalent to that carried by the Amazon River would almost certainly diminish the salinity of surface waters in the northern Atlantic enough to disrupt the deep-water formation process. One might say that the Younger Dryas was not only a warning about the manner in which climate reacts when pushed but also clearly showed that the coupling between the transport of fresh water across the earth's surface and the transport of salt within the sea is a critical element in the earth's response to climate change.

If this reading of the paleoclimatic record is correct, then we must face up to the reality that our climatic system does not operate in an orderly manner. As the greenhouse gases we produce build up, the ocean-atmosphere system may leap to yet another mode of operation. Unfortunately, the paleoclimatic record provides no clues as to how the earth's climate system responds when warmed beyond its prevailing state. Over the period for which our paleoenvironmental records are sufficiently detailed to permit such reconstructions, climate has not been significantly warmer than today's. So we are pushing the earth into an unknown realm. We have no way to predict how the great ocean conveyor will respond, nor can we be sure of other important elements of the system, which are subject to dramatic change.

The computer simulations that have greatly improved our ability to predict weather have also told us some important things about the possible response to the greenhouse buildup. But because of their basic design, these computer models cannot tell us anything about the ocean-atmosphere system and leaping climates. At present no one knows how to incorporate the oceans into these simulations. Decades may pass before this can be done. Even then I doubt if computer simulations will offer much insight into the changes in climate that might be triggered by the greenhouse buildup.

The upshot is that we must take our greenhouse experiment more seriously. Rather than treating it as a cocktail hour curiosity, we must view it as a threat to human beings and wildlife that can be resolved only by serious study over many decades. We must expand our efforts to understand the operation of each of the units of the earth's climate system and how they interact.

Only in this way will our grandchildren be able to prepare wisely for the changes that are bound to be wrought by our great experiment.

THE CLIMATIC AND OTHER GLOBAL EFFECTS OF NUCLEAR WAR[4]

A nuclear war would be totally unlike any previous form of warfare in its immeasurably greater destructive power. Atom bombs of the type used at Hiroshima and Nagasaki represented an increase in explosive power from the equivalent of tons of trinitrotoluene (TNT) to thousands of tons (kilotons). Hydrogen bombs, developed about a decade later, represented an increase from thousands of tons to as much as millions of tons (megatons). More than 50,000 nuclear weapons now exist throughout the world amounting to an estimated total yield of some 15,000 megatons (about 5,000 times greater than that of all the explosives used in World War II).

The publication in 1982 of "The Atmosphere after a Nuclear War: Twilight at Noon" marked a turning point in the consideration of the indirect effects of a large-scale nuclear war. The authors realized that large quantities of light-absorbing smoke particles would be injected into the atmosphere by fires ignited by nuclear explosions. The incoming sunlight, which warms the Earth's surface and provides the energy that drives atmospheric processes and biological production, would be reduced by the smoke and soot, altering the weather and influencing climate. Further calculations on the amounts of combustible material, smoke emission, and radiative properties of the smoke supported the hypothesis. Significant potential effects on natural ecosystems, fisheries, and agriculture were recognized. Agricultural supplies for the survivors of the direct effects would be jeopardized. . . .

[4]Reprinted from the first chapter of UN Document A/43/351, June 1988.

Progress on Key Scientific Issues

Earlier estimates of the amount of combustible material (fuel loading) have been refined by successive analyses of production and inventory, such as a recent detailed survey of a representative set of targets in the United States. While global estimates that up to 150 million metric tons of smoke could be released into the atmosphere remain generally credible, recent work has indicated that these amounts are in the upper range. On the other hand, estimates of the components of smoke emissions produced by burning materials such as petroleum and plastics in large fires have increased substantially. Moreover, arising from recent measurements in laboratory work and in small-scale fires, estimates of the ability of smoke produced in urban fires to absorb sunlight have increased by as much as three times over some earlier calculations. This dark, sooty component of smoke emissions is now recognized as the most important factor with regard to effects on the atmosphere and climate and, accordingly, much of the recent research has focused on the characteristics of soot particles.

This large amount of smoke and soot would absorb a substantial fraction of incoming solar radiation over much of the Northern Hemisphere. Estimates of the reduction of insolation vary considerably, depending on the scenario; in instances of concentrated smoke, the available light at the Earth's surface might be only 1 percent of normal for periods of a few days and less than 20 percent of normal for a few weeks or more.

Smoke injected by large fires can initially reach altitudes of as high as 15 kilometers, although most will be in the 5- to 10-kilometer range. The rising smoke eventually stabilizes, allowing the smoke to spread laterally at the stabilization height. Subsequent heating of the smoke by absorption of solar radiation can result in the further ascent of the smoke particles. Recent modeling studies indicate that such large-scale lofting from midlatitudes during the Northern Hemisphere summer may carry a large fraction of the smoke as high as 30 kilometers. The self-induced lofting of nuclear war smoke suggests that its residence time in the stratosphere could be greatly increased, that substantial quantities of smoke could be transported to the Southern Hemisphere, and that the integrity of the stratospheric ozone layer could be threatened.

The removal efficiency of smoke by clouds and precipitation ("scavenging" and "removal") is presently assumed to be in the range of 30 to 50 percent during the first few days following smoke generation, although uncertainties are large and the actual amounts removed could be greater or lesser. The removal processes include the prompt scavenging in "black rain" directly over the conflagrations expected after a nuclear exchange, as well as subsequent scavenging by precipitation downwind of the fires. Scavenging of the smoke would decrease the potential for light reductions, and patchiness would produce lighter and darker regions locally. Recent laboratory and field measurements of smoke properties suggest that the removal efficiency for the blackest, sootiest smoke may be smaller than is currently assumed. Accordingly, further refinement of the smoke (soot) scavenging estimates is needed.

New laboratory studies indicate that soot reaching the stratosphere (by direct injection and self-lofting) is not likely to be rapidly decomposed by reacting with ozone and that decomposition may take about a year or more. This important result implies that soot layers could be quite stable in the upper atmosphere, allowing them to spread globally, with the potential for long-term effects on the global climate.

Although still highly simplified, significant advances have been made in modeling the atmospheric response to massive smoke injections. The laws governing relevant atmospheric processes are cast in mathematical form and the resulting equations solved on high-speed computers. Such computations, using advanced general circulation models, are now capable of representing in detail the changes in solar and thermal infrared radiation transfer, the hydrologic cycle, as well as atmospheric circulation and dynamics. Such models, adapted for simulation of "nuclear winter" conditions, have been developed at the Los Alamos National Laboratory, the National Center for Atmospheric Research, and the Lawrence Livermore National Laboratory in the United States; the Computing Center of the USSR Academy of Sciences in the Soviet Union; the United Kingdom Meteorological Office; and the Commonwealth Scientific Industrial Research Organization in Australia. Work on these models has led to significant general advances in climate modeling capabilities. These models confirm the possibility that subfreezing temperatures may be reached in localized regions even in summer. They also show substantial reductions of precipitation and suppression of the summer monsoon, even with relatively small amounts of smoke. Moreover, the potential for climatic effects lasting for a period of one year or more has been recognized, with the possibility of average global temperatures decreasing by several degrees, which could have a major effect on agriculture.

There is now ample observational evidence that the smoke from natural forest fires and dust, if present in sufficient quantities, can cause decreases of several degrees in daytime temperatures in a matter of hours to days. These reductions are reproduced well by the models, which means that the basic physical processes are sufficiently understood. This also increases confidence in the model results showing more severe temperature reductions if very large quantities of smoke were injected into the atmosphere by fires started after a nuclear exchange.

The injection into the stratosphere of the nitrogen oxides produced in a nuclear fireball and of air from the lower atmosphere, which is low in ozone, the displacement of the ozone-rich lower stratospheric air, and the dependence of chemical reaction rates on the anticipated temperature increase of the stratosphere are also being studied with respect to their potential for reducing the amount of stratospheric ozone. Ozone depletion would imply increased damaging ultraviolet solar radiation reaching the Earth's surface for several years following a nuclear exchange. Current estimates are that ozone reduction could be very substantial, on the order of 50 percent. Because of the great potential importance of this problem, it urgently needs further study.

The electromagnetic pulse, caused by high-altitude nuclear detonations, can disrupt and damage a wide variety of electrical and electronic components and devices, leading to the loss of power, of communications, and of other services out to distances of thousands of kilometers. This would represent a significant additional disruption to the infrastructure on which survivors would have to rely.

Early radiation, along with blast and heat, would kill many people in the immediate vicinity of the explosions and destroy the housing, sanitation, transportation, and medical facilities. Beyond the areas of devastation, nuclear fallout from the explosions themselves and from the destruction of nuclear installations would spread globally and be a source of continuous radiation exposure for years. The long-term consequences (including cancers, malformations, and possibly genetic effects) among the survivors of the initial radiation burst and those exposed to fallout would be significant, but their importance would be considerably smaller than consequences of the early effects and those resulting from disruption of basic infrastructures, including medical and food distribution services, for months and perhaps years after the event.

Findings and Conclusions

The group's examination of the evolution of scientific thought on the global environmental consequences of a nuclear war reveals a clear convergence toward consensus. The criticisms and objections that have been raised from time to time—mostly concerned with uncertainty and limitations of early models— have been reviewed by this and other expert groups and do not invalidate the conclusion that a large-scale nuclear war could have a significant effect on global climate.

The scientific evidence is now conclusive that a major nuclear war would entail the high risk of a global environmental disruption. The risk would be greatest if large cities and industrial centers in the Northern Hemisphere were to be targeted in the summer months. During the first month solar energy reaching the surface in midlatitudes of the Northern Hemisphere could be reduced by 80 percent or more. This would result in a decrease of continental averaged temperatures in midlatitudes of between 5° and 20° C below normal within two weeks after the injection of smoke during summer months. In central continental areas individual temperature decreases could be substantially greater. Three-dimensional atmospheric circulation models with detailed representations of physical processes indicate regional episodes of subfreezing temperatures, even in summer. These temperature decreases are somewhat smaller than suggested by earlier, less complex atmospheric models, but the agricultural and ecological impacts are no less devastating. Recent work presented at the workshop in Moscow of the Scientific Committee on Problems of the Environment (SCOPE) study group on the environmental consequences of nuclear war (ENUWAR) suggests that these impacts might be compounded by a decrease in rainfall of as much as 80 percent over land in temperate and tropical latitudes. The evidence assessed to date is persuasive that residual scientific uncertainties are unlikely to invalidate these conclusions.

Beyond one month agricultural production and the survival of natural ecosystems would be threatened by a considerable reduction in sunlight, temperature depressions of several degrees below normal, and suppression of precipitation and summer monsoons. In addition, these effects would be aggravated by chemical pollutants, an increase in ultraviolet radiation associated with depletion of ozone, and the likely persistence of radioactive hot spots.

The sensitivity of agricultural systems and natural ecosystems to variations in temperature, precipitation, and light leads to the conclusion that the widespread impact of a nuclear exchange on climate would constitute a severe threat to world food production. The prospect of widespread starvation as a consequence of a nuclear war would confront both targeted and nontargeted nations. This would be aggravated by the increasing dependence of food production on inputs of energy and fertilizers and the dependence of food distribution and availability on a smoothly functioning societal system of communications, transportation, trade, and commerce. The human impacts would be exacerbated by an almost complete breakdown of health care in targeted countries and the likelihood of an increase in damaging ultraviolet radiation. The direct effects of a major nuclear exchange could kill hundreds of millions; the indirect effects could kill billions.

The socioeconomic consequences in a world interconnected economically, socially, and environmentally would be grave. The functions of production, distribution, and consumption in existing socioeconomic systems would be completely disrupted. The severe physical damage from blast, fire, and radiation in the targeted countries would preclude the type of support that made recovery possible following World War II. The breakdown of life-support systems, communications, transportation, the world financial system, and other systems would compound the difficulties caused by food shortages in nontargeted countries. Long-term recovery would be uncertain.

The immediate and direct effects of nuclear explosions and the global environmental consequences of a major nuclear war constitute a continuum. Each would exacerbate the other. Moreover, there would be synergy within each aspect as well as between them, so that the integrated total effect of fire, blast, and radioactivity would be greater than their sum. Similarly, temperature decreases, brief subfreezing episodes, diminished precipitation, suppressed monsoons, and increased ultraviolet radiation would interact in a manner that would compound their separate effects. The global environmental disruption resulting from a major nuclear war would be inseparably related to its direct and localized effects. Both should be considered in resolving policy issues of nuclear weaponry and should be the concern of all nations.

The possibility exists that further global environmental consequences of a major nuclear exchange may yet be identified. The United Nations study group believes that the cooperative, international scientific effort that has identified this new dimension of nuclear warfare should be continued to refine present findings and to explore new possibilities. For example, there is a need to resolve the emerging issue of a possibly massive depletion of ozone as a result of a major nuclear war and the ensuing increase in ultraviolet radiation with potentially serious consequences for exposed living organisms.

The scientific advances that have led to a clearer understanding of the global consequences of a major nuclear war should be pursued internationally. They should also interact strongly with the analysis of public policy decisions on these issues that have potential implications for noncombatant nations as well as for nations that might be in conflict. The discussion of these matters has underscored the importance of the dialogue between the world scientific community and public policymakers—a dialogue that has illuminated this general issue during the 1980s.

APOCALYPSE AGAIN[5]

Some say the world will end in fire,
Some say in ice.

—ROBERT FROST

[5]Article by Peter Shaw. Reprinted from *Commentary*, April 1989, by permission. Copyright © 1989 by Peter Shaw. All rights reserved.

Predictions of the end of the world, as old as human history itself and lately a subject of scholarly inquiry, have by no means abated in our own time. Nor are those who believe in such predictions confined to isolated religious sects, as was the case as recently as the 19th century. While such sects do continue regularly to spring up and disappear, predictions of catastrophe have become the virtual orthodoxy of society as a whole. Journalists, educators, churchmen, and philosophers daily endorse one or another script foretelling the end of individual life, of human civilization, or of the entire earth. Some say the world will end in fire—through the conflagration of a nuclear holocaust; some say in ice—through the same event, this time precipitating a "nuclear winter."

Fire and ice. We need only add earth and air to include within the apocalyptic genre all four of the elements understood as basic by the Greeks, and water to include the biblical account of the flood. Contemporary prophecies of flood are stated in apparently scientific terms: as a result of global warming, the polar ice caps will melt and inundate the world's major cities. As for earth and air, we anticipate the disappearance of the one thanks to the erosion of farmland and shorelines, while the other is to be depleted of its ozone, if not first saturated with carbon dioxide or poisoned by man-made pollutants.

Pagan man projected his fears outward; contemporary man internalizes. Like biblical man (at least to that very limited extent) he holds himself, or more accurately his own society, responsible for the coming end of the world. Not only the disaster allegedly threatened by pollutants but every prospective modern apocalypse stipulates man rather than the gods or nature as the primal cause. And the charge is always the same: whether it is to be by fire or by ice, mankind faces extinction as a punishment for its impiety.

The continuities and discontinuities between ancient and modern imaginations of disaster would amount to no more than curiosities if it were the case that superstitious fears had been replaced by rational ones. But it is not the case. On the contrary, given the best scientific understanding of reality available to early man, it made sense for him to ascribe natural disasters, present and future, to the gods. Later, it made sense for the Greeks to ascribe such disasters to some wayward or even malign characteristic of matter itself. Nor was Empedocles a simpleton for regarding the personification of the elements by gods as a persuasive account of reality. Would that our own conceptions of apocalypse were similarly founded on the best available scientific understanding. Instead, most if not all of the disasters currently being predicted have gained widespread credence *despite* a lack of scientific basis, or even in the face of definitive counterevidence.

Without question the most spectacular example of such a wholly suppositions theory has to do with the so-called greenhouse effect. The greenhouse effect itself, as every schoolchild knows, is simply the process by which the earth's atmosphere traps enough heat from the sun to create a habitable planet. As for the disaster scenario that bears the same name, it posits, in the words of a New York *Times* editorial, an increased "warming of the atmosphere by waste gases from a century of industrial activity." The *Times* goes on:

The greenhouse theory holds that certain waste gases let in sunlight but trap heat, which otherwise would escape into space. Carbon dioxide has been steadily building up through the burning of coal and oil—and because forests, which absorb the gas, are fast being destroyed.

Now, aside from the mistaken assumption that forests worldwide are decreasing in size (they are not), the theory of a runaway greenhouse effect, otherwise known as global warming, presents even its advocates with a variety of internal contradictions. In the first place, the earth has a number of mechanisms for ameliorating fluctuations in global temperature: a significant rise in temperature, for example, leads to increased evaporation from the oceans; this is followed by the formation of clouds that shield the sun and then by a compensating drop in temperature. Too, if the greenhouse theory were valid, a global warming trend should be observable in records of temperatures soon after the jump in man-made carbon dioxide that is the result of modern industrial activity. Yet if there has been such a rise over the past one hundred years, it does not follow but precedes the onset of modern industrialism, and anyway it amounts to a barely detectable change of no more than one degree Fahrenheit over the entire period.

Here is a particularly significant problem for any hypothesis—the lack of evidence. Purveyors of the global-warming theory counter it by pointing to computer projections which show a catastrophic upward trend in the *next* century. Once again, however, a knotty problem presents itself: computer models, writes Andrew R. Solow, a statistician at Woods Hole Oceanographic Institution, "have a hard time reproducing current climate from current data. They cannot be expected to predict future climate with any precision."

Does any of this detract from the persuasive power of the global-warming theory? Apparently not. As in certain forms of religion, the less evidence, the more faith. And in the resultant climate of belief (as it deserves to be called), not only the lack of evidence but even outright counterevidence can work to a theory's benefit. According to the late Leon Festinger, Henry W. Riecken, and Stanley Schachter, the authors of the classic study, *When Prophecy Fails* (1956), "Although there is a limit beyond which belief will not stand disconfirmation, it is clear that the introduction of contrary evidence can serve to increase the conviction and enthusiasm of a believer." So it has been during the most recent phase of prediction, which itself represents a revival of the great irruption of ecological warnings that dominated the early 1970's.

The central document in that earlier wave was *Limits to Growth*, a report issued by the Club of Rome in 1972 foretelling a worldwide doom brought on by the combined forces of "resource depletion," overpopulation, pollution, and starvation. The future conjured up by computer simulation in *Limits to Growth* bore a certain resemblance to the still more spectacularly stated predictions of Paul Ehrlich in his 1968 book, *Population Bomb*. Ehrlich had offered specific dates for specific catastrophes: 1983, for example, would see a precipitous decline in American harvests and the institution of food rationing, by which time a billion people worldwide would have already starved to death. The Club of Rome, more cautiously, assigned likely years for the exhaustion of specific resources: petroleum (1992), silver (1985), natural gas (1994), mercury (1985), tin (1987).

In 1982 one of the authors of the Club of Rome report had to admit that his predictions were not coming true. Yet he was not repentant. There may have been a postponement, a temporary reprieve, but man and the earth still remained poised on the brink of cataclysm. Presumably Paul Ehrlich, who never recanted, felt the same way. Just so have members of religious sects always responded when their confidently predicted apocalypses pass without incident.

True, the general public and even some members of the sect begin to fall away after such disappointments; in our time, both Paul Ehrlich and the Club of Rome did fade out of the spotlight. But instructively, and in contrast to the sects studied in *When Prophecy Fails*, they did so without having been exposed to the full glare of adverse publicity and ridicule that used to attend the collapse of prophecy. Perhaps that is why so little time elapsed before the public could be brought to credit similar predictions.

For even as the "population bomb" failed to explode on schedule, or ecological disaster to strike, new predictions of not only global but galactic proportions were being prepared. By the late 1980's these were receiving the same respectful, credulous hearing as their forerunners, and were being promoted just as avidly by the press. In the case of nuclear winter, the most publicized apocalypse, the cycle from prediction to publicity to disconfirmation took only a few years, from approximately 1985 to 1988; yet once again the end came without bringing ridicule or discredit to the theoreticians.

Nuclear winter was at once a prediction of what would happen after a nuclear war and the claim that an identical disaster, never detected in the geological record, had already taken place once before, in the age of the dinosaurs. A giant explosion, the theory went, had been caused on earth by a "nemesis" or "death star" wheeling in from far out in the universe and returning so quickly whence it had come as to be invisible to the most farseeing of modern telescopes. The clouds of dust kicked up by that explosion had shielded the sun and thus caused the earth's vegetation to wither, bringing about the extinction of the dinosaurs by cold and starvation. The lesson for the mid-1980's was clear: intermediate-range nuclear missiles should not be emplaced in Western Europe and disarmament should commence forthwith.

As chance would have it, not long after the nuclear-winter theory gained currency there was a giant volcanic eruption at Mount St. Helens in the state of Washington. It was followed by the spreading of just such dark clouds as had been described— but without any hint of the predicted effect on vegetation or climate. At about the same time, too, paleontologists demonstrated that the dinosaurs could not possibly have been the casualties of a single, catastrophic event, since they had disappeared over a period of some thousands of years. Finally, a check of some of the nuclear-winter projections exposed gaping errors of math and physics.

As a result of these and other refutations of the theory, nuclear winter died its own death-by-theoretical-starvation. But so quickly was its place taken by similar predictions, similarly linked to geopolitical issues, that the event seems to have almost entirely escaped notice. Nuclear winter remains today in the public mind as a proven hypothesis, vying for popularity with its mirror opposite, the greenhouse effect.

Actually, not so long ago (as the journalist John Chamberlain has pointed out) we were being assured that we were living not in a warming but in a "cooling world." In the 1970's, as *Science* magazine reported in 1975, meteorologists were "almost unanimous" that such a trend was taking place, and that its consequences, especially for agriculture, were potentially disastrous. Climatologists, according to *Fortune* magazine, warned that the cooling trend "could bring massive tragedies for mankind." A decade later, all of this quite forgotten, the opposite theory of global warming has drifted past the rocks of evidentiary lack, tumbled safely through the falls of skepticism, and sailed triumphantly onto the smooth lake of public respect.

The status of global warming as an unassailable, self-evident truth was recently confirmed by the reaction to a scientific report that challenges its assumptions. This report, compiled at the National Oceanic and Atmospheric Administration and duly described on the front page of the New York *Times* and other newspapers, traces U.S. temperatures since 1895. It shows that the putative one-degree rise in temperature worldwide over the past hundred years, a figure widely accepted even by many of those skeptical of the global-warming scenario, is wrong for the United States. As the *Times* headline put it: "U.S. Data Since 1895 Fail to Show Warming Trend."

The reaction was immediate. All of the experts consulted by the *Times* were in agreement that the report does not set back the global-warming theory by so much as an iota. Prominent among these experts was Dr. James E. Hansen, director of the National Aeronautic and Space Administration's Institute for Space Studies in Manhattan, a leading proponent of global warming and the man who produced the data showing a one-degree rise in global temperature. "We have to be careful about interpreting things like this," he warned, and went on to explain that the United States covers only a small portion of the earth's surface. Besides, the steadiness of the temperature readings could be a "statistical fluke." Note the implicit distinction here: we must be "careful" in interpreting data that appear reassuring, but it is virtually our duty to indulge any strongly felt premonitions of disaster even if they are based on the flimsiest evidence, or none.

The concept of the "statistical fluke" could easily be applied to many current predictions, but is not. Thus, the acidification of a number of fresh-water lakes in the eastern United States is considered not a fluke but a definite trend, even though it might be taken to fall well within the range of natural fluctuations. Similarly, the disturbing deaths of numerous dolphins during the summer of 1988 were traced to the same pattern of human depredation of the environment supposed to be causing acid rain and other ecological catastrophes. Later, it developed that the dolphins were killed by a so-called "red tide" of algae—itself first seen as a man-created scourge but then conceded to be a natural phenomenon. Here, in other words, was a genuine statistical fluke; but it was never labeled as such since it exonerated industrial man.

It does not give pause either to the catastrophists or to their credulous promoters in the media that some predictions cancel out others. Dr. Hansen, for example, suggests that the absence of a warming trend, as shown by the new study, might be "the result of atmospheric pollutants reflecting heat away from earth." Yet these are the same pollutant particles supposedly responsible for global warming in the first place. Now it develops that the particles they carry with them counter the greenhouse effect. In fact, Dr. Hansen is worried that "anti-pollution efforts are reducing the amount of these particles and thus reducing the reflection of heat" away from the earth. It is surely a measure of the power of catastrophic thinking that what may have been the first public revelation of an actual decrease in man-made atmospheric pollutants should prompt the fear that such a decrease itself portends the direst consequences.

What all this suggests is that we have come to depend at any given moment on a constant degree of threat. When times are bad—because of war, depression, or real natural disasters—proximate fears tend to dominate the imagination. When times are good—through the conquest of disease and famine, the achievement of high employment, prosperity, and an upward curve of longevity—apprehension has to be supplied from without. And during extended good times, a supply of fresh disasters is required as each one comes progressively to lose its appeal. Air pollution, rising to disaster proportions in the Club of Rome report, declines in importance but is soon succeeded by loss of the ozone layer, which will supposedly leave mankind vulnerable to the unfiltered rays of the sun and a consequent plague of, among other things, skin cancers and blindness. Continent-wide poisoning of fresh water through the eutrophication of lakes and streams from fertilizer runoff is forgotten only to be replaced by the threat of acid rain. Direct incineration of all mankind by atomic war cedes to a secondary stage of destruction by nuclear winter, and nuclear winter in turn to global warming.

This persistent and insistent imagining of disaster might be no more than a sideshow were it not for its political dimension. But in the 1970's and 80's, successive waves of catastrophism followed and reflected episodes of defeat for radical political movements. The 70's wave succeeded the collapse of the New Left and engaged many of that movement's disillusioned supporters (as well, of course, as many people opposed or indifferent to the New Left). That of the 80's followed the worldwide discrediting of the economic, political, and moral record of Communism. It was as if sanguine hopes of an end to the cold war required a compensatory new fear, one that natural catastrophe alone could supply. And thus, soon after James Baker's nomination as Secretary of State, a bipartisan memorandum from members of the Senate Foreign Relations Committee called his urgent attention to the leading foreign-policy issue he would have to face, a "global problem of unprecedented magnitude." The issue was global warming.

It goes without saying that clean air and water, the retention of farmland and forests, a satisfactory ozone layer, and the avoidance of nuclear war are all desirable things. But the pursuit of these goals through the rhetoric of hellfire renders more immediate political concerns mundane and secondary. Many are the societies that have been distracted from the actual dangers they faced by the allure of disasters wholly imaginary. That consideration aside, though, our obsession with distant and unprovable catastrophe is so stultifying, from both the moral and the intellectual point of view, as to constitute a cultural disaster in its own right.

III. THE POLITICS OF ECOLOGY

EDITOR'S INTRODUCTION

If the technological fixes for many ecological problems are not at all clear, the political ones are often even harder to achieve, especially when the problems are international in scope. A classic case is the acid rain dispute between Canada and the U.S. The Canadians have complained long and bitterly about emissions from U.S. smokestack industries acidifying Canadian waters. During the Reagan years, the U.S. government gave lip service to reducing acid rain, but did nothing about it under pressure from industries that did not want to bear the cost of switching to cleaner fuels or investing in emission-cleaning technologies. It was the desire for a comprehensive trade agreement with Canada that finally brought movement on the acid rain issue—although even now relatively little is being done to enforce new clean air standards. An even more intractable problem is presented by forest preservation efforts in Peru. The high Andean forest is being cleared by cocaine farmers for their crops; they are being protected both by drug traffickers and by Shining Path Marxist rebels, who see drugs as a way to bring down capitalist governments. Saving the Andean forest requires solutions to Peru's internal political instabilities and the U.S. drug problem before ecologists can even begin their work.

The global environment may replace arms control as the dominant international political issue of the coming decades. As former U.S. environmental official Richard E. Benedick notes in the speech that leads off this section, environmental degradation, overpopulation, and resource depletion contribute to political instability as much as racial, religious, economic, and ideological conflicts, a point reinforced by Norman Myers in his article on the environment and national security. A detailed case study of environmental politics in Great Britain by Timothy O'Riordan shows how even within one country it can be difficult to fashion rational environmental law from the competing interests of national and local governments, business, and environmental groups. The fourth selection, "Tropical Chic" by Peter P. Swire, targets the essential hypocrisy of the developed nations when they preach to the third world about ecological preservation; any pleas must be couched in terms that are economically appealing and ideologically flexible.

ENVIRONMENT IN THE FOREIGN POLICY AGENDA[1]

Last week, at Georgetown University, I encountered an eminent statesman, Kenneth Rush, under whom I had served quite a few years ago, when I was a junior Foreign Service officer and he was U.S. Ambassador to Germany. He inevitably asked me what I was doing now, and when I told him, his face brightened with enthusiasm and interest. We both realized that when we were in Germany, my present position did not even exist in the State Department; environment was simply not on the foreign policy agenda. And this distinguished diplomat, the architect of the famous accord that finally guaranteed the freedom of West Berlin, clearly recognized the contemporary importance of environmental isssues for U.S. foreign policy—and was delighted to learn that I was in the middle of them.

It is certainly true that this is not traditional diplomacy. Although, like Kenneth Rush, we negotiate treaties with foreign countries, we are not redrawing frontiers but, rather, are dealing with exports of hazardous chemicals or protection of wetlands. We go to the United Nations to argue not about border conflicts but about possible damage to the marine environment from ocean disposal of radioactive waste. And when the professional diplomats in this new field sit down at the negotiating table, we are flanked by a new breed of international lawyers, as well as by an imposing array of atmospheric physicists, zoologists, or molecular biologists. In the course of a week, my personal portfolio can range from the ocean depths to stratospheric ozone; from recombinant DNA [deoxyribonucleic acid] to African rhinos; from sewage treatment in Tijuana, Mexico, close to our border, to the

[1]Address by Richard E. Benedick, then Deputy Assistant Secretary for Environment, Health, and Natural Resources, before the *Ecology Law Quarterly* Symposium on Environmental and International Development on March 27, 1986. Reprinted from *Department of State Bulletin*, June 1986.

impact of population resettlement on the tropical rainforests of the outer islands of Indonesia.

A New Dimension of Diplomacy

Why is it that such esoteric themes are now on the foreign policy agenda? To answer that question, let me share with you an impression from last year's meeting of the UN Environment Program's (UNEP) Governing Council in Nairobi. The highlight of this meeting was the joint appearance of an American astronaut and a Soviet cosmonaut to inaugurate a new UNEP program utilizing space technology to monitor global environmental trends. The audience—which comprised seasoned UN and government officials from all over the world, international press, and Kenyan schoolchildren—was universally transfixed by the simplicity and sincerity of the message of the space voyagers. For both the American scientist and the Soviet Air Force major made vivid, for all of us in that hall, what is possibly the most inspiring and poignant image of our century: planet Earth as seen from outer space—this beautiful blue sphere, radiating life and light, alone and fragile in the still vastness of the cosmos. From this perspective, the maps of geopolitics and diplomacy vanish, and the underlying interconnectedness of all the components of this unique living system—animal, vegetable, mineral, water, air, climate—becomes evident.

It is this sense of interdependence that has fostered a growing realization in foreign ministries around the world that many international activities—trade, industrial investment, development assistance—have profound implications for the environment. Nations share a responsibility to protect human health and to preserve the common natural heritage. In the State Department, we have come to recognize that U.S. national interests in promoting human freedom and economic growth can be undermined by instability in other countries related to environmental degradation, population pressures, and resource scarcity.

Thus, a new dimension has been added to our diplomacy. This is reflected in the growing number of international agreements concerning the environment: efforts to promote cooperation in scientific research and exchange of data; to develop internationally accepted guidelines or principles; to harmonize regulatory measures.

The negotiations on such accords are heavy in scientific and legal content; indeed, international environmental law is itself a rapidly growing field. Negotiations are monitored closely—and frequently attended—by representatives of Congress, industry, and citizens' groups.

For the issues are complex, sensitive, and often emotionally charged. Human health may be at stake, but so, too, are jobs. Trade patterns can be affected. The quality of life and the esthetics of flora and fauna and landscape are also involved.

Against this background, I would like to highlight for you today five aspects of U.S. international environmental policy, illustrated by examples from our current agenda. These are:

• Maintaining the tradition of U.S. leadership;

• Reconciling economic growth with environmental protection in the Third World;

• Working to improve the international system;

• Promoting, and relying on, the best possible science; and

• Pursuing a balanced, nonconfrontational approach that engages the private sector.

U.S. Leadership

The United States has been the leader among the world's nations in recognizing—and acting upon—environmental problems. Following passage of the Clean Air Act, for example, emissions of sulfur dioxide declined by 28% from 1973 to 1983. Over the past 15 years, approximately $70 billion has been spent on stringent motor vehicle emission controls, which have substantially improved the air quality of our cities, whereas Europe is just beginning this process. U.S. laws regulating pesticides, industrial chemicals, and toxic wastes—originating in the 1970s, or even earlier, and continually amended to reflect newer science—have served as models to other countries.

This leadership is also reflected in our participation in some 20 international treaties, ranging from the Convention on International Trade in Endangered Species to the Cartagena Convention for the Protection and Development of the Marine Environment of the Wider Caribbean Region.

The United States cooperates with over 70 countries through 275 bilateral agreements which either are wholly environmental

in scope or which have significant environmental components—
for example, one with China on acid rain research, another with
Nigeria on water quality. The United States also contributes
funds or support in kind to 70 specialized environmental or natural resource programs carried out in 40 international or regional
organizations, such as the International Register of Potentially
Toxic Chemicals and the International Union for the Conservation of Nature.

Leadership also implies involvement in environmental issues
at the top. This was exemplified in the headlines last week describing President Reagan's full endorsement of the report and
recommendations on acid rain produced by Special Envoy Drew
Lewis and his Canadian counterpart. The President also joined
with other leaders of the major industrial countries at the Bonn
economic summit last year in a formal declaration which began,
"New approaches and strengthened international co-operation
are essential to anticipate and prevent damage to the environment, which knows no national frontiers," and concluded, "We
shall work with developing countries for the avoidance of environmental damage and disasters worldwide."

Environment and Development

Thus, my second theme, environment and development—
the subject of this symposium—is clearly on the agenda of world
leaders. This was also a dominant issue at the 1972 UN Conference on the Human Environment, in Stockholm, which was an international landmark in drawing attention to the need for
reconciling economic growth with protection of the environment.

Unfortunately, it is all too easy to find discrepancies between
the well intended rhetoric of Stockholm and the environmental
reality in many developing countries today: deforestation in
Thailand and Honduras, massive soil erosion in Haiti and Nepal,
hazardous air quality in Mexico City and Ankara, the advance of
the deserts in Sahelian Africa, destruction of wildlife habitat in
the Amazon rainforests, industrial pollution of the Nile—these
are only a sampling.

On the other hand, there is incontestably an evolution in attitudes toward environment in the Third World. The South was
initially suspicious that warnings from the North about the envi-

ronment were a disguised attempt to limit economic growth—
and hence the industrial competitiveness—of the poorer countries. Now, there is a new appreciation among Third World
governments of the enormous human and financial costs if environmental considerations are ignored in the headlong rush for
industrialization.

Since Stockholm, many developing countries have established
new ministries to look after the environment; some of these have
achieved reasonable prominence and effectiveness within their
governments. Environmental education and training have much
improved; better data have been compiled and disseminated;
some legislation is in place. There is even growing awareness
among the public in the Third World: citizens in Egypt are pro-
testing against pollution, and a few weeks ago a local conservation
group in Bolivia denounced—and was able to reverse—a government decision to sell monkeys of a threatened species to the U.S.
Agency for International Development (AID) for malaria research.

Lest this last mentioned anomaly leave a false impression of
AID, let me hasten to add that this development agency contributes significantly to environmental protection in the Third
World, with programs involving biological diversity, guidelines
for pesticides, environmental training, national conservation
strategies, and support for nongovernmental organizations.

A particularly important development since Stockholm is the
special attention being focused on the world's tropical forests.
The Administrator of AID, Peter McPherson, sent a personal
message to all overseas missions in November 1984, warning that
"destruction of humid tropical forests is one of the most important environmental issues for the remainder of his century." The
cable provided strong policy guidance for efforts to help other
countries in preserving and properly managing their forests.

The World Resources Institute, a private, U.S.-based organization, released several months ago a meticulously documented
study entitled "Tropical Forests: A Call for Action." This study,
prepared in collaboration with the World Banks and the UN Development Program, stimulated the UN Food and Agriculture
Organization (FAO) to produce a "Tropical Forestry Action
Plan," which the United States strongly supports. The State Department has also encouraged UNEP and FAO to further improve data on the state of the world's forests, and we are giving

tropical forest research highest priority within the U.S. Man and the Biosphere Program. I would also note that the State Department, together with the U.S. Forest Service, reconstituted this year an interagency task force to update U.S. strategy for this sector. Finally, we are working much more closely with the World Bank and regional development banks to ensure that their lending is consistent with sound environmental management of forests.

Having mentioned the development banks in the forestry context, I should note that there is a growing recognition that their loan programs generally must take much greater account of the environment than has been customary in the past. Currently, the State Department, together with the U.S. Treasury Department and AID, uses an early warning system involving our overseas missions to uncover potential environmental problems in proposed loans. Meetings are being held with World Bank staff on such lending sectors as irrigation and forestry. And, evidencing the high level of attention to this issue, Secretary of State George Shultz sent a cable last October to all U.S. ambassadors requesting their personal involvement in efforts by American embassies to monitor the environmental implications of proposed development bank projects.

Let me conclude this consideration of environment and development linkages by stressing the ultimate responsibility of the Third World governments themselves for securing an environmentally sound future for their people. We have seen from international efforts on desertification in Africa that external assistance, technology, plans, and rhetoric are not enough—if the governments of the affected countries themselves will not pursue environmentally sound national economic, agricultural, and development policies.

International Organizations

A third aspect of our agenda is active U.S. participation in key multilateral organizations which deal with environmental issues. UNEP, mentioned earlier, is our principal forum for programs involving developing countries. In the OECD [Organization for Economic Cooperation and Development], we consult with the major Western industrialized countries. The UN's Economic Commission for Europe (ECE) is our forum for East-West dealings on transboundary environmental issues. In addition, we work on environmental problems in such other international organizations as the UN Food and Agriculture Organization, International Maritime Organization, World Health Organization, World Meteorological Organization (WMO), and many others.

Our basic philosophy in these organizations is to improve their effectiveness in solving environmental problems. We encourage sometimes overeager international secretariats to focus on a limited number of high priority areas and to avoid duplication of effort with other organizations. We seek to prevent proliferation of new agencies. We try to upgrade program quality and administration and to place qualified Americans on the staffs of these organizations.

There have been notable successes. Within the last 12 months alone, negotiations have been concluded under UNEP auspices on two important and complex subjects: the Convention for Protection of the Ozone Layer and a South Pacific convention on the marine environment. The ozone convention represents the first time that the international community has acted in concert on an environmental problem before there are actual and costly damages. The OECD is about to release a report on safety considerations in biotechnology, over 2 years in the making, which has been lauded by scientists and policymakers as a major contribution to assessing and managing risks in this dynamic new industry. The ECE is bringing East and West together to reduce transboundary air pollution by sulfur dioxide and nitrogen oxides. The World Meteorological Organization is leading an expanded international research effort on the "greenhouse effect"—the possibility of global climate change caused by growing concentration in the atmosphere of carbon dioxide and various trace gases, much of it resulting from industrial processes.

The Scientific Basis

All of these activities underscore the crucial nature of my fourth theme: the necessity for our international negotiating positions to have the best possible scientific basis—especially if regulations are involved. In order to achieve broad consensus for rational policies to protect the environment, it is essential, in my view, to eschew emotional appeals and to establish the scientific rationale for addressing any potential threats to environment or health.

Unfortunately, this is often easier said than done: there are gaps in the data, and there are varying interpretations. What are the causes of tree damage in the Black Forest? (Even the Germans are less certain of the answer than they were a few years ago.) How safe is incineration of highly toxic wastes in special ships on the high seas, as opposed to land disposal? Why have many lakes in New York and New England become heavily acidified, while others have actually declined in acidity? How can experiments with genetically engineered organisms, which have such enormous potential for medicine, agriculture, and industry, be kept safe in ways which do not stifle innovative research? What are the sources of increasing methane in the atmosphere, and how will it interact with other gases?

In order to face such questions, the State Department, not a scientific institution itself, maintains close working relationships with such bodies as the Environmental Protection Agency (EPA), National Academy of Sciences, Smithsonian Institution, National Aeronautics and Space Administration (NASA), Rand Corporation, National Oceanic and Atmospheric Administration, and many other scientific agencies. We administer the U.S. Man and the Biosphere Program and encourage its multidisciplinary research on a range of natural ecosystems. In order to support our ongoing international negotiations on protecting the ozone layer, we helped promote the most up-to-date and comprehensive assessment ever made of the state and prospects of stratospheric ozone—a study cosponsored by NASA, WMO, UNEP, and others and completed just 4 months ago. We participate in the National Acid Precipitation Assessment Program, a multiyear interagency research effort into the causes and effects of acid rain, with a budget this year alone of $85 million. We met with microbiologists and chemists from several countries to aid us in our successful OECD negotiations on the biotechnology report referred to earlier. And we are leading a U.S. Government interagency committee to develop policies for addressing the growing international concern over global climate change.

But, as mentioned earlier, the scientific basis for our work is frequently ambiguous. We are not dealing with black-and-white choices; we must realistically assess risks, probabilities, and costs—in an imprecise world.

A Balanced Approach: The Private Sector

Which leads to my final theme: the need for a balanced approach to environmental protection. By this I mean that in considering these many-faceted issues, we must avoid exaggerating either the risks of not regulating or the costs of regulating. We must neither act overhastily nor refuse to consider acting. And we must engage in reasoned debate rather than confrontation.

What this means in practice at the State Department is that we seek counsel from both environmental and industrial groups. It was, for example, the concern of such organizations as the Sierra Club and the Natural Resources Defense Council that helped alert both Congress and the executive branch to environmentally poor projects of the multilateral banks.

We recongnize, moreover, that private industry can make significant contributions to environmental protection; many industrial leaders are also dedicated environmentalists. Such environmental organizations as the Conservation Foundation and the World Resources Institute have reached out to establish linkages with private industry and have found an encouraging response. The industry-financed World Environment Center, for example, in cooperation with AID, is sending American experts to Third World factories to help improve environmental performance. When I testified last week before the Senate Foreign Relations Committee to urge ratification of the Convention to Protect the Ozone Layer, representatives of both environmental groups and the chlorofluorocarbon manufacturers also supported this treaty. And, when a U.S. scientific agency announced last month that, for budgetary reasons, it was grounding a satellite which monitored the upper atmosphere, there were immediate appeals both from EPA and the Chemical Manufacturers' Association—even though data from this satellite could be used to justify future controls over certain chemical products.

UNEP deserves particular recognition for its initiatives to involve industrial leaders more closely in Third World problems. I represented the United States last January at a followup meeting to UNEP's successful 1984 World Industry Conference on Environmental Management. This small, high-level meeting was sponsored jointly by the executive director of UNEP and the president of the International Chamber of Commerce and included environment ministers from such places as Indonesia, Ivory Coast, and China, as well as chief executives of multinational companies. Its result will be the establishment this year of a special bureau, financed by private industry, to provide assistance to developing countries on environmental management.

Conclusion

To conclude, environment is now very much on the U.S. foreign policy agenda. And while our constituents on one side or the other of a given environmental issue may not always entirely agree with our ultimate position, we hope that at least they will acknowledge that they had a fair hearing and that we acted in good faith. On the international scene, we need constantly to balance environmental concerns with economic and political realities. To some, it may seem that we act slowly, but I maintain that a measured, patient strategy is more effective in the long run than a hasty overreaction. In dealing with these issues, we must try not to let the perfect be the enemy of the good.

It seems hardly necessary to emphasize before this assembly that the challenges of protecting the global environment are formidable. Yet, there is no place for either complacency or despair. Governments cannot do it alone, especially in the current era of budget-tightening. New coalitions must be forged, involving citizens' groups, academic and research institutions, legislators, multilateral organizations, and private industry.

And I am just optimistic enough to believe that, with the support of individuals and institutions such as those participating here today, we will work together ever more effectively to promote both the betterment of the human condition and our stewardship of this planet for the generations to come.

ENVIRONMENT AND SECURITY[2]

The world is increasingly interdependent environmentally as well as economically. Pollution, whether air- or waterborne, is readily transported from one country to another, as is the case between the United States and Canada, between the Soviet Union and its neighbors, among the countries of Western Europe, and across the Mediterranean basin. The effects of soil erosion on agricultural productivity are a legitimate cause for international concern, whether the erosion occurs in India or in Indiana. Mass extinction of species affects all countries through agriculture, medicine, and industry, all of which depend to varying degrees on the genetic resources inherent in wild plants and animals. The global atmosphere is shared by all as well. Following the build-up of carbon dioxide and other gases that increase the retention of the sun's radiant energy in the earth's atmosphere—known as the greenhouse effect—all countries will suffer the vagaries of changed climate. If the ozone layer continues to be depleted, exposure to enhanced ultraviolet radiation will pose serious health threats to all populations. Similar observations can be made with regard to tropical deforestation and the spread of deserts. These two latter problems, like certain others, are closely connected to rapid population growth in the Third World, a problem related in turn to pervasive poverty and to associated issues of massive unemployment, overburdened cities, and refugees from environmental degradation.

Some of these problems affect the United States directly and immediately. For example, acid rain from the United States and Canada destroys animal and plant ecosystems in both countries, and refugees flee environmental disasters in the Caribbean basin. Other problems, such as population growth and mass extinction of species, have more indirect, long-term consequences for the United States. Some—climatic change, for one—may not exert their full impact for a few decades yet. But all will prove significant for a United States increasingly involved in developments around the world by virtue of its economic and security relationships.

[2]Article by Norman Myers, a scientist and environmental consultant. Reprinted with permission from *Foreign Policy* 74 (Spring 1989). Copyright 1989 by the Carnegie Endowment for International Peace.

The problems most significant to America probably will prove to be those with effects that are diffuse and often deferred, making them difficult to discern right away. Many Third World countries depend greatly for their development prospects on the natural-resource base—soil, water, and vegetation—that sustains much of their economic activity. For instance, in Central America about one-fourth of gross domestic product is based on natural resources; these resources also account for more than one-half of all employment and for most export earnings.

As cropland soil erodes, water supplies fail, and forests and grasslands are depleted, Third World economies start to falter or stagnate, even to decline. This process can have serious adverse consequences for the United States. Already more than 40 per cent of American exports go to the Third World, a figure that is projected to reach 50 per cent by the year 2000 provided developing countries achieve sustainable economic growth. In addition, repayment of the approximately $400 billion in outstanding loans made to the Third World by American banks depends on improved economic performance in the debtor countries.

The repercussions for the United States of inadequate development in the Third World extend beyond the loss of markets and investments. When economic growth slows or stops, social strains emerge and political systems become destabilized. All too often the result is civil turmoil and outright violence, either within a country or with neighboring countries. This process is of particular interest with regard to countries in which the United States has salient economic and security interests. As then Secretary of State George Shultz stated in 1984: "In our world today, there can be no enduring economic prosperity for the United States without sustained economic growth in the Third World. Security and peace for Americans are contingent upon stability and peace in the developing world." This statement highlights the pragmatic interests at stake for the United States: By helping key Third World countries with their environmental needs, the United States is helping itself. This hard-nosed approach, posited on a rationale of What's in it for the United States? is likely to prove more productive in policy terms than an appeal to "environmental conscience" or some similarly vague motivation.

Of course, a number of other factors in addition to environmental problems can hinder Third World development—faulty development policies, inflexible political structures, oligarchic regimes, and oppressive governments. But environmental issues present a novel and increasingly important set of challenges for U.S. foreign policy. The United States has scant experience dealing with the environmental linkages to foreign policy. Worse, many of the linkages operate in slow and covert fashion; they do not generate month-by-month headlines. Yet their unregarded workings are important nonetheless, so much so that policymakers cannot pursue national, economic, and security goals coherently without a basic understanding of what environmental trends are at work. As the cases presented below reveal, U.S. interests are increasingly caught up in the decades-long deforestation in the Philippines, water deficits in the Middle East, land degradation in El Salvador, and rapid population growth in Mexico.

The Philippines

The United States maintains a substantial security interest in the Philippines. Clark Air Base and Subic Bay Naval Base stand at the center of American military operations in the Pacific Ocean, serving as a springboard for the projection of American power throughout much of Asia. They have become still more important since the communist victory in Vietnam.

The United States also has a commercial stake in the Philippines. In mid-1988 the Philippines owed $4 billion—out of a total foreign debt of $29 billion—to private American banks. The prospect of repayment remains uncertain as long as interest servicing absorbs 21 per cent of the country's export earnings. The Philippine economy is still shaky in several respects, and political stability remains elusive. Unless an extended period of sustainable development can be achieved, there could eventually be more support for the New People's Army (NPA) and other dissident groups that would like to see an end to the American presence.

But the economic outlook is unpromising in part because of environmental mismanagement. A sizable share of the economy is environmentally based. The sectors of agriculture, forestry, and fisheries contribute more than one-fourth of the Philippine gross national product, earn two-fifths of export revenues, and employ one-half of the labor force. Yet the natural-resource base is severely overburdened. Productive hardwood forests, which once covered most of the country and generated 32 per cent of export earnings as recently as 1967, have been reduced to 22 per cent of land area and generate only 5 per cent of export revenue. A "timber famine" is imminent even though domestic demand for wood in the year 2000 is projected to exceed the 1985 level by 69 per cent and export opportunities will be at least double the 1985 mark.

The closing of the agricultural frontier (available cultivable lands) in the Philippine lowlands has spurred a steady migration of landless peasants into the uplands. These upland forests provide critical cover for catchment zones that supply water for much of the country's hydropower energy and irrigation needs. But because of progressive deforestation, water flows are being reduced and becoming irregular. As a result, erosion-derived sedimentation is cutting short the operational lives of major hydropower reservoirs by one-half or more. And heavy sedimentation in water bodies affects the most productive sector of agriculture—irrigated crop cultivation. The sedimentation also reduces usable water flows in many areas, even though the government hopes to increase irrigated areas by 43 per cent during the last quarter of this century as a crucial part of its plans to expand agriculture. Output of the most widely irrigated crop and the country's leading staple, rice, no longer keeps pace with population growth. Although the country reached rice self-sufficiency in 1974, it reverted to being a net importer in 1985.

The future is even less promising. In the wake of growing migration, the uplands population is projected to increase from 17.8 million in 1988 to 28.8 million by 2005. Even with greatly intensified agriculture, the provision of more off-farm employment, and other measures, a halt in the migratory push into ever steeper parts of the uplands seems unlikely, leading to the eventual demise of the remaining forests. The single most helpful measure would surely be a vigorously expanded family-planning program. The Philippines is the only country in Asia where the birthrate has risen persistently through the 1980s. The population of 63 million is projected to surge to 86 million in the year 2000 and to 115 million in 2020. Nor are there signs that the government is inclined to do much to reduce the growth rate. Its new population policy prescribes no education campaigns, tax incentives, or other fiscal inducements to promote smaller families.

Certainly other variables are at work besides environmental factors and population growth. These include the inequitable distribution of farmland, inappropriate development policies, bureaucratic inertia, and corruption. But environmental and population problems make other problems worse—and seem set to make them much worse in the future. If there remains little prospect of economic advancement for the majority of Filipinos (real per capita income fell by 16 per cent between 1980 and 1986), growing throngs of disaffected peasantry may increase popular support for insurgents like the NPA. The rebels now control 20 per cent of the countryside and mount growing attacks despite intensified government operations.

The Middle East: Israel, Jordan, and Syria

In much of the Middle East, with its vital American interests, water presents an environmental source of conflict. The competition for water is greater in this region than virtually anywhere else in the world, and shortages are projected to grow even more acute. Israel consumes roughly five times as much water per capita as its less industrialized and intensively farmed neighbors. So critical are assured water supplies to Israel that one reason it went to war in 1967 was that Syria and Jordan were trying to divert the flows of the Jordan River. Israel still occupies the Golan Heights and the West Bank in part because it wishes to safeguard its access to the river's water. While Israel receives about 60 per cent of its water from the Jordan River, only 3 per cent of the river's basin lies within the country's pre-1967 territory.

However, Jordan also seeks a greater share of the river's water. Even with agronomic inputs matching U.S. levels, the country will not be able to feed itself from its own land by the year 2000, meaning that it will have to purchase increasing amounts of food overseas. Between 1974 and 1984 Jordan's food imports in terms of value jumped by 431 per cent; yet in 1984 its terms of trade were only 95 per cent those of 1980. Servicing Jordan's external debt of $4.1 billion in 1986 consumed 29 per cent of its annual export earnings. Compounding its problems, Jordan's annual population growth rate of 3.7 per cent—the third highest in the world—means that the present population of 2.9 million is projected to more than double early in the next century. The country's great need for irrigation water demands that it maintain a powerful interest in the river. Jordan's water needs are projected to exceed supply by 20 per cent by the year 2000, but Israel, which already recycles an unusually large share of its water resources, could face deficits as high as 30 per cent by then.

The upper Jordan River is already developed to its maximum capacity. Its main tributary, the Yarmuk River, is only partly tapped, but Syria plans to use this water by building a dam at Maqarin on the Jordanian-Syrian border. Eventually Syria aims to construct an entire series of dams on the Yarmuk, diverting 40 per cent of the river's flow. This would induce severe shortages in Jordan and Israel.

Plans for the Euphrates and Tigris rivers, which run through Turkey, Syria, and Iraq, could mean further trouble in the region. Through its huge Anatolia Project, Turkey hopes to construct 13 hydroelectric and irrigation facilities on the upper reaches of both rivers. The Ataturk Dam is sufficient to irrigate almost 7,000 square miles of land—an area about the size of Isreal—enabling Turkey to double its farm output. But the project would divert as much as one-half of the Euphrates water that currently crosses into Syria and two-thirds of Euphrates flows into Iraq.

Syria, too, entertains ambitious irrigation plans for the Euphrates, intending to divert one-half of the water now entering the country. The downstream neighbor, Iraq, would be hard hit. In 1975, after Syria built its al-Thawrah Dam, the Iraqi government claimed that the resultant loss of water threatened the livelihood of 3 million farmers. The two countries came close to hostilities over the dispute.

It is not inconceivable that future interstate violence in the Middle East might arise not from the region's most plentiful resource, oil, but from its scarcest, water. Long after the oil wells run dry, competition for water will continue to increase.

These frictions over river flows in the Middle East suggest the scope of water-related conflicts around the world. Of 214 first-order river systems, 155 are shared by 2 countries and 59 by 3–12 countries. Already these major rivers support 40 per cent of the world's population, and about two-thirds of these people are located in developing countries, which often have fewer per capita water resources than do developed countries. Tensions and violence over water-use rights and river-diversion projects have already erupted in the river basins of the Mekong, which is shared by Laos, Thailand, Cambodia, and Vietnam; the Paraná, which is shared by Brazil and Argentina; the Lauca, which is shared by Bolivia and Chile; and the Medjerda, which is shared by Tunisia and Libya.

The Middle East: Egypt

Equally significant with regard to river-related conflict in the Middle East is the case of Egypt. Egypt is especially important to the United States because of its moderating influence throughout the Arab world. Two decades ago Egypt was self-sufficient in food, but today, mainly because of population growth and land mismanagement, it is experiencing quickly mounting difficulties in feeding its population. Urban riots and other domestic upheavals have already resulted from rising food prices and related food-supply problems. In 1986 Egypt had to import 121 million tons of cereal grains—55 per cent of its food needs—at a cost of $4.1 billion. This volume could well double by the year 2000, when Egypt's population is projected to reach 71 million from 55 million in 1988. Moreover, Egypt's external debt reached $44 billion in 1988; service of just nonmilitary debt consumed 31 per cent of export earnings. If Egypt cannot reduce its debt through increased trade revenues—unlikely unless it can reverse the recent steady decline in its terms of trade—it may not be able to buy all the grain it needs.

What prospect, then, is there for Egypt to produce more of its own food? Primarily because of rapid population growth, but also because of environmental problems, grain output per person declined by 18 per cent from 1971 to 1985. Of 363,250 square miles of national territory, less than 10,000 are cultivated in a strip averaging 6 miles wide along the Nile River. Farming is critically dependent on irrigation, but by 1982 one-half of all irrigated croplands were suffering from salinization and the rest were considered at risk. About 10 per cent of annual agricultural production is now lost because of a decline in soil fertility. Another 8 per cent is lost to desert encroachment.

Nor does population planning hold out much hope. Little reduction in the population growth rate has been achieved since 1980; and with plenty of demographic momentum built in to present growth trends, even a vigorous birth-control campaign would have little effect for the better part of a generation. By that time the population is likely to double.

In this tightly constrained situation, Egypt could face worsening water shortages. Eight successive drought years in the watershed areas of Ethiopia and equatorial Africa reduced the Nile flows by mid-1988 to the lowest level since 1913. Storage water in Lake Nasser was for a time deemed likely to prove adequate only for the 1988 harvest, after which the early 1989 planting season would have been so curtailed through lack of irrigation water that Egypt would have had to import a further 15 per cent of its food needs. The ambitious programs to expand the irrigation network and to reclaim desert lands would also have come to a halt. Fortunately the upstream drought broke in August 1988 and the immediate crisis was relieved. But according to the minister of public works and irrigation, Isam Radi Abd el-Hamid Radi, two additional above-average flood years will be needed to replenish the water reserves depleted by drought.

Should the 1980s drought in the upstream catchments return, as many climatologists anticipate in light of long-standing climatic cycles soon to be exacerbated by the greenhouse effect, the results would be, according to Sarwat Fahmey, director of the Nile Water Control Authority, "a calamity." The water shortages would affect not only agriculture. By mid-1988 the low flows into the Aswan High Dam's hydropower turbines, which supply 40 per cent of Egypt's electricity needs, reduced power output by 20 per cent. Even before the drought Egypt was failing to meet a 10 per cent annual growth in demand for electricity. A new drought could easily lead to still more serious power cuts than in mid-1988, possibly as high as 60 per cent, at a cost of millions of dollars of lost output each month. Since the energy deficit would have to be made up primarily with oil, the river-flow problem would all but eliminate Egypt's oil-export revenues—and thus induce further restrictions on Egypt's ability to buy food overseas.

An even greater threat to Egypt's water supplies is emerging. Upstream countries are now claiming a greater share of the Nile's waters. The other countries within the river's drainage system—Sudan, Ethiopia, Uganda, Kenya, Tanzania, Zaire, Rwanda, and Burundi—are shifting from dependence on rainwater to reliance on irrigation systems for their croplands. This applies notably in Ethiopia, which controls the Blue Nile tributary that is the source of approximately 80 per cent of the Nile water entering Egypt. Ethiopia has never joined Egypt or the other downstream country, Sudan, in a legal agreement to regulate the share-out of the

Nile's waters. On the contrary, Ethiopia has regularly asserted that it feels at complete liberty to dispose of its natural resources in whatever manner it decides. The Ethiopian government is re-settling 1.5 million peasants from the degraded highlands in the Welega province and other sectors of the fertile western part of the country. To supply irrigation water for the new settlements, Ethiopia plans to eventually divert up to 39 per cent of the Blue Nile's waters.

This prospect alarms Egypt. In 1980 then Egyptian President Anwar el-Sadat declared ominously, "If Ethiopia takes any action to block our right to the Nile waters, there will be no alternative for us but to use force." And in 1985 then Foreign Minister Butros Ghali stated: "The next war in our region will be over the waters of the Nile, not over politics. . . . Washington does not take this seriously, because everything for the United States re-lates to Israel, oil, and the Middle East."

El Salvador

El Salvador is the most troubled country in a region about which former President Ronald Reagan stated, "The national se-curity of all the Americas is at stake in Central America." Former Secretary of State Henry Kissinger has observed about the region that "if we cannot manage in Central America, it will be impossi-ble to convince threatened nations in the Persian Gulf and in oth-er places that we know how to manage the global equilibrium."

El Salvador has endured more civil strife, political upheaval, military activity, and pervasive violence than any other country in Central America. It has also suffered more environmental im-poverishment than any other country, notably through soil ero-sion, deforestation, and depletion of water supplies. These two concurrent trends can hardly be coincidental—even though the putative connection was scarcely noticed in the 1984 report of the National Bipartisan Commission on Central America (Kis-singer commission). To be sure, various other factors come into play, particularly inequitable land-tenure systems, disparities of wealth and income, and repressive government. But the environ-mental dimension to El Salvador's predicament deserves greater attention than it has received.

Within a country the size of Vermont, which has a population of 535,000, live 5.4 million people, about one-half of them farmers. So important is the natural-resource base to the economy that almost 67 per cent of export revenues in 1982 derived from agricultural commodities. Yet soil erosion is extensive and often severe. Salvadoran forests are a matter of history; watershed deterioration is the rule rather than the exception; and water flows from upland catchments are increasingly erratic, with adverse repercussions for irrigation agriculture. As a result of general degradation of agricultural resources, among other factors, El Salvador is increasingly unable to feed itself. Per capita grain production declined from 312 pounds in 1950 to 284 pounds in 1983, and cereal imports were rising sharply until 1984.

Agriculture is also beset with maldistribution of farmlands, associated problems of land-tenure systems, and pressures of high population growth. Cropland per person has fallen by two-thirds since 1950, and agricultural advances—agrarian technology, credit systems, and extension services—have not nearly compensated for such a steep falloff. Almost one-half of Salvadoran farmers are confined to a mere 5 per cent of agricultural lands, and the average small holding is one and one-fourth acres or less. Almost two-thirds of the farming community can be categorized as nearly landless or landless. As a result, throngs of impoverished peasants are pushed into marginal environments, often steeply sloped areas where the friable volcanic soil erodes easily.

Meanwhile, the overall economy has weakened seriously. Per capita gross domestic product in constant 1982 dollars amounted to $610 in 1960, rising to $785 in 1970 and to $855 in 1980 but falling to $708 in 1984 and to $690 in 1987. Salvadorans today are economically worse off than they were in 1970 and little better off than in 1960. The economic decline is forcing large numbers of people to return to a state of semisubsistence in which their main option is to exploit the meager natural resources available.

El Salvador's population density now exceeds India's and is well over 650 people per square mile. Its population density is between 3 and 10 times greater than that of other countries in the region and is projected to reach 1,120 per square mile as soon as the year 2000. So El Salvador experiences by far the most acute land pressures in the region, even disallowing the skewed distribution of farmlands.

Whether population growth and environmental decline are chiefly at fault, or whether the main problem lies with the maldistribution of land and unjust distribution of economic and political power, the resultant pressures have caused a steady migration of Salvadorans into neighboring countries. By the late 1960s, when El Salvador had an average of 410 people per square mile and, by comparison, Honduras had only 57, one out of eight Salvadorans had gone to that country next door. Tensions over this migration erupted in 1969 in so-called Soccer War. Since then more than 500,000 Salvadorans have migrated to other Central American countries before migrating to countries farther afield, notably the United States. By the mid-1970s, migration to the United States was accelerating; by 1982 an estimated 500,000 Salvadorans had entered the country, many of them illegally. All told, some 20 per cent of Salvadorans, counting internally displaced as well as international refugees, have fled their homelands. While political repression and inequitable social factors have often played a role, many of these migrants can legitimately be called environmental refugees.

Nor is the future any more promising. Such are the population pressures that even if the government's land reform program begun in 1980 were fully successful, about one-third of the rural poor would not have secure access to farmland. The population is projected to reach 7.8 million by the year 2000 and to exceed 10 million by 2020. Yet according to a 1984 report by the Food and Agriculture Organization of the United Nations, El Salvador could not support more than 10 million people through its own land resources even if it could fully employ high-technology methods of agriculture. Prospects for purchasing food abroad are also poor. Even projecting a highly optimistic economic growth rate of 3.9 per cent per year, the World Bank does not expect Salvadorans to enjoy the standard of living they had in 1979—before the outbreak of the current civil war—until the year 2006. With a more realistic growth rate for the economy of between 3 and 3.5 per cent per year, per capita income would continue to decline, never able to regain its poor 1979 level. To make matters worse, one-half or more of new entrants into the job market would remain unemployed in the year 2006, thus adding further pressures to the natural-resource base if they opted for a semisubsistence lifestyle in marginal lands. Such economic dislocation could only exacerbate El Salvador's instability, probably fueling pressures for radical political change.

Mexico

With 87 million people today, Mexico has the second largest population in Latin America. It has a 2,000-mile common border with the United States. Mexico is the third largest trading partner of the United States; its economic importance to America is seen in its enduring economic crisis and austerity program, which have led to reduced imports that cost some 200,000 American jobs in 1983 alone. American banks still hold about $45 billion of outstanding debt in Mexico, out of a total Mexican debt of $105 billion. If Mexico were to default, the backlash would reverberate throughout the American banking system. Long-term economic stresses could lead to political upheavals of a scope exceeding those with which the United States now grapples in Cental America. As the Mexican political scientist Jorge Castañeda stated in the Fall 1986 issue of *Foreign Policy*: "The consequences of not creating [nearly 15 million jobs in the next 15 years] are unthinkable. The youths who do not find them will have only three options: the United States, the streets, or revolution."

So the common border—the world's most extensive conjunction between a developing country and a developed country—highlights the "special relationship" the United States conducts with its troubled neighbor. Approximately 150,000 Mexicans each year are legal migrants to America, while another 150,000—350,000, and possibly many more, are illegal and traveling to stay; still larger numbers cross the border for temporary purposes. The cumulative total of both legal and illegal immigrants is between 2.5 million and 4 million. In a few more years the number could readily top 10 million with no end in sight. Whatever the ultimate impact on American society, it surely will be significant.

Among the mix of factors that impel Mexicans northward, two of the most important are environmental decline and population growth. Mexico has limited agricultural lands because much of the country is dry. In at least 70 per cent of the good lands soil erosion is deemed significant. Spreading deserts claim 865 square miles of farmland each year. At least one-tenth of irrigated areas has become highly salinized, and almost 4,000 square miles need urgent and expensive rehabilitation if they are to be restored to productivity.

Moreover, Mexico's remaining forests total well under 50,000 square miles and are falling victim to large-scale ranchers and small-scale peasants alike. The loss of the forests' "sponge effect" disrupts river flows. Water supplies constitute the main factor limiting agricultural productivity in two-thirds of arable lands. Thus failing water availability and soil erosion lead to the abandonment of about 400 square miles of farmland each year. From the late 1950s to the early 1970s, the area cultivated under staple crops—corn, wheat, rice, and beans—expanded by almost 50 per cent, extending into marginal lands with highly erodible soils. (At least 45 per cent of farmers occupy the 20 per cent of croplands that are steeply sloped.) By the mid-1970s these newly farmed areas began to experience declining crop yields— precisely when the population growth rate peaked. Domestic calorie production as a percentage of total supply reached 105 per cent in 1970, but by 1982 it had slipped to 94 per cent, and by 1986 Mexico had reverted to being a net importer of food.

In addition, the distribution of agricultural lands is becoming ever more skewed as large farmers buy out smaller ones and engage in capital-intensive cash cropping for export. The growing concentration of peasants imposes greater strains on overworked croplands, reducing their carrying capacity; migrating farmers are pushed into the marginal lands most susceptible to degradation.

The agricultural debacle also spurred an upsurge in migration from Mexico's rural areas to its cities. Having grown at 5 per cent or more per year since 1960, the cities are even less able to absorb new arrivals. For every two rural Mexicans who move to the city, one now crosses the border into the United States, drawn partly by the prospect of a better life there but also pushed by poor and deteriorating conditions in Mexico.

As for perhaps the biggest problem of all—population growth—the outlook must be considered bleak because Mexico cannot support its present population of 87 million, let alone greater numbers. Despite some recent success in family planning, the Mexican populace has a youthful profile and hence a built-in demographic momentum. Thus the year 2000 could well see 109 million Mexicans. Of the 27 million in the work force in 1987 at least 14 million were considered unemployed or underemployed, a total that is expected to exceed 20 million by the year 2000. The work shortage is worst in rural areas where the rate of unemployment and underemployment often reaches 65 per cent, and where the rate of near landlessness and outright landlessness reaches 60 per cent of all farming households.

The United States must ask itself a basic question: What are the prospects for future Mexican immigration? By the year 2000, Mexico is projected to have almost one-half as many people as the United States, but an economy only one-twentieth its size. Average real wages in 1987 were below the 1970 level, and the economy has generally stagnated and sometimes contracted since 1980. Neither the economic outlook nor development policies presage much improvement. A realistic outlook, then, is that Mexicans in the year 2000 might well be poorer than they are today. It is an optimistic estimate that foresees "only" 20 million Mexicans without proper employment in the year 2000. At least one-half of these will be living in rural areas where they will be joined by an additional 2–4 million landless peasants, creating a sizable pool of potential migrants.

These trends make for a plausible prospect of instability and insecurity. It is realistic rather than alarmist to envisage the possibility of a revolution. The makings of revolution—declining living standards, rising unemployment, soaring aspirations—all have been gathering force throughout the 1980s. Should a revolution occur, the outflow of Mexicans who now are seeking economic survival in the United States would be joined by those seeking physical safety. It ought to be recalled that the 1910 revolution led at least 500,000 out of 15 million Mexicans to seek sanctuary north of the border. If a revolution today had a comparable impact, it would drive 2.9 million Mexicans across the border. And in 1910 the great majority of Mexicans lived far from the border, whereas today several million live within 10 miles of it.

Policy Implications

This review of environmental problems facing a sample of countries where important American interests are at stake raises a key question: What should the United States plan in the way of policy responses?

First of all, U.S. policymakers can take cognizance—systematic and comprehensive cognizance—of the fast-changing character of international relations with regard to environmental factors. Without a clear comprehension of these emergent factors, policymakers will be less able to safeguard U.S. interests from new threats. Environmental issues are exceptionally interwoven in both their causes and their consequences. Policymakers thus need to apprehend not only the range of accumulating problems but their multiple interrelationships as well. Many of these diverse interactions appear set to grow more numerous and significant and to exert a greater impact on Third World development.

Regrettably, international environmental issues do not often lend themselves to ready and concise analysis. The myriad interlocking webs of cause and effect simply do not permit a linear interpretation of discrete relationships among members of the international community. It cannot be asserted that environmental problem X will necessarily lead to economic consequence Y that postulates policy response Z. It cannot be predicted precisely how these factors will interact among themselves, nor the specific ways in which they will interact with other factors, such as the growing means of violence manifested in the global traffic in arms, the prevalence of terrorism, and the proliferation of nuclear devices to countries or subnational organizations. But it is realistic to suppose that tensions and conflicts, whether domestic or international, will escalate and multiply.

The difficulty of perceiving connections between the environment and instability may say less about the nature of the connections than about the limited capacity of policymakers to think methodically about matters that have long lain outside their purview. In addition, the connections that are more apparent may not lend themselves to quantification—in contrast with "conventional" connections such as trade and investment flows, whose effects are readily measurable and thereby carry greater weight with policymakers. What can be counted should not be emphasised to the detriment of what also counts.

Notwithstanding these difficulties, some emergent factors of the "environmental dimension" to international relations can be defined. Prudent policy dictates an effort to anticipate new problems—however meager the data base and the analytic methodologies that lead to tentative conclusions. When connections are difficult even to define, policymakers should remember that, as in other situations that combine uncertainty with high stakes, it will be better to have been roughly right than precisely wrong.

Within this conceptual framework, the United States might well appraise its present policy measures to protect its interests abroad. In the case of Egypt, for instance, the United States in 1986 supplied $1.4 billion in security assistance and $1.3 billion in development assistance and economic support funds (formerly known as security supporting assistance). Only a small part of this aid was directed at environmental measures to safeguard Egypt's capacity to feed its fast-growing population. Therefore, the question is whether military or environmental outlays would purchase more real and enduring support for U.S. interests in Egypt and, because of Egypt's international role, in the Middle East and the Arab world generally.

Equally illuminating is the case of U.S. support for El Salvador. In 1986 the Salvadoran government, with the U.S. government's ostensible approval, spent $211 million on military activities. Just one-fifth of that amount could have done a great deal to shore up the country's environmental foundations. For example, it could have reforested some 400 square miles of land (out of a national territory of 8,260 square miles). Such reforestation could have begun to rehabilitate watershed functions and conserve topsoil, thus enhancing the agricultural resource stocks that sustain much of El Salvador's economic and populace, notably the peasants who depend on marginal land and supply much of the support for the insurgents. Also in 1986, the U.S. government supplied El Salvador with $122 million in military aid; that figure can be compared usefully with $21 million for environmental measures in South and Central America and the Caribbean basin. Yet a strong case can be made that an environmentally impoverished country may well experience the very economic and social problems, followed by the political upheavals, that the United States seeks to contain through its conventional support of El Salvador.

So in these and the other cases discussed above there is a need to incorporate an environmental dimension into security planning. The conventional approach to security interests surely reflects an overly narrow perception of security problems and of available responses, largely military, to security threats. Could the time be coming when as much lasting security can be purchased through trees as through tanks?

Additional initiatives are also available to the United States, notably on the multilateral front. For instance, Washington can influence the World Bank and other international lending agencies to invoke tougher environmental criteria for those loans that affect the natural-resource base of Third World countries. Partly because of U.S. pressure, the World Bank has dramatically modified, if not suspended, its loans for road-building projects in the Brazilian Amazon and for the Transmigration Program in Indonesia, both of which have contributed significantly to deforestation. But the Bank should also establish more stringent environmental requirements for such projects as dams in tropical forests, ranching in Botswana savannahs, and cash crops for export in the semiarid lands of the Sahel countries. The World Bank has set up an entire environment department, partly as a result of American lobbying. But the Bank still has much to do in institutionalizing environmental concerns in its operations.

Above all, U.S. policymakers should bear in mind that environmentally induced change will come, whether the government pursues it positively or not, and whether it arrives by design or by default. Fortunately there is still time—though often only just time—for policymakers to choose productive responses. Through immediate and incisive action, the United States can generate a sizable security return for itself by protecting its interests in the global environment.

THE POLITICS OF ENVIRONMENTAL REGULATION IN GREAT BRITAIN[3]

The British display an apparently schizophrenic approach to environmental matters. As a people they have always been very sensitive about scenic beauty and their architectural heritage of castles, country houses, and cathedrals. They love animals and, over the generations, have produced a great variety of dedicated amateur naturalists. For over a century, literally thousands of public-spirited groups have campaigned long and hard for envi-

[3]Article by Timothy O'Riordan, professor of environmental sciences at the University of East Anglia, Norwich, U.K. *Environment.* 30:4+. O. '88. Reprinted with permission of the Helen Dwight Reid Educational Foundation. Published by Heldref Publications, 4000 Albermarle St., N.W., Washington, D.C. 20016. Copyright © 1988.

ronmental cleanliness and peace and quiet in their communities. Yet the British government, purporting to act for the nation but in effect reflecting certain economic interests, actively resists the establishment of international agreements aimed at reducing acid emissions and the dumping of toxic wastes at sea, reluctantly subsidizes an excessively expensive agricultural industry that is also the source of widespread environmental pollution, and systematically underfinances its regulatory agencies and professions until their effectiveness is noticeably diminished. It is not surprising that the country is called "the dirty man of Europe."

The many facets of contemporary British environmental politics cannot be covered adequately in a brief article. So I have chosen to look at how environmental policies are formed, how public opinion is changing, and what the main political parties are advocating. I shall also emphasize the growing significance of the influence of the European Community (EC) on British environmental regulation. Finally, I shall examine the link between national economic strategy and technological development on the one hand, and the emergence of new environmental thinking on the other, in what is now popularly known as "the enterprise culture."

Great Britain's Governing Style

In constitutional terms Great Britain experiences an unusual form of what is known as an "elected dictatorship." In theory parliament is meant to represent the democratic voice of the British people. But members of parliament (MPs) are elected on the basis of the greatest number of votes cast in each constituency. In a two-party system, this should produce a parliament that is fairly representative. In modern multiparty British politics, however, where an MP who receives as little as 35 percent of the total vote can be elected, the resulting composition of parliament does not reflect the popular voting pattern. In the 1987 general election, for example, the Conservatives won a 101-seat majority in the 649-seat House of Commons with 42.3 percent of the popular vote. Thus a minority party in terms of the popular vote enjoys in effect dictatorial power by virtue of a large parliamentary majority. Although ministers are nominally accountable to parliament, in practice they tend to be more answerable to their own restive backbenchers—the nonministerial MPs who form the majority of the parliamentary party. The official opposition is divided and feeble and likely to remain that way for the foreseeable future. Nowadays, legislation of all kinds is the prerogative of the prime minister and cabinet, the outcome of their own ideologies and prejudices checked and executed by a mostly supine civil service. Unlike members of Congress in the United States, MPs rarely created their own bills and, when they do, few bills survive the parliamentary grinding mill unless they are supported by the government. British courts are constitutionally weaker than their U.S. counterparts, so intervention through litigation is rare, expensive, and chancy. Because there is no Bill of Rights, aggrieved individuals or groups cannot look to the courts to defend their basic well-being, let alone their environmental health.

The point here is that while a majority of the British people may prefer one line of approach, the state, in the form of governmental will, may pursue another. This political arrangement helps to explain the apparent schizophrenia referred to earlier. It also clarifies why public opinion polls consistently indicate a preparedness to pay for cleaner vehicle emissions and power station discharges, objectives that are thwarted by the Thatcher administration's anti-inflation policy of holding down consumer prices even at the expense of increasing environmental pollution. Similarly, less than a fifth of even Conservative voters support an increase in nuclear power generation. Yet the Conservative government, aided and abetted by both the industry and the civil service departments responsible for energy strategy, is vigorously pursuing a policy of encouraging the electricity industry to construct a small family of pressurized water reactors.

The government promotes this policy by deliberately manipulating the finances of the electricity industry and lowering the cost of borrowing for large capital investment in nuclear power stations as compared to the availability of cash for technological investment in the conservation of electricity use. These nonmarket interventions not only clash with the government's stated market-oriented philosophies, they also isolate the nuclear industry from competition with coal-fired and combined-heat-and-power schemes that are becoming more cost effective as coal prices fall and small, purpose-built, gas-fired turbines become increasingly economical. Indeed, in recent policy statements the government has made it clear that up to 20 percent of future power stations must use non-fossil-fueled sources (meaning nuclear power).

Part of the reason for this paradox between popular will and state policy lies in the method by which environmental policy is developed in Britain. It is normally formed through a consensual, consultative approach that allows established interests a major say in decisions on proposals. For example, the 1974 Control of Pollution Act, still the most important antipollution statute in the United Kingdom, was shaped by industry and local government despite over 150 amendments tabled by environmental pressure groups. For the most part, these consultants are the emitters and regulators of the majority of common pollutants. Similarly, the 1981 Wildlife and Countryside Act, by far the most influential legislation affecting the protection of rural scenery and seminatural wildlife habitats in the United Kingdom, was virtually dictated by the powerful farming and landowning organizations against the challenge of a vigorous but strikingly unsuccessful wildlife and landscape lobby.

In both these instances, and also for other crucial pieces of environmental legislation, the public-interest environmental groups in Great Britain (those that are approximately equivalent to organizations like the Environmental Defense Fund or the Sierra Club in the United States) are politically active but only sporadically influential. Any clout they have is a product of their respectability and campaigning credibility. The majority of modern environmental activists dress professionally, cultivate civil service and industry contacts, placate suspicious trade unions, and rely extensively on favorable media support. In short, for the most part they have tended to acquire the attire, reasoning, and behavior of the establishment.

Because Great Britain is officially a highly secretive society, where all government information, including the color of the canteen walls, is technically confidential until a minister specifically authorizes disclosure, the environmental lobbies depend to an unreliable extent on judicious leaks, anonymously supplied envelopes containing photocopied sensitive documents, and insider whistle blowing for their political effectiveness.

Official secrecy is one of the greatest impediments to environmental lobbying in the United Kingdom. But in characteristic British fashion, it is so often sidestepped that responsible pressure groups can exploit officials' ready willingness to turn a blind eye. This maneuvering, however, is all part of the co-opting process. Truly radical environmental opposition in the United Kingdom is steadily decreasing.

This secrecy is not an appropriate basis on which to develop public faith in environmentally sound government. Indeed, good environmental practice depends on trust and full disclosure. It is hardly surprising that the prestigious Royal Commission on Environmental Pollution, established by royal warrant in 1970 to oversee Great Britain's environmental problems, called for consistency in the provisions covering the public's right to know and for a legislative change that would place the burden of proof on a minister if information was withheld in the public interest. So far, the government has not amended the notorious Official Secrets Act, which makes the unauthorized disclosure of *any* official information a criminal offense. Reform is on the political agenda, but it is highly unlikely that a general right to know will ever be sanctioned, despite strong public sentiment in favor of liberalizing this important aspect of public affairs and the opposition parties' forceful supporting arguments.

Environmental politics in the United Kingdom is not especially radical, in the sense that novel, visionary, and unconventional ideas get much airing. The nonconformism in matters of no-growth economics, animal rights, third-world economic and environmental stabilization, and adequate safeguards over public health and safety that most far-sighted environmentalists crave is all but nonexistent outside of rhetoric and polemics, and the state's biases together with its powerful alliances and capitalist influences dominate the political agenda. Environmental politics in the United Kingdom is essentially reactive and accommodative to prevailing political realities. It is not the visionary politics of far-sighted ecological housekeeping.

The Greening of British Politics

The unrepresentative electoral arrangement that neither of the two major political parties (Conservative and Labour) wishes to change guarantees that minority parties attract far fewer votes and even less political influence than they deserve or than they would receive under an alternative electoral system of proportional representation. In Great Britain, the timing of elections is determined by the prime minister, so a ruling party can soften electoral opinion before calling an election. The British Green Party gathered about 1.3 percent of the national vote in the 1987 election, but in West Germany, where minority parties can win seats in proportion to the vote they obtain—as long as that vote exceeds 5 percent—the Die Grünen (Green) Party gathered 8.3 percent of the vote in January 1987. Unless some form of proportional representation comes to the United Kingdom, the British Green Party will never become a serious political force. The party has painfully developed reasonably coherent policies across the spectrum of public affairs, but it is seriously handicapped by internal disorganization, crippling underfunding, and a low-profile public image. At the local level, however, half a dozen Green local councilors have been elected, and there are many active and articulate grassroots groups with small but enthusiastic memberships.

Both the broadly socialist Labour Party and the former Alliance Party (the former Social Democrat and Liberal parties), which support more decentralized forms of government with an emphasis on cooperative enterprise, took environmental issues seriously in the 1987 election.

Both the Labour and the old Alliance parties called for a more environmentally sustainable pattern of economic growth guided, where necessary, by governmental intervention through taxes (imposed by a government levy), charges (collected as a price on a service), and nonstatutory but voluntarily binding codes of practice and performance audits. Both parties also advocated a new ministry of environmental protection, headed by a minister of cabinet rank, that would encompass not only all regulatory activities covering pollution and hazard but also wildlife management and land-use planning to protect and enhance scenic beauty. Both parties agreed to a moratorium on nuclear power, and Labour, backed by the majority of trade unions, advocated the abandonment of the whole nuclear program, including nuclear weapons systems. Both parties argued for greater public access to the open, mostly privately owned countryside and for fiscal policies aimed at reducing agriculture's dependence on chemicals.

POLLUTION CONTROL

These points are stressed because the 1987 general election was heralded as the first that would be influenced by the "Green vote." Private polls commissioned by the major parties suggested considerable voter sympathy for Green issues. Before the June election, the ruling Conservative Party also made distinctive but opportunistic concessions to the Green lobby by creating a combined pollution control agency, known as Her Majesty's Inspectorate of Pollution (HMIP), a very pale shadow of the U.S. Environmental Protection Agency but at least an embryonic attempt to establish a unified approach to pollution abatement. One of a number of factors that prompted that move and certainly influenced the timing of the announcement was the active pamphleteering in 1985 and 1986 by the two opposing political parties, which proposed reforms to the administration of environmental protection.

The aim of HMIP is to ensure that every large or, in emission terms, awkward environmental discharger is regulated by a single inspector whose duty is to find the best practicable environmental option (BPEO) for disposal of effluent onto land, into air, or via water. The concept of BPEO originated from a proposal by the independent Royal Commission on Environmental Pollution, the only permanent body of its type in Great Britain today. The commission reports to the Queen via parliament and carries much prestige. It has published twelve reports, four of which emphasized the BPEO approach. That approach has recently been accepted by the government as an approved method of comprehensive pollution control. No other European country is so committed to this linked air-water disposal strategy for pollution abatement.

The practical implementation of the BPEO approach will be a daunting and challenging task. It will not prove easy to determine the environmental consequences of differing quantities and qualities of effluent streams in different receiving media. For example, how can one compare the effects of minute concentrations of a toxic substance in atmospheric dust with its concentration in a sludge disposed of in a landfill site? Two pilot studies conducted by HMIP to see how best to make these judgments show that regulatory inspectors can think and act in an integrated manner and that many industries welcome the comprehensive, single-inspector approach because it saves regulatory time and money. However, even with a willing client, preparation of a good BPEO study absorbs so much time and costs so much for an agency already burdened by public expenditure controls that future surveys may have to be the responsibility of licensees. This change in responsibility may reduce the effectiveness and practicability of the BPEO concept, unless or until the regulatory regime in the

United Kingdom is changed in favor of a comparable and consistent statutory basis to air, water, and land disposal. At present the powers available to the licensing (regulatory) authorities vary enormously and there is no relationship between guidance at the center and implementation.

Radioactive Waste Disposal

The government also abruptly changed its policy with respect to radioactive-waste disposal in the month before the June 1987 election. It had encouraged the official waste management agency, the Nuclear Industry Radioactive Waste Executive (NIREX) to search for two sites in which to dispose of intermediate and low-level radioactive waste. The existing facility at Drigg, near the Sellafield nuclear reprocessing plant in Cumbria in northwest England, was filling up and a new site had to be found. Such is the public antipathy to nuclear waste, even among those who do not live adjacent to proposed sites, that the government told NIREX to look for possible sites without prior public discussion. It also encouraged NIREX to choose only two sites for exploratory drilling, one for low-level waste and the other for intermediate-level waste.

Subsequently the industrial private landowners of the site that had been selected for possible disposal of intermediate-level waste refused to give permission for the exploratory drilling program, and that site had to be abandoned. The government allowed NIREX to consider codisposal dumps for both low-level and intermediate-level waste in relatively shallow clay areas, although the search for an intermediate-level waste location also continued. To placate objectors at the remaining selected site, the government asked NIREX to find three additional locations for codisposal in suitable areas in lowland England.

These site investigations were conducted exclusively for scientific purposes. Any subsequent proposals for actual disposal would be subject to rigorous and extensive public examination. But the antagonism to and deep distrust of NIREX in the areas selected were so strong that the government added insult to injury by bypassing the normal planning process, which would have required an independent public inquiry for the test drilling phase, and obtaining planning permission for the investigative program by pliant parliamentary vote.

Opposition at the four selected sites was so intense that the four sitting Conservative candidates, including the party parliamentary organizer (chief whip) of the Conservatives, were in danger of losing their majorities. The local authorities involved, together with local scientific experts, presented an admittedly self-serving but plausible case for the deep disposal of low-level radioactive wastes in hard rock, rather than shallow disposal in clay where all the NIREX sites were located. The scientific and political opposition to the government-backed NIREX proposals was tough, articulate, and coordinated.

Ostensibly because of a NIREX report that the costs of shallow drilling were not significantly less than the costs of deeper drilling—a surprising judgment in the light of virtually no experimental information on the former and none at all on the latter—the government abandoned the four test sites ten days before the election was called.

Consequently, NIREX has embarked on a costly and extensive public consultation exercise aimed at sounding out reaction to three disposal options for a "superdump" of low- and intermediate-level radioactive waste—on land, on the ocean floor, or via a coastal site into the sea bed. A fourth possibility, strongly advocated by all antinuclear groups, is to retain the waste above or below ground at all existing nuclear facilities. This is not an official policy option and is not included in the NIREX consultation exercise. The omission could create major problems for NIREX, whose carefully constructed consultation may well come to be regarded as an expensive charade if a particular routeway is seen to be closed off before the debate begins. At stake is an important issue of credibility in an environmental arena of considerable political sensitivity.

Nuclear Politics and Tax Reform

This cameo history of the mismanagement of radioactive-waste disposal in the United Kingdom demonstrates both how the politics of nuclear issues are handled and how public suspicion of nuclear-related decisions can become inflamed simply through appallingly inadequate public relations. The government wants a steady-growth nuclear power program and has consistently backed the nuclear industry with state-supported research and development, beneficial borrowing arrangements, and political patronage. Until recently the industry enjoyed unqualified governmental support despite serious errors of management, poor public relations, and inadequate prior consultation. Public disaffection with matters nuclear in the United Kingdom is at least as much the result of perceived incompetence and economic prodigality as it is of environmental and safety considerations.

The industry is slowly learning its lesson. The NIREX initiative is one of a series of more open and honest attempts to discuss tactics and compensatory packages of community aid. Yet serious accusations of perceived preferential treatment and political patronage remain to plague the entire industry. It is also unlikely that the present government will ever sanction payment for local community compensation schemes, despite their success in France and Sweden. This unwillingness is partly a matter of political ideology, but it is also embroiled in the controversial proposals to reform local government income. Normally the local taxes paid by large industry such as nuclear facilities go to the national exchequer and are subsequently disbursed through a complicated formula to the local community. The proposed government legislation on a local community charge (through which everyone will pay a set fee for local government services, with some dispensation for the very poor) will not change this essentially unfair practice and is too politically contentious (because of the alleged unfairness of a set fee virtually irrespective of wealth or income) to allow any changes in the meantime. So local people faced with nuclear developments in their midst will probably receive no sweeteners. This situation has heightened local antagonism.

Post-Electoral Quiescence

Since the 1987 election, environmental politics in the United Kingdom has become very quiet. The opposition parties are licking their wounds and undergoing painful and prolonged reorganization. It will be many years before any coherent Green thinking emerges from that quarter. The new government has lost its most effective environmental minister, William Waldegrave, in a cabinet shuffle that split environmental protection from planning and housing. These ministerial responsibilities should be interlinked in a nation where land-use planning and environmental protection are so closely connected. To fragment them is a cruel blow that still further weakens coherent environ-

mental policymaking. Waldegrave was the only British minister
in modern times who substantially understood the complexities
of environmental science and the all-important relationships between scientific certainties, scientific uncertainties, and public
opinion on environmental hazards. He was ably supported by his
chief scientist, Martin Holdgate, who has also departed. That formidable combination has been replaced by a secretary of state
with an often outspoken distaste for environmental matters and
environmental activists and by junior ministers who sit in the
House of Lords and have no special environmental expertise. At
least on first sight, official British environmental interest is on the
wane.

European Community Policies

In the light of this declining governmental interest, arguably
the single most important influence on contemporary British environmental politics is the European Community, the political
collection of twelve member states administered by the Commission of European Communities in Brussels. When it was originally
created through the Treaty of Rome in 1957, the EC, then with
only six members, had no environmental policy, and any initiatives had to be put through vague and legally challengeable articles of the treaty. But since 1972 the EC has embarked on a series
of environmental action plans in the wake of the all-important
UN Conference on the Human Environment held in Stockholm,
at which the international obligation for good environmental
houskeeping by nation states was endorsed by all participants. So
far there have been four environmental action plans, each more
comprehensive, aggressive, and proactive than its predecessor. In
1985, the EC amended its governing legislation to give it specific
powers in the area of environmental protection.

The EC enacts its policies by a number of means, of which the
most important for the environmental arena is the commission directive. Directives require member states to create or amend
their own legislation according to how member states believe
they can best meet the spirit and purpose of the directive.

EC environmental directives are extremely important. One of
their purposes is to standardize environmental-quality targets
and objectives throughout the EC. In time this may reduce the
likelihood of pollution havens (regions of slack enforcement that

ignore illegal environmental damage) in the poorer Mediterranean countries where, generally speaking, environmental issues are less enthusiastically embraced. EC law also makes it difficult for individual member states to pursue their own, tougher regulations, especially where a product or a process associated with cross-border trade is involved, because the EC obliges member states to harmonize trading practices and avoid unfair competitive advantage or disadvantage through the use of specific national policies. Hence, it is impossible for an individual member state to set, for example, higher emission removal standards for motor vehicles (unlike the case for U.S. states), or to place an excessive tax on nitrogenous fertilizer, even though both actions would be in accord with the "polluter-pays principle" so hallowed by the EC.

In general, British governments have resisted EC-inspired environmental initiatives for four major reasons. The first is geographical. British governments believe they are blessed with large turbulent seas and gusty Atlantic gales that can dilute or disperse, up to a point, almost anything that is directed into them. The second is cultural. The British prefer regulation to be based on flexible objectives rather than on legally binding standards and they prefer purpose-built emission controls to regulations. The third is economic. British governments have always been wary of the cost of environmental regulation; they want controls to include some formal sense of cost-effectiveness. The continental Europeans prefer "technology-forcing" compliance—namely, strict targets for emission controls that stimulate improved abatement technologies. This may result in overall economic savings through improvements in processes or recovery of by-products.

The fourth factor is scientific. The official British view is that too much of the justification for EC environmental directives is based on scientific hearsay, too readily accepted by a commission that does not know how to marshal and evaluate scientific evidence. Accordingly, the British claim that many regulations are either unnecessarily expensive, because they are based on a false picture of the environmental dangers to be removed, or else premature, in the sense that better and more coordinated scientific research should be completed before legal commitments are made. This situation was very much the case over the removal of sulfur dioxide and nitrogen oxides from cars and coal-fired generating stations, and was originally the line the United Kingdom adopted over cleaning up the southern North Sea.

There is some justification to these criticisms. But such claims do not justify inaction or procrastination when environmental damage is manifestly evident. This is the special target for those who dislike Great Britain's political ploys. The West Germans in particular have become enthusiastic about technology-forcing environmental protection strategies based on the precautionary or anticipatory principle, the *Vorsorgeprinzip*. The Germans already spend about 20 billion DM (about $107.5 million) annually on pollution abatement technology and regard this as a healthy growth industry with considerable export potential. The British have yet to learn this lesson—an unfortunate state of affairs because the market will soon be saturated. The *Vorsorgeprinzip* established the rule that where scientific knowledge is still being gathered, but there is a threat to the human or nonhuman environment, then, as a precautionary measure, the best available technology should be instituted. This principle applies to maintaining the intrinsic health of ecosystems such as forests, lakes, and seas that should remain ecologically viable for their own sakes. The Germans believe that persistent and toxic pollutants should therefore be removed and safely disposed of under controlled conditions, not dispersed in the hope that they will disappear, which tends to be the belief of the British scientific establishment.

The *Vorsorgeprinzip* provides the basis for three important recent EC environmental initiatives. One is the 1984 framework directive for combatting air pollution from industrial plants. That directive requires all member states to meet agreed-upon targets for reducing emissions of sulfur dioxide and nitrogen oxides from coal-fired plants over the period from 1992 to 2003 and should prove significant in altering British regulations on coalfired emissions. The second directive is the 1987 North Sea Protocol, and the third, due to be announced in late 1988, is the so-called "red list" of toxic substances that will apply to water pollution control in rivers and estuaries.

Under the "red list" directive, the technology-forcing approach to the reduction of discharges, based on adoption of the best available technology, will in every case precede the cost-effectiveness analysis, which is defined in the directive as "not entailing excessive costs." This policy should drive the point of leverage in pollution control "up the pipe" into process design, maintenance and management, and by-product recovery. The aim is to reduce, but not eliminate, these substances to the lowest possible concentrations. It appears that Great Britain may adopt the "red list" directive for only 25 substances, although it is used for over 100 substances in continental Europe.

New regulations are to be imposed on sewage and industrial effluent being discharged into rivers that drain into the North Sea. By the mid-1990s, these regulations will bring to an end the controversial practice of dumping sludge residues and incinerating toxic wastes in specially designed ships, practices that were the special target of a campaign by Greenpeace in 1987. As a result, Great Britain will have to find other disposal routes for some 350,000 metric tons of toxic wastes, most of which are being produced without regard to the possible need for a land disposal pathway. Safe disposal on land of that thoroughly heterogenous and largely unlicensed material will prove quite a headache for British waste disposal authorities who have a little over five years to sort it out.

The EC has also finally adopted a directive on environmental impact assessment (EIA). Originally modeled ten years ago on the U.S. National Environmental Protection Act, this directive was steadily diluted, mostly by British pressure, over the course of six years of hard bargaining. The British line, backed by industry and supported by local government planning authorities, was that because of the comprehensive nature of British town and county planning procedures there really was no need for formal EIAs, especially if the EC commission in Brussels was to examine them for content and effectiveness. In any case, the British argued, EIAs would add to industrial development costs and frustrate and delay the essentially collegiate planning process. The EC modified its proposals so that EIAs would be mandatory for a small class of development projects, while a second, much larger group would be subject to EIAs only at the discretion of the member state. However, the European Commission could require that an EIA be undertaken where a proposed scheme would significantly affect the environment.

One arena in which this "significance" aspect of EIA activity will specially apply in the United Kingdom is in large agricultural development and afforestation schemes that currently lie outside the formal local authority planning process. Agricultural and afforestation projects have already resulted in unacceptable alteration of the landscape and habitat, yet at present both kinds of development can take place without adequate public scrutiny except in the national parks and a few prominent nature conservation areas. Together, these designated zones cover only 12 percent of the United Kingdom. The significant-environmental-effect clause in the EIA directive could change all this, but developers will try to devise schemes that they will claim fall below the threshold of "significance." Doubtless one such scheme will be challenged as a test case in the national courts and possibly even in the European Court, which can look at national performance under EC directives to establish just where this all-important distinction occurs. But for the first time, the expensive burden of proof will lie with the intervenors.

The Enterprise Culture

Of the many features of Margaret Thatcher's administrations since 1979, the application of her vision of the "enterprise culture" stands out. Never formally defined, this concept applies to the privatization of nationalized industries, increasing the emphasis on individual responsibility in private and social behavior, and encouraging self-reliance and entrepreneurial spirit. Captured in this philosophy of enterprise are four key ideas: voluntarism, self-regulation, competition, and diminished governmental control.

What does all this mean for environmental politics in the United Kingdom? Assuming, as seems likely, that Thatcher policies will continue to evolve over another ten years, one can speculate as follows.

PRIVATIZATION

The aim is to sell off all major public corporations involved in resource management to a share-owning democracy that in effect will be controlled by the major national and international financial institutions. Planned privatizations include the water and electricity industries within the next two years, after that the coal industry, and possibly some, if not all, of the publicly owned assets such as local authority parks and national nature reserves. The prospect of the transfer of huge public resources of enormous environmental significance to private, profit-seeking hands has filled the environmental movement with horror.

Environmentalists won a minor victory over the government's proposals for privatizing the water industry. Originally the proposal was to sell off the regional water authorities in their entirety, which would have transferred responsibilities for water quality management and environmental protection in general to the private sector. EC law and British public opinion forced the government to change its mind. Now water supply and sewage treatment (including the collection of industrial effluent for treatment) will be privatized, but all the environmental functions, together with land drainage and flood protection, will be transferred to a new public agency, the National Rivers Authority. Whether that body will have sufficient cash and clout to preserve Britain's water environment remains a matter of much speculation.

SELF-REGULATION

As public-sector budgets continue to be cut, the official regulatory agencies are reduced in manpower, stripped of funds for long-term research and development, scrutinized in a way that inhibits individual initiative and career development, and generally demoralized. Only the nuclear inspectorate is receiving sufficient money to provide adequate salaries for officials. The balance of regulatory responsibility for environmental protection is steadily shifting to the licensee—the private industry or the privatized former public corporation. It remains to be seen how far those who are regulated will adopt an environmentally responsible, self-policing line, no matter how strong the paper regulations.

Given the continuation of secrecy, weakened environmental intervention, and inadequate legal safeguards, the signs are not good. Because the still-public water industry is underfunded, water pollution is getting worse. A 1987 survey found that 10 percent of the rivers and estuaries in the United Kingdom had deteriorated, some seriously, since 1979, and prosecutions for illegal discharges were increasing. Similarly, sulfur dioxide emissions from coal-fired power stations are likely to rise because the shortly-to-be-privatized electricity corporations will probably be forced to spend too little on pollution control in order to keep prices down. Landfill management is in a deplorable state, with as many as 1,000 sites subject to migrating methane emissions and inadequate policing. Local-authority environmental health departments (comparable to city and county agencies in the United

States) are also underfunded and demoralized. Although some local authorities are competent, monitoring is virtually at a standstill, and enforcement is often weak, hit or miss, and ineffective.

Cost-Recovery

In the longer term, the Thatcher government's aim is to uncouple executive government from policy government. This means freeing whole ministries from the inflexible grip of civil service codes of practice, recruitment, and career paths, and establishing free-standing public agencies, made corporate under private-sector management regimes. The agencies would be able to run their own ships, within policy guidelines set by policy directorates that would remain centrally located. The new agencies, which could embrace all the environmental regulatory and custodial bodies, should have the flexibility to charge for their services. At present the idea is simply to operate on the basis of cost recovery. Fees for licensing effluent discharges—or, for example, fertilization practices in areas where groundwater nitrate levels are too high—are likely to be set on the basis of the administrative cost of preparing and executing a license.

But this narrow line hardly deals with the "polluter-pays principle." The golden opportunity could be lost to establish charges that relate to environmental damage and to build up revenue to finance long-term research and development and monitoring programs. These charges could have far-reaching implications for environmental protection, opening the way for much initiative and more adventurous revenue generation within the environmental protection services. The major snag is the policy control machinery that will still remain in the central government. Under tough ministerial direction, that state-dominated bias could suffocate a truly imaginative regulatory enterprise spirit.

Green Capitalism

A new spirit of Green capitalism is emerging in four forms: the manufacture and production of pollution abatement technology; the introduction of new process technologies that are efficient in their use of energy and materials; privately sponsored development of and investment in the rehabilitation of environmentally degraded areas, notably old industrial sites and parts of the dilapidated inner cities; and the sponsorship or environmental initiatives such as new wildlife parks, exhibitions, charitable trusts (including voluntary environmental restoration groups), and advice on how to incorporate good environmental practice in all aspects of business. There is even a new ecological investment trust, specializing in environmentally ethical business investment, that already has an impressive portfolio and steadily attracts new funds.

The future of Green capitalism is circumspect. Many suspicious environmental groups talk of "greenspeak"—ostensibly sound practices that in reality cover up for old-fashioned commercial profit and public relations of dubious sincerity. Certainly Green capitalism is no panacea. In a thoroughly competitive world it is still a very tender shoot. On the one hand, Green capitalism is the product of much good will and personal conviction, and in an important way it is linking part of the enterprise culture to modern environmentalism. But on the other hand, it is setting a potentially dangerous precedent that could further blunt the knife of truly radical environmentalism in the United Kingdom. There is a danger of incorporating environmental reform within a pattern that is dictated by an enterprise culture and an uninformed industrial ethos.

Public Accountability

Environmental protection is, in essence, a public good. Generations of economists have preached market failure and the impracticality of relying on the profit motive to ensure good environmental housekeeping practices over the long term. The question at the heart of the modern environmental dilemma in the United Kingdom is: Can an enterprise culture be guaranteed to be farsighted, socially responsive, and environmentally accountable? The *Vorsorgeprinzip* is not a peaceful bedfellow for the enterprise culture. As ministers become less responsive to parliament and steadily fail to control the everyday actions of their own agencies, as public money is removed from formerly state-supported research and development agencies, and as competitiveness and self-regulation dominate environmental responsibility, the future of British environmental politics may well lie in the changing character of the EC and the public spiritedness of the British people. By 1992, the EC will operate as a single, competitive market, with no barriers to the flow of trade, people, finance, or pollutants. This may weaken the harmonizing aspects of the environmental directives, but it could also provide an opportunity for more imaginative, nationally inspired political initiatives to establish good environmental practice. The onus of responsibility will increasingly fall on the British public. In the years to come citizens will have to learn how to assert their environmental conscience.

Two Cultures

Environmental politics in Great Britain is heavily dominated by EC issues and the realities of cooperative and responsible international action. Just as the Reagan administration could not throw off the environmental lobby, the Thatcher government will continue to be haunted by the strident political demands of environmental groups. The problem is that these demands tend to be more parochial than millenial, much more NIMBY (not in my back yard) than global, and more concerned with financial well-being than ecological health. The spirit of British environmentalism is in danger of being lost to an alien morality of neo-Victorian liberalism and a willingness to tolerate two cultures, one permanently affluent and one selectively impoverished. Environmental concerns are dominated by the protests of the wealthy. The more valid claims for revitalization of the land and for upgrading the quality of life in the poorer communities are only faintly heard. On the international stage, the link between environmental disruption and development hardly surfaces on the political agenda, despite the tragedy of the Ethiopian famine and the worldwide spontaneous response to help arising from the Live Aid charity.

Hope lies in the inner sensibilities of the British people, who are steadily realizing that all is not well with the world and that the environmental account is turning red at a pace that could affect the quality of life for today's generation of children. That is a chilling prospect. Environmentalism will come of age in the United Kingdom, even in a hostile political climate, but its day of dawning will be too long delayed, and much unnecessary suffering will first have to be experienced.

TROPICAL CHIC[4]

In case anyone is wondering where Peter Max has been since the early 1970s, the answer is "in creative retreat," according to a spokesman. But now Max is back, and he's determined to use his art "to show his concern for planetary issues," especially the preservation of tropical forests. For instance, Max has produced a "quality line of sportswear" that features shirts saying "Save the Rainforest" and "Hug a Tree." The proceeds will be donated to Peter Max's bank account. But don't get the wrong idea; Max says he plans to hold a $1 million auction of his work, and *that* money will go to the Rainforest Action Network, a San Francisco–based organization devoted to linking rain forest activists.

That's a lot of linking. Max is but one of many cultural heroes who have lined up for the hottest political cause since world hunger. The British rock star Sting has done a rain forest benefit concert at the Kennedy Center. And the Grateful Dead, though long known for consciousness raising, had never raised it for any specific political cause until last September's benefit concert for tropical forests at Madison Square Garden. The audience received an extensive information kit, including ready-to-send postcards to officials at the World Bank, at the United Nations Environment Program, in Congress, and in Brazil. Also: quotes from band members, including drummer Mickey Hart's meditation on "a profound understanding of man's biochemical relationship with nature." Suzanne Vega and Roger Hornsby sang at the concert, and Kermit the Frog was featured in a "Save the Rainforests" film.

Tropical chic is particularly evident in Washington, D.C. The Smithsonian is featuring a major exhibition on rain forests, the National Zoo in raising money to start its own tropical forests, and environmental groups are staffing up on lobbyists and grassroots activists in the area. Among politicians, tropical forest preservation has moved up the charts to rate mention not only by members of Congress, but by former presidents Ford and Carter and President-elect Bush.

[4]Article by Peter P. Swire, a Washington, D.C., attorney. *New Republic*. 200:18+. Ja. 30, '89. Copyright 1989 by The New Republic, Inc. All rights reserved. Reprinted by permission.

There is one problem with all of this. Backers of the rain forest movement are mostly in the United States or other modern industrialized countries. The rain forests are not. They're mostly in developing countries, which face other, more pressing issues, such as feeding their growing populations. So two questions must be answered. First, why is it our business to tell Brazil, Indonesia, and other forested countries what to do with their forests? And, assuming there's an answer to that question, how can we in developed countries convince the forested countries they should listen to us?

The standard answer to the first question is that the whole world is affected by tropical deforestation, so everyone should have a say in what happens to the forests. The best-known spillover effect is global warming, caused by emission of carbon dioxide and other gases. Deforestation (often to create farmland or ranch land, or just for the lumber) contributes to the greenhouse effect in two ways: burning the trees releases carbon dioxide into the environment, and cutting them reduces the number of trees on hand to convert carbon dioxide back into oxygen. The effect of deforestation on warming is substantial, perhaps one-third of the effect of all burning of fossil fuels. Estimates of the rate of tropical deforestation vary from 27,000 square miles per year (a bit larger than West Virginia) to 77,000 square miles (Nebraska). At the latter rate, the tropical forests, now covering about seven percent of the world's land surface, will disappear by 2050. Recent satellite photos that show thousands of fires in Brazil, ruining 31,000 square miles of virgin forest per year, suggest the higher number may be more accurate.

Unfortunately, the problem of global warming can seem abstract and distant to political leaders struggling with crises of debt, hunger, population growth, and urbanization. More to the point, even if, say, Brazil does recognize the gravity of the greenhouse effect, why should it sacrifice for the entire world? After all, northern countries don't have a long history of such sacrifice. They got rich by cutting their forests and exploiting their minerals. In fact, even since the environmental toll of economic development became evident, northern nations haven't posted a strong record. The United States, for example, has been blocked by political bickering from taking strong action on acid rain. So Third World leaders can justifiably tell us to clean up our own back yard before telling them to clean up theirs. In particular, they can demand that we cut our own, sky-high consumption of fossil fuels, which contributes substantially to global warming.

In short, demanding unilateral action from the Southern Hemisphere in the name of the greenhouse effect is unlikely to do any good. And it may backfire, since U.S. pressure is easily seen as Yankee imperialism.

To be sure, in trying to drive home the urgency of saving the rain forests, we can always note, correctly, that the greenhouse effect is not the only problem. Consider the loss of "biodiversity." Tropical forests hold over half of all terrestrial species, and perhaps over 90 percent. Deforestation, at current rates, will lead to a greater extinction of species than accompanied the demise of the dinosaurs. It is hard to reduce this issue to costs and benefits. Ecologists warn about the large and unpredictable effects that would follow such a mass extinction. Scientists worry about losing the world's most complex ecosystems before most species there are even catalogued, much less studied. Genetic engineers will feel cheated by the loss of their chief feedstock, new genes, just when biotechnology is opening the tropics' genetic diversity to myriad new uses. And many people find human-caused extinctions wrong for moral and aesthetic reasons (which, of all the concerns about biodiversity, turn out to carry the greatest political clout).

Still, with biodiversity as with the greenhouse effect, the question arises: Why should southern nations especially care? Clearing the forests bring them short-term economic gains—at least to their cattle ranchers and governing elites—even if it impedes sustainable economic development. But the long-term, more abstract benefits of saving the forests accrue mostly to the north. That's where the bioengineering and pharmaceutical companies are, and that's where most of the biologists and taxonomists and National Geographic photographers are.

Given that moral suasion is largely unconvincing and ineffective, how are we to get tropical nations to do what we want? Some have proposed boycotting imports of beef raised on burned-out forest plantations, or wood logged in non-sustainable ways. This approach may sometimes work, but it also risks trade retaliation, and it suggests a moral high ground that we may not, in fact, have. Suppose the tropical countries, or other countries, started boycotting U.S. products whose manufacture entailed the burning of fossil fuels (i.e., most U.S. products). How would we feel about that?

The fact is that if the world wants southern nations to stop burning their tropical forests, the world is going to have to pay them to do it. It can either pay them in the same currency, by forging some international environmental agreement under which all nations cut their various contributions to the greenhouse effect, or it can pay them with money. For now, the latter is simpler. And the mechanism for it already exists. The World Bank and the other multilateral development banks (MDBs), such as the Inter-American Development Bank, make more than $24 billion in loans and credits available each year to developing countries. These agencies have been criticized for funding projects that cause great environmental harm. Because the United States and other developed nations provide the funding, they can require the MDBs to pick projects that preserve the forests. There are signs that this is starting already.

The idea of subsidizing the preservation of rain forests has been picked up by some environmental groups in the form of "debt-for-nature swaps" that have offered an attractive deal to debtor nations including Costa Rica, Bolivia, and Ecuador. In these swaps, environmental groups buy up debt in hard-to-get dollars. In return, the debtor government agrees to make conservation investments in the local currency. The symbolism is apt: rather than "borrowing" short-term from their natural resources, the nations reduce debt by preserving those resources. The swaps expand parklands, sponsor environmental education and research, and provide funding for maintaining parklands that otherwise often exist only in theory.

But debt-for-nature swaps remain tiny compared with the economics of the overall debt problem. A far greater help to the rain forests would be an aggressive debt reduction plan that would directly ease the pressure on developing countries to exploit their resources so rapidly. Tropical forest preservation can become a major issue in LDC debt negotiations, joining traditional concerns about promoting democracy and maintaining economic stability. Environmental groups are pushing for such a solution, and Latin American governments are starting to see how effective the greenhouse effect could be in getting them more debt relief than they receive under the Baker Plan's renewed loans.

As the debt-for-nature swaps illustrate, environmental groups have done a fair amount of hard-nosed thinking about saving the rain forests. And the statements attributed to their celebrity patrons, for the most part, have been strikingly well informed. But it's important to remember that conscience alone won't save a single tree, and the forested countries are unlikely to respond favorably to stirring moral pleas or self-righteous demands.

Resisting faddish rain forest proposals is a particular challenge for Congress. A bill introduced by Representative Claudine Schneider of Rhode Island would require a forest conservation plan from every tropical country (a significant bureaucratic burden for some countries), and *all* activities supported by direct U.S. foreign assistance would then have to be consistent with the plan. Saving the rain forests is important, but not important enough to trump all other goals of foreign aid.

Among the better congressional proposals: part of the Agency for International Development (AID) appropriation has been earmarked for rain forest projects, with good results. The next step is to increase the overall level of aid and use it as leverage in the rain forest issues.

And what will professed environmentalist George Bush do? He has promised to convene a global conference on the environment in 1989, and to place tropical forest preservation high on the agenda. Sounds fine. But remember: presidents go to Moscow to duck tough domestic issues. Similarly, perhaps Bush will want to go to the international conference rather than tackling the tough, expensive, and controversial environmental issues that await him at home.

Be that as it may, the Bush administration can help save tropical forests through AID and the MDBs, by its support on debt-for-nature issues, and by starting to see forest preservation as integrally tied to the debt crisis. Bush can also use his bully pulpit to educate Americans about environmental issues. Perhaps a joint appearance with the Grateful Dead at the Kennedy Center?

IV. PRESERVING THE FUTURE

EDITOR'S INTRODUCTION

Many environmental activists claim that scientific or political efforts to preserve the environment aren't enough; what's needed is a new ecological ethos that puts the well-being of the Earth ahead of all other concerns. Without this philosophical foundation, as Norwegian prime minister Gro Harlem Brundtland and social theorist Ivan Illich note in the interviews that begin this section, environmental issues will usually take a back seat to short-range economic, political, or social needs. Brundtland offers the concepts of "sustainable development"—economic growth that proceeds no faster than the environment can handle—and "intergenerational responsibility"—accepting the task of handing a viable world to our children—as the linchpins of the budding "green" era in environmental awareness.

Two articles on forest restoration and preservation follow. Ariel E. Lugo, a tropical forest expert with the U.S. Forest Service, describes how reforestation can begin to heal ravaged forestlands. But the inhabitants of the forest must take primary responsibility for their own environment. The Kuna tribe of Panama is doing just that by establishing their homeland as a nature preserve, as described by Norman Myers in his article for *International Wildlife*. Americans who have taken similar responsibility for their local environments are profiled in the next essay.

Sometimes it can take decades for poisoned lands to return to life. Surprisingly, while we are willing to expend great effort to restore the ecological balance, we may still feel nostalgic for our own works, even destructive ones. So feel the people profiled in Wilton Barnhardt's essay on Ducktown, Tennessee, a former copper-mining community laid waste a century ago. Carefully planted trees now grow on the town's spectacularly barren copper-red hills, but as one Ducktown resident puts it, "They ought to leave it to show what men can do to nature, as well as what man can undo."

THE TEST OF OUR CIVILIZATION[1]

GRO HARLEM BRUNDTLAND: Ms. Brundtland is the prime minister of Norway and chair of the UN World Commission on Environment and Development. She is the first environment minister in any nation to have become a head of government.
In the following interview, conducted by NPQ Editor Nathan Gardels in Oslo, Prime Minister Brundtland outlines the ecological issues which will frame international affairs after the Cold War.

NPQ: As the Cold War winds down and the atmosphere heats up, the environment is rising to the top of the global agenda. George Bush, Margaret Thatcher, François Mitterrand and even Mikhail Gorbachev are espousing ecology. *Realpolitik* has turned Green.

What's happened all of a sudden?

Gro Harlem Brundtland: A revolution is taking place in 1989. For those of us who have been pressing ecological concerns for fifteen years, it is astonishing to see the leading political figures of the world compete over who holds the most important meetings on the ozone layer or the greenhouse effect. It's fantastic.

The changes began in 1987 and 1988. In those years, scientific evidence about the rapid and irreversible destruction of the support systems for life on this planet—from ozone depletion to deforestation—finally sifted into the power circles of industry, the main transformer of resources on the globe, and from there into the political centers of decision-making. I only hope this rapid shift in sentiment is enduring, not fleeting.

NPQ: Back in the 1970s, when you were environment minister, ecology was becoming a major issue. There was even discussion in those days about entering an "era of limits."

Then, with the revival of the Cold War and bi-polar conflict in the late 1970s and early 80s, these issues fell into eclipse and languished at the margins of political debate. Issues of growth and military buildup dominated the agenda.

With the arrival of Mikhail Gorbachev's *perestroika* and Ronald Reagan's happy stroll in Red Square, the Cold War lost its impetus. Now, it seems, the vital issues of the future can emerge.

Do you see it this way?

[1]Interview with Norway's Prime Minister Gro Harlem Brundtland. *New Perspectives Quarterly.* 4+. Spring '89. Copyright 1989 by the Center for the Study of Democratic Institutions. All rights reserved. Reprinted by permission.

Brundtland: Yes, I do. I feel we have just passed through a period where everything was frozen, a black age.

Environmental issues have *re-emerged*, in a sense. There was much more multi-lateral concern on the environment in the late 1960s through 1975 than from 1975 onward, when the conflict between the superpowers eclipsed the vital issue of ecological destruction. When there is a fear war is pending, everything else is pushed aside in the minds of political leaders. Thoughts turn to arms buildups and military security. After all, it was not easy to imagine cooperation on acid rain between East and West in Europe when each side was installing a new round of intermediate range missiles. But this diversion has now passed.

Already, a new awareness of global ecological interdependence is filling the political space which used to be occupied by divisive Cold War concerns. The fact that our own life, and the lives of our children, is in danger wherever we live on this globe, helps us all see that we need to find solutions to our common problems in a cooperative, global framework.

NPQ: Will the environmental issue replace the Cold War as the main framework of international affairs?

Will we turn from an agenda of military security to ecological security? Will we start counting refrigerators, air conditioners and cars instead of missiles?

Brundtland: Yes, I hope so and I think so.

I also believe this will provide a framework for new political thinking; the opportunity for a "global *perestroika*" in the way we think about how states work together to deal with the common and interrelated problems of ecology and development.

No nation has gotten itself into a rut on the environment issue. There are thus no ideological barriers to finding solutions. There is no preconceived Truth on ecological matters, whether one is from Africa, Asia, North America or Europe. Everything can start anew. For the first time in nearly a century, we can make a fresh start in global politics.

NPQ: Your 1987 World Commission report introduced the concepts of "sustainable development" and "intergenerational responsibility" into the debate.

What do you mean by these terms?

Brundtland: Fundamentally, "sustainable development" is a notion of discipline. It means humanity must ensure that meeting present needs does not compromise the ability of future generations to meet their own needs. And that means disciplining our current consumption.

This sense of "intergenerational responsibility" is a new political principle, a virtue, that must now guide economic growth. The industrial world has already used so much of the planet's ecological capital that the sustainability of future life is in doubt. That can't continue.

The inhabitants of this industrialized and industrializing planet must begin to think like the farmer in a stable community. He realizes that his small plot of earth must also be used by his children and grandchildren. So he grows food in a way that preserves the fertile capacity of the land.

That is not the way we have lived in the modern world. Particularly since the emergence of the money economy, we have adopted a way of thinking which places only a *present* value on resources. The value of a natural resource is priced by market forces of supply and demand only in a very short-term time frame. That kind of thinking is no longer possible when the depletion of finite resources—including our precious atmosphere—threatens to ruin our own long-term life basis.

We have to change. I'm sure we can have a market economy in the future. But new scientific and political frameworks at the international level must redefine the boundaries of economic growth within which the market operates.

The Montreal Protocol of 1987, in which most industrial nations agreed to cut the production and consumption of ozone-destroying chlorofluorocarbons (CFCs) and halon gases 50% by 1999, is an example of how a political framework can set limits on economic growth. In London recently, environmental ministers from Europe agreed to cut CFCs 95% by 1995. A meeting in Helsinki in May will try to bring all the signatories of the Montreal Protocol, as well as key nations in the developing world, in line with the more rapid action of the London meeting. Prime Minister Michel Rocard of France, Prime Minister Ruud Lubbers of the Netherlands, and I are working, along with some 21 other heads of state and government, to develop a system of measures against nations who don't act to cut CFC use.

As responsible leaders, we must be able to defend the future we are leaving to our children. This is really what sustainable development and intergenerational responsibility are all about.

NPQ: When you strip away all the politics, aren't we really saying that, if the planet is going to make it, future generations simply cannot enjoy our same rates of consumption growth?

Brundtland: Yes, in the end, that is inescapably true. The key word is *rate* of growth in consumption. There is that no doubt we must reduce levels of consumption and change the pattern of consumption, particularly our wasteful use of energy.

I do think it is possible to have economic growth, but at a lower and more steady rate; growth defined more in terms of quality of life than simply more and more material goods.

An analogy may be helpful here: Many people in the Western industrialized countries not only eat more than they need; they eat more than is healthy. Generally speaking, our whole culture crossed the threshold from affluence to overconsumption.

This is bad not in moral terms, but in self-interest terms. To use one example from my experience as a medical doctor, too much meat and too much fat reduces life expectancy. The same is true of overconsumption of resources at the societal and global level: it reduces the life expectancy of the species. It is an unsustainable pattern of growth.

And, of course, equity issues are also involved. In many parts of the developing world and in the poorer reaches of the industrialized North there are cultures and individuals that have hardly reached the threshold of overconsumption. My point is that the discipline of sustainable development inescapably places an upper limit on consumption.

NPQ: Let's look at the equity issue:

The Chinese now produce less than 10% of the CFCs that Europe and the US produce. Yet, while we plan to cut out all CFC production by the year 2000, the Chinese have already built 12 CFC factories and plan to put a refrigerator in every Chinese home by the year 2000.

Liu Ming Pu, the vice-chairman of China's Commission for Environmental Protection, argues that Europe and the US took the "quick growth route" to vast wealth, flooding the atmosphere with carbon dioxide and CFCs in the process. "Why should China's standard of living suffer as a result?" Liu asks.

India's environment Minister, Z. R. Ansari, says his poor nation can't "wait" for development without facing a social explosion.

Brundtland: I think these statements are very typical and also very understandable. If those of us in the rich nations don't realize we need a serious answer to these questions, then the industrializing countries will not feel obliged to join any international accords that will save the white-skinned peoples of the Northern Hemisphere from melanoma.

Indira Gandhi made this point to me some years ago. For her, stopping development to save our white skins was unacceptable, especially since poverty, in her view, was the main cause of environmental destruction in India. It is simply not possible for us to say, "we will keep what we have and you shall have no more."

I think it is incumbent upon the industrialized nations of the North to use some of the wealth we have accumulated to finance alternative technologies—for example other chemicals besides CFCs that can be used in refrigeration—and the retooling of industry so places like India and China can enjoy certain benefits of development without the destructive side-effects. Debt relief can also help lift the burden of rapid growth to meet bank payments.

We also have to shift to resource-efficient, low-waste technologies in the developed world to, in effect, allow room for the poorer nations to develop.

NPQ: So technology is what will make development sustainable?

Brundtland: . . . And political decisions. Otherwise, the technological solutions will not be forthcoming. Politics forces technology. If we set the restrictions, market-driven technological innovation will rise to meet them. That is why the present revolution in the environmental awareness of political leaders is so crucial.

NPQ: What about alternative paths to development in India, China, Africa or Latin America? It make little sense for the financial centers of the Northern industrial world to provide petro-dollar debt relief if the result will be to flood the atmosphere with even more carbon dioxide and chlorofluorocarbons.

Brundtland: This is true, but unless we first realize our obligations to shift toward a low-waste, low-energy, resource-efficient growth path our preachings are sure to have little impact. It would be very difficult, for instance, for us to say to Mexico, "You should not follow our same stupid path of development, which we have seen is unsustainable, but should build your infrastructure in a completely different way."

If choosing an alternative path puts a more expensive price on development in Mexico, it is in our own interest to see they get the technology, financing and investment necessary. In this interdependent world, there is no escaping the fact that we in the North must internalize some of the costs of a cleaner model of economic growth in the South.

NPQ: The World Commission report also stressed the necessity of democracy, participation and decentralization of power in the developing world as a pre-condition for sustainability.

Brundtland: The important point here is not the type of democracy, but that democratic processes are set in place. If people have no say in constructing their future they will have no commitment to it. As a political principle, intergenerational responsibility obviously cannot work without a commitment to the future.

Human behavior is not apt to be reasonable or sound, or capable of thinking about the long-term, unless people believe that the institutions of a society are working on their behalf and on the behalf of their children. If a person doesn't think that her child will grow up or that there is the possibility of a happy life, why cooperate? Why conserve?

Also, the pressure of public opinion and social movements like the Greens is necessary to force governments to act. The need for participation and democracy extends to the international level as well. Without the pressure of multi-lateral efforts and international opinion, it is difficult to make the nations most irresponsible about pollution and environmental destruction act responsibly.

NPQ: As the newfound environmental awareness takes center stage, it can develop in two directions: the technological fix or cultural transformation.

Having dealt with this issue for so long, especially from the unique perspective as chair of the World Commission, what is the crux of the matter? Ultimately, is your faith in technology or in a new cultural ethos, perhaps the virtue of *enoughness*?

Brundtland: A new cultural ethos is the main thing. That ethos, I believe, is intergenerational responsibility. If that ethos is not accepted almost as a religious belief, we cannot convince anyone that we must change the way we live. If we cannot make people realize that living as we do will make it impossible for their grandchildren to live at all, they won't change. If people believe this is true, it is a premise that can reach both minds and hearts.

Having said that, if people adopt this ethos only to find the proposed solutions too out of reach in their own lifetimes, too impossible, they will stick to their old habits. They will continue to dream their own dreams at night and write novels about Utopia.

That is why the link between ecology and economy is so essential. The present world is so dominated by economic thinking it is not possible to change this basic reality, at least in my lifetime.

What is possible is to move people to think ahead a decade or two. Businessmen must see the opportunity to sell non-leaded fuels or non-petroleum energy sources or air conditioners without halon gases or fruits and vegetables without pesticides. If we can nudge a large portion of the dominating economic structure in these directions, then we can build the momentum to sustain a cultural change in a way that no longer seems utopian. Our objective should not be to rely on technology, but to utilize resource-efficient technology as the passageway to a low-energy infrastructure in the 21st century.

That's why I insist on the link between economy and ecology. One without the other will not succeed in taking us toward a sustainable way of life.

NPQ: China again comes to mind as I think about the need for a new cultural ethos. If we press for democracy and participation in a land where the new slogan is "to be rich is glorious" the result will be consumer demand for 1 billion refrigerators! What if that demand arrives before new technologies dispense with the need for chlorofluorocarbons and electricity generated by burning coal?

Brundtland: You are right. We have little time to find the new technological solutions, especially in the energy field.

There is already a gap between need and energy supply on a global level. If we can't find a way to fill that gap with resource-efficient technologies, it will be filled by wasteful, polluting technologies.

That is the unavoidable, disheartening reality. It is all the more reason why the already developed countries must, without delay, place the global environment issue at the top of their agendas. The research and investment in alternative energy and benign chemicals should have started two decades ago.

NPQ: Which type of society poses the toughest challenge to sustainability: the acquisitive consumer societies of Europe, America and Japan; the authoritarian bureaucracies like China or the Soviet Union; or the "catch-up" industrializing nations like Brazil or Mexico?

Brundtland: The acquisitive consumer societies of the West. People in our part of the world are satisfied with the lifestyle made possible by continuous economic growth. They have little interest in changing.

That is why it is so important to drive home this point: "Look, are you going to deliberately avoid making tough decisions even though you know that if you or your children move away from pollution, because you have enough money to pay for a nicer neighborhood or for a country home, it doesn't help? Don't you know there is no escape from the damaged atmosphere?"

To counter consumer complacency about the future we need to use the other strength of our culture: the ability to spread information and knowledge. Our future rests in this hope.

As for the other societies you have mentioned, I think they are still dominated by Western models of science and development. If we take the lead in an ecological direction, in changing ourselves culturally, it will have an enormous impact.

Europe was the birthplace of the Industrial Revolution. We were the ones who polluted the atmosphere on a massive scale and initiated the plunder of the earth's resources. It seems to me that the historical obligation to break a new path toward sustainable development thus also falls on us.

NPQ: In our modern time, almost by definition, the future has no political constituency. Especially in consumer societies, politics is beholden to the interests of the present.

Our ability to import the future into present politics is, as you have stated, the test of our civilization.

Are we going to meet that test?

Brundtland: The new urgency about the environment convinces me we are moving in the direction of meeting that test. I truly sense it has dawned on our species that our problems can't be left for tomorrow, for the next generation. We seem to have grasped, instinctively, that the future is now because, if it is not, there will be no future.

THE SHADOW OUR FUTURE THROWS[2]

IVAN ILLICH: Because of his groundbreaking critique of industrial society well over a decade ago in such books as *Energy and Equity*, *Medical Nemesis* and *Toward a History of Needs*, the philosopher Ivan Illich is widely regarded as a founding thinker of the ecology movement. He is often thought of as the "prophet of an era of limits."

NPQ Editors Nathan Gardels and Marilyn Berlin Snell recently spoke with Illich at his home in a small village on the slopes of the Sierra Madre some seventy miles from Mexico City.

NPQ: Because of your radical critique of industrial society fifteen and twenty years ago, you are widely regarded as a founding thinker of the environmental movement.

Now, many of your concepts have entered the vocabulary of the established institutions of industrialism and development: the World Bank now talks about "sustainable development" and incorporates ecological concerns into their sponsorship of economic development; George Bush, Margaret Thatcher and Mikhail Gorbachev worry publicly about the ozone layer and promise "an environmental agenda."

What's changed?

Ivan Illich: What has changed is our common sense has begun searching for a language to speak about the shadow our future throws.

The central thesis that ran through much of my early work was that most man-made misery—from the suffering of cancer patients and the ignorance of the poor to urban gridlock, housing shortages and air pollution—was a by-product of the institutions of industrial society originally designed to protect the common man from the environment, improve his material circumstances and enhance his freedom. By breaching the limits set on man by nature and history, industrial society engendered both disability and suffering in the name of eliminating disability and suffering!

In this early critique, I recalled Homer's warning of the doom of *Nemesis*. Driven by *pleonexia*, or radical greed, Prometheus transgressed the boundaries of the human condition. In *hubris*, or

[2]Interview with social philosopher Ivan Illich. *New Perspectives Quarterly.* 20+. Spring '89. Copyright 1989 by the Center for the Study of Democratic Institutions. All rights reserved. Reprinted by permission.

measureless presumption, he brought fire from the heavens and thereby doom onto himself. He was chained to a rock, an eagle preyed on his liver and heartlessly healing gods kept him alive by regrafting the liver each night. The encounter of Prometheus with Nemesis is an immortal reminder of inescapable cosmic retribution.

Common to all pre-industrial ethics was the idea that the range of human action was narrowly circumscribed. Technology was a measured tribute to necessity, not the implement that would facilitate mankind's chosen action. In more recent times, through our inordinate attempt to transform the human condition with industrialization, our whole culture has fallen prey to the envy of the gods. Now Everyman has become Prometheus and Nemesis has become endemic; it is the backlash of progress. We are hostage to a lifestyle that provokes doom.

Man cannot do without his CO_2-belching cars or the chlorofluorocarbon deodorant sprays that destroy the biosphere. He can't do without his radiation therapy, his pesticides or his nonbiodegradable plastic bags at the supermarket. If the species was to survive, I argued in my early work, it could do so only by learning to cope with Nemesis.

For a seminar in the summer of 1970, I gathered a reading list on "environmental issues." It included several of the first studies on genetic changes in children born into the fallout from atomic experiments at the Bikini Atoll; a study on the pesticide residues in the human liver; and the very first study of its kind on DDT residues in mothers' milk. At that time, I was widely criticized for engaging in "apocalyptic randiness."

Now, nearly two decades later, a woeful sense of imbalance has dawned on the common sense. The destruction of the ozone layer, the heating up of the earth's atmosphere, the non-reversible and progressive depletion of genetic variety—all these things bring to consciousness the consequences of our Promethean transgression.

There is a generalized sense now that the future we expected is not working and that we are in front of what Michel Foucault has called an "epistemic break"—a sudden image-shift in consciousness in which the unthinkable becomes thinkable. Until the French Revolution, for example, it was simply not thinkable that a king could be beheaded. Then, suddenly the king was beheaded and a dramatically new image of the common man's role in society emerged. A language was invented which spoke in new, previously unimaginable, terms about the order of society.

Similarly, it is no longer tolerable for us to think of nuclear bombs as weapons; now they are known as tools of self-annihilation. The disintegrating ozone layer and warming atmosphere are making it intolerable to think of industrial growth as progress; now it appears to us as aggression against the human condition. Perhaps for the first time, we can now imagine that, as Samuel Beckett once put it, "this earth could be uninhabited."

What is new is not the magnitude, not even the quality, but the very essence of the coming rupture in consciousness. This rupture is not a break in the line of progress to a new stage; it is not even the passage from one dimension to another. We can only describe it as a *catastrophic* break with industrial man's image of himself.

NPQ: When Norwegian Prime Minister Brundtland's World Commission on Environment and Development calls for "sustainable development," they are both contributing to and detracting from a language which speaks to the future's shadow.

"Sustainable" is the language of balance and limits; "development" is the language of the expectation of *more*.

Illich: Although Brundtland exposes the detrimental side- effects of industrial progress and tells the rich nations they must bear the burden of saving the planet, she remains firmly within the "development" discourse. While Ms. Brundtland is quite capable of delinking the pursuit of peace and justice from the 19th century dream of progress, the underlying critique of the concept of development still remains outside her thinking. The outer forms are crumbling, but the conceptual underpinnings of "development" remain vigorous.

The pressing questions today are: "After development, What? What concepts? What symbols? What images?"

In order to find an alternative language, one must return to the past—discover the history of those invented certitudes that are the mythological crystallization points around which modern experience is organized, certitudes like "need," "growth," "participation," "development."

To paraphrase the Chilean poet Vicente Huidobro, insight into alternatives not chosen can be found by remembering "those hours which have lost their clock."

For example, before Cortez, there was a unique Indian corn seed made up of at least 150 distinct genetic strains. It was uniquely adapted to the micro-climate of the area where I live. When ground into meal, the corn was the characteristic blue color of local flowers, different from those ten miles east or west of here. Religious festivals, marriage customs, ovens and diet were shaped by that crop.

Then came Dr. Borlaug's "miracle" seed, with government subsidies for fertilizer, insecticides and fungicides. In the first few years, the fields produced fantastic returns. But then, within less than a decade, the terraces which covered this region from pre-Columbian times, left uncultivated, were all washed out. Now, the young people here no longer work in the fields. They seek work in larger towns, repair old cars or try to earn some money peddling household appliances. The tools of their fathers have disappeared. These changes occurred so rapidly that the "blue corn" festivals are still celebrated.

Only by re-entering the present moment with knowledge of the lost time of the blue tortilla—to extend this example—will it be possible to establish a new way of seeing and a new set of terms that can guide sustainable "policies" without recourse to "development."

NPQ: What is the history of the term "development?" How has it transformed our relationship to nature?

Illich: The "human condition" once described a way of life bound by immutable necessities. Each culture cultivated commonly shared desires or projects of a symbolic nature. In the instance I just described, before transportation and refrigeration, or scientifically produced seed strains, great varieties of food, like blue corn, were grown, complex diets formalized, and seasons ritualized. "The Good" was defined within the "commons"—life bounded by accepted limits.

"Development," on the other hand, is one of those modern terms which expresses rebellion against the "necessity" that ruled *all* societies up to the 18th century. The notion of "development" promises an escape from the realm of necessity by transforming the "commons" into "resources" for use in satisfying the boundless "wants" of the possessive individual.

"Development" combines a faith that technology will free us from the constraints which bound all past civilizations with the root certainty of the 20th century: evolution. As interpreted by optimistic politics, "evolution" becomes "progress." The term "under-development," in fact, was first used by Harry Truman in 1949, when the colonialism shattered by World War II "revealed" a world that was not on the track of industrial growth.

Parallel to the construction of this idea of industrial progress, another concept, which implied the assent of the "masses" to development, came into vogue: participation. Since development reduces the constraints of necessity, people must, for their own good, transform their vague and sometimes unconscious desires into "needs," which then must be fulfilled.

"Needs" redefine "wants" as "lacks" to be satisfied by "resources." Since "wants" are boundless, resources become "scarce" because of the value "lack" places upon them. This is the basis for the insatiable demand for *more*.

"Needs" are not "necessities." They are "wants" that have been redefined as claims to commodities or services delivered by professionals from outside the vernacular skills of the community. The universal appearance of "needs" during the past 30 years thus reflects a redefinition of the human condition and what is meant by "the Good."

For example, in Mexico City today, the burgeoning population *needs* to be provided with food because fewer people in absolute numbers can grow their own food. More people in Mexico City *need* public transport or recycled American cars because they have no choice but to commute in order to work in the market economy. More housing, with water and electricity, *needs* to be provided by borrowing from North American banks because there is less space suited for self-built shacks, and because people have lost the skills necessary to pour a roof slab.

NPQ: So, at the root of environmental destruction and depletion of finite resources is a drive for economic growth stimulated by transformation of the human condition ruled by necessity into a reign of "needs."

If that is so, then the path "after development," in your view, would involve a return to subsistence and restoration of the commons?

Illich: Yes, exactly. Sustainability without development, or subsistence, is simply living within the limits of genuinely basic needs. Shelter, food, education, community, and personal intimacy can all be met within this framework.

NPQ: A renunciation of economic growth hardly seems capable, at the moment, of garnering much political support. And, in modern times, where political will lacks, technology substitutes.

Indeed, one wonders why we can't move on to "post-scarcity" instead of "subsistence." Why not go the route of ecological modernization?

If energy is finite, why not resource-efficient technology? If petroleum powered cars pollute, why not switch to methanol? If passenger miles are excessive for the commute to the office, why not stay at home and work on the computer?

Illich: The Information Revolution has injected new life into what would otherwise have been the exhausted logic of industrialization. It encourages expectations that, through his tools, man can escape the limits of his human condition.

On the other hand, subsistence assumes a context of commonly defined needs balanced against the limits of nature. The social awareness that distinguishes between post-scarcity and subsistence rests upon historical knowledge that the human condition is precarious.

NPQ: With the technologies of the Information Age, especially bio-engineering, I suppose it is even more crucial to see attempted escape from the human condition as a trangression. In your terms, this delusion is all the more dangerous for seeming all the more possible.

Does this make you more or less hopeful about the future?

Illich: I distinguish between the attitudes of hope and expectation. "Expectation" is based on a belief in instruments and the naive acceptance of socially constructed certitudes. "Hope" is based on historically-rooted experience. To face the future freely, one must give up both optimism and pessimism and place all *hope* in human beings, not *trust* in tools.

I, for one, see signs of hope in the lifestyles of subsistence peasants or in the network of activists who save trees here, or plant them there. But, I admit that I am still unable to envisage how, short of a devastating catastrophe, these hope-inspiring acts can be translated into "policy."

NPQ: Surely, when the revenge of the cosmos crystallizes in the ruin of an ancient metropolis like Mexico City—where the fetuses of the unborn are poisoned by lead from the air their mothers breathe—its ruins will stand, like Prometheus, as a testament to the curse of Nemesis.

Then, perhaps, "policy" will desert development and new forms of organizing life will take hold.

Illich: Mexico City is beyond catastrophe. It is a metaphor for all that has gone wrong with development. That ancient city, founded on a lake in the pristine air of a high mountain valley, will have no clean air or water by the year 2000.

But what is marvelous about Mexico City is *why* the city survives at all.

Why are people there not dying from thirst? Of the enormous amount of water pumped over the mountains from the countryside, 50% goes to less than 3% of the households and 50% of the households gets less than 3% of the water. That means the latter 50% gets only enough water to drink, cook and wash, and then flush away only every seventeenth shit!

The fact is that dilution of feces in water is totally unfeasible in Mexico City. Yet, the 5.5 million people who have no stable place for shitting somehow keep even this aspect of their life under control.

So, Mexico City is also a symbol of the stability of neighborhood equilibrium beyond catastrophe. In such a world as this, I see frightening but effective forms of self-government emerging that keep government and the development institutions out of people's everyday affairs. Most of this new activity emerged after the earthquake in 1985 when the government was paralyzed and unable to aid recovery.

Today, demands for self-governance are formulated routinely by the Assembly of *Barrios* (neighborhoods) in discussions like these:

"How can there be enough water in Mexico City for everyone? Let us build the water tanks, fill them, and then we will distribute the water in our own barrio."

"How to avoid gridlock and traffic jams and lower the lead level in the air? No trucks on Mexico City streets during the day. During the night, food can be brought to central markets in each of the barrios and then hauled from there to neighborhoods by pushcart."

Now, there are even demands for the self-management of their own shit! And, in many barrios, there is an increasing number of places where the police are barred because they are considered a menace.

These are practical indications that people can invent alternatives to a concept of development that has thrown the whole nation into a debtor's prison. Self-management of genuinely basic needs is what occurs here.

NPQ: So, new forms of living emerge out of the ruins of development?

Illich: Some novelists, like Doris Lessing in *The Fifth Child*, create a sense of the emergent future, of what kinds of relationships are possible in the ruins. There is a sense in Lessing's writings of the frightening beings who have survival capacity.

It is fascinating to discover this shared experience of outsiders in post-earthquake, pre-ecological-apocalypse Mexico City. There is something here of the taste of the gang, the ragpicker, the garbage dump dweller. Our difficulty is finding a language to speak about this alternative, because , contrary to professional wisdom, people with unmet basic needs are surviving with new forms of conviviality.

Perhaps we can think of them as the *technophagic majority* of the late 20th century—people who feed on the waste of development. This population comprises half of Chicago's inner-city youth who have dropped out of school, as well as two-thirds of Mexico City's dwellers whose excrement goes untreated. From New York's underclass to Cairo's "city of the dead" where people live in the cemeteries, these survivors are the spontaneous architects of our post-Modern "future."

NPQ: *Roadwarriors* is the image that springs to mind. . . .

Illich: Guilty of the crime of "social disillusionment," these survivors reassert unsquashable hope with the chilling character of the gang. As outlaw communities without diplomatic consistency, their experience is barred from the Brundtland discourse except as recalcitrant, "needy" clients who require the kindness of strangers.

Yet, as living renunciations of the "future," these survivors somehow show the way forward. Their willingness to engage in communitarian exercises, outside "development," makes us smile about the pompousness of professionals plotting humanity's next step.

NPQ: You've sketched a path beyond development and outside the dominant debate now shaped by the Brundtland Commission. What is the next move within that discourse?

Illich: It is clear to me that an administrative-intensive global ecology follows logically from the utilitarian ethic of management that undergirds Brundtland.

Originally, utilitarianism was conceived as an attempt to give the most good to the largest number of people. Then, sometime in the 1970s, it came to mean the least pain for the largest number of people. This medical metaphor illuminates the next step after Brundtland: not the greatest good, nor the least pain, but the greatest *pain management* for the species.

NPQ: In effect, hooking up the earth to a respirator and supplying it with drugs. . . .

Illich: Precisely. After Brundtland, I envision management of the depletion of the commons, not restoration of the common environment to culturally bounded, politically sanctioned limits to growth. In this ectopia, we will see the technologically-assisted management of man from sperm to worm, including rates of reproduction.

NPQ: Would you then welcome the emergence of a new ecological worldview that focuses man's attention on restoring the natural equilibrium? Might that be the new universal ethos which ties this fragmented planet together?

Illich: You must understand that the concept of ecology is deeply related to the concept of life. "Life" cannot be understood apart from the "death of nature." In a continuous thread which runs back to Anaxagoras (500–428 BC) and up through the 16th century, an organic, whole conception of nature was a constant theme in the West. God was the pattern that connected the cosmos. With the Scientific Revolution, however, a mechanistic model came to dominate thinking. As the object of man's will, nature was transformed into dead material. This death of nature, I would argue, was the most far-reaching effect of the radical change in man's vision of the universe.

Now, this artificial character of "life" appears with special poignancy in the ecological discourse. The pattern which connects living forms and their habitat—God—is dissolved into the cybernetic concept of an "ecosystem" which, through multiple feedback mechanisms, can be regulated scientifically if the inputs are chosen properly by intelligent man. Man, the agent of disequilibrium, projects upon himself the grand task of restoring equilibrium to nature. Ecological man protects "life" and defends resources from depletion.

The self-regulating system of "life" thus becomes the model for opposing industrial destruction. It is a very seductive idea and it simplifies everything. In an attempt to come to grips with Nemesis, man expands his presumption to managing the cosmos! In the name of nature, ecology idolizes Promethean man.

THE FUTURE OF THE FOREST[3]

Among the Earth's regions, the tropics have been considered the most stable and least disturbed. Half of the world's forests, as well as the largest area of mature forests in the world, are located in the tropics. Tropical lands are, on average, 42 percent forested and support the world's most complex ecosystems. Because of their complexity and apparent pristine condition, tropical forests are considered to be "cradles of evolution," or the regions where most species evolved.

The highest current rates of land-use change in the world are also found in the tropics, where human populations are growing rapidly. Each year more than 10 million hectares of mature tropical forest cover are converted to other uses. Simultaneously, about 5 million hectares of secondary forest and 6 million hectares of deforested agricultural lands are created annually. Such dramatic changes in land use have been linked to changes in the increase in the carbon dioxide content of the atmosphere, species extinction, declining environmental quality, and direct threats to human welfare. In short, reduction of forest cover in the tropics is generally considered detrimental to the long-term productivity of the land resource.

However, not all forest conversions are negative. Some lead to sustainable land uses that are beneficial to human survival. For example, the establishment of agroecosystems in rich soils with humid climates and the potential for sustainable food production should not be construed as a negative change in land use.

[3]Article by Ariel E. Lugo, director of the U.S. Forest Service's Institute of Tropical Forestry in Puerto Rico. *Environment.* 30:17+. S. '88. Reprinted with permission of the Helen Dwight Reid Educational Foundation. Published by Heldref Publications, 4000 Albemarle St., N.W., Washington, D.C. 20016. Copyright © 1988.

It is very difficult to separate changes that are induced by humans from those induced by natural phenomena. For example, in pristine regions of the tropics, natural catastrophes such as hurricanes, fires, or drought can cause devastations that the untrained observer may attribute to human causes. It is also possible to blame natural causes for devastations caused by floods, when in fact the blame may fall squarely on people because of poor land use.

It is also difficult to understand the many temporal and spatial scales at which such changes occur in the world. Changes may occur in areas as small as a few square meters or in areas as large as millions of hectares. Further, changes can be instantaneous or can occur over millions of years. Factors that cause change in vegetation and soils interact at each temporal and spatial scale through gradients of intensity and duration.

Vegetation Changes in the Tropics

Today's tropical forests are a result of past changes induced by humans and by natural phenomena. Periodic natural events triggered by fires, hurricanes, changes in river channels, and landslides and earthquakes have all been shown to affect large areas of tropical vegetation, so mature tropical forests are not as stable and pristine as previously thought. Past human-induced changes include deforestation of large areas in Central and South America by Inca, Mayan, and Aztec civilizations, followed by natural reforestation as these civilizations disappeared. Mayan manipulation of forests in the Yucatán Peninsula of Mexico resulted in self-sustaining forests with physiognomy and species diversity similar to the so-called climax, or natural, rain forest.

The notion that once people take over an area of forested land the forests disappear is not completely accurate. Forestlands have been rehabilitated following human destruction in specific areas such as the Caribbean, El Salvador, Africa, and throughout much of the tropics generally. These rehabilitations occurred through natural succession after humans migrated from overcrowded areas. However, these rehabilitated forests are not identical to the original ones: the species composition and physiognomy have changed. It is not known if ecosystems in these rehabilitated lands are inferior to those they have replaced in terms of their geochemical and biotic roles in the landscape.

Ecosystem rehabilitation involves the management of succession, which is the direction and speed of change involving all components of ecosystems including vegetation, soils, animals, and microbes. Through ecosystem rehabilitation, humans attempt to convert land that has been damaged by either human or natural perturbations to land that can have productive uses. The idea behind rehabilitation is to manipulate successional processes so that the end product of the successional change will be useful.

If large areas of today's mature tropical forest ecosystems are the result of past human intervention and/or periodic natural disturbances, what is the goal of rehabilitation? No one can be certain what a desirable species composition for a tropical forest rehabilitation project is, and it is necessary to be flexible when determining the objectives of such a project. The goal should be sustainable forest productivity, with species composition a secondary concern. If the project aim is to derive usable forest products, one group of species will be required. But if the aim is to achieve species diversity rather than product yield, a different group of species will be called for.

Damage to Tropical Forestlands

It is impossible to determine categorically how seriously damaged tropical forestlands are because data are generally not available. Furthermore, efforts to assess soil degradation on a global scale have resulted in very little information regarding the tropics.

Damaged lands have been defined as *derelict*—land so damaged by industrial or other development that it is incapable of having beneficial use without some treatment—or *disturbed*, where the land has some residual ongoing use. Reviews elsewhere discuss in detail the problems of rehabilitating derelict lands and possible solutions. Most techniques for rehabilitation of vegetation on derelict lands have been developed for temperate zones, but the principles should also apply in the tropical biome because of the overriding effect of poor site conditions on plant growth.

The condition of most deforested tropical lands fits the disturbed category because plant growth and some human uses are still possible after forest removal. Some deforested lands, however, are not capable of supporting direct human use and should be considered derelict. For example, lower plants, ferns, and other herbaceous vegetation invade highly eroded, steep slopes in the wet tropics. These plant communities grow slowly and require time before they can support human use. Frequently burned pastures on highly compacted soils support grass cover and shrubs, but mature tropical forest tree species fail to regenerate in these areas.

Clearly, a scale is needed to rate ecosystem degradation in the tropics for at least three reasons: to guide collection of statistics on land use and conditions, to set priorities for rehabilitation work, and to advance basic understanding of the natural phenomena involved in the interaction between humans and tropical ecosystems. Examples of damaged forestlands that may require rehabilitation include overlogged forests; secondary forests with poor species composition; damaged agricultural lands; forests dominated by exotic species; arrested successions; drained forested wetlands; abnormally flooded soils; eroded hillsides; overgrazed, compacted, or repeatedly burned pastures; and burned forests.

However, as stated earlier, lands that appear to qualify for rehabilitation may in fact be beneficial for humans and need not be included in rehabilitation schemes. For example, productive, sustainable agriculture—arrested successions—can be carried out in drained wetlands; exotic species (crops) may also be used. Rehabilitation projects should focus on lands whose net value to society can be sustainably enhanced through human intervention.

Rehabilitation and Redevelopment

It is very difficult to control with certainty the direction of a rehabilitation project. This is particularly true of complex tropical ecosystems, where there are a staggering number of possible states and species compositions. For example, 72 possible conditions for rehabilitation result if three levels of damage to forestlands are recognized in three rainfall zones with four temperature conditions and two kinds of substrate. Furthermore, a succession may proceed at varying speeds and directions, even in the absence of human intervention. This problem is compounded by the immense diversity of environments in the tropics, each with its characteristic suite of ecosystem types, rates of processes, and resiliency. Damage to tropical forestland can be derelict, deforested, or impoverished, and annual rainfall can vary tremendously among different areas, as can mean temperature and nutrient levels in soils. Clearly, different rehabilitation strategies are required for each alternative case and for local conditions.

One model describing rehabilitation options in the Great Lakes region of the United States and Canada included four alternative pathways that also apply to tropical conditions: restoration, further degradation, replacement, and rehabilitation. Restoration implies a return to the original state; further degradation involves a do-nothing approach by which the land continues to suffer chronic human and/or natural stress; and replacement is independent of the original state and might lead the system further away from the original state, perhaps by adding desirable human-made features and suppressing undesirable ones (enhancement). Alternatively, replacement may lead the system to a less desirable state (impoverishment) if conditions no longer permit the development of any additional biotic complexity. Rehabilitation involves a mix of nondegradation, restoration, and replacement strategies.

A more inclusive concept is redevelopment, a broad term that implies a redoing of development schemes that have somehow deteriorated the natural resource base of society. In the tropics, where development has traditionally been dissociated from ecological considerations, there is a great need for redevelopment ideas.

An example of a tropical redevelopment project is the 1985 Tropical Forestry Action Plan of the Food and Agriculture Organization (FAO). This program addresses five areas of tropical forest management in an effort to change the traditional focus on tropical forest exploitation. The areas are forestry land use, forest-based industry development, fuel wood and energy, conservation of tropical forest ecosystems (including their rehabilitation), and institutions.

Forestry is extremely important to the economy and development of tropical countries, and positive tropical redevelopment will occur if FAO's Tropical Forestry Action Plan is implemented. In 1988 the general assembly of the International Union for the Conservation of Nature and Natural Resources concluded that FAO's plan "represented the best available mechanism for influencing aid to forestry and forest conservation both quantitatively and qualitatively."

Rehabilitation is defined in this article as a component of re-development. Most redevelopment schemes will require rehabilitations and restorations of ecosystems and institutions. Here the term is limited to strategies for natural ecosystems; the broader subject of redevelopment needs in the tropics is not addressed.

Rehabilitation is the preferred strategy for damaged tropical forestlands because it is the most realistic approach for dealing with complex tropical systems. Pragmatism is necessary if the most limiting factor in any strategy of ecosystem rehabilitation, cost, is to be addressed realistically. The significance of the cost factor can be illustrated with the restoration of a flood plain after the Kissimmee River in south Florida had been channeled. In 1978 the cost of partially restoring the river's original meanders was estimated to be U.S. $48 million, $15 million more than the original cost of channelization. By 1986 the estimated cost of the restoration had soared to between $97 million and $134 million. Yet the restoration is needed to avoid water shortages and reduced water quality in Miami and the Everglades region.

Experience with plantation forestry in the tropics suggests that while tropical lands respond to intensive management (for example, site preparation, fertilization, irrigation, and use of vegetative propagation techniques), the cost of such manipulations usually limits the extent of their applications, even though plantations do not require intensive management after seedling establishment or after trees grow above competing vegetation. Rehabilitation projects face similar problems. Therefore, a cornerstone strategy for tropical forest rehabilitation is the use of natural processes and natural subsidies (such as wind and animals for plant dispersal) rather than human inputs (such as planting or application of fertilizers) to the greatest extent possible. There is a need for research to quantify the long-term economic significance of using natural versus artificial approaches in rehabilitation projects.

Examples of Rehabilitation

If nature is to perform most of the work of ecosystem rehabilitation, what should be done if the natural process is too slow or too fast, or if it takes an unfamiliar or undesirable path? What examples of the success or failure of rehabilitation projects are available?

Rehabilitation of tropical systems has been most successful in simple ecosystems, such as mangrove stands, *Thalassia* meadows, and reforestation or afforestation of damaged lands with exotic tree plantations. In these cases the strategy has been to replant the dominant plant species (usually one or a few species) in conditions optimal to their growth. Only tree plantations and pastures have benefited from intensive management before and after planting.

Another example of rehabilitation occurs in coastal areas, where "islands" are created by depositing enough dredged material to reach the mean low-water mark. The strategy is to create habitat and allow flora and fauna to colonize naturally. Such projects have been successful in Florida and illustrate the importance of geomorphology and birds in the establishment of vegetation: birds influenced vegetation cover by transporting seed (usually exotic tree species) and improving the phosphorus and ammonium concentration in soils. Island geomorphology (for example, elevation relative to sea level) was critical in regulating plant zonation and species composition in these islands.

The best example of the rehabilitation of tropical ecosystems is subsistence agriculture as practiced by indigenous people on all tropical continents. Schemes vary from region to region, but they all have in common the manipulation of succession, so that over several decades monocultures, polycultures, and natural and planted forest fallows occupy the same site without apparent degradation of soil conditions.

In one study investigators established multispecies agroecosystems that mimic natural successions and simultaneously provide yields for human consumption. The succession was also enriched to see if the complement of species in an area undergoing natural succession could be increased. Periodic assessments showed that after the first year the natural succession accumulated more species than the mimic ecosystem and had about the same number of species as the enriched succession. The number of species in all systems increased dramatically. Beginning with no plant species (everything had been cut down), after 47 months the enriched succession had 268 plant species, the natural succession had 238, and the mimic had 151. Twenty-six percent of the species in the enriched succession were introduced by the investigators. The leaf area index was proportionally higher in the species-rich systems. The herbivory rate was similar in all ecosystems (in including monocultures), but because of differences in species richness and leaf area index, plants in the complex ecosystems experienced proportionally less herbivorous impact than those in simpler ecosystems.

Experience with tree plantations in Puerto Rico shows that tree cover can be re-established quickly in moist and wet sites that were previously used intensively for agriculture. These plantations do not degrade soil conditions and do not prevent the regeneration of native species. On the contrary, plantation understories support rich floras of native species. Plantations also enhance soil organic matter and nutrients in degraded sites.

The naturally established secondary forests on abandoned and damaged lands that had been used intensively for agriculture in Puerto Rico and elsewhere in the Carribean are case studies of natural rehabilitation. Initially, vegetation composition in these areas is dominated by species associated with human use of the land (for example, fruit trees, coffee shade trees, or plantation species). Later, naturalized and native tree species regenerate and grow rapidly in the secondary forest understory.

The fact that ecosystems can recover from chronic human impacts does not mean that the temporal cost of such human activities is low. The costs of careless use of the land can be extremely high and are usually paid back in terms of time—for example, the period of time during which lands are not usable or productive. In Puerto Rico it took about 30 years of fallow for soil organic matter to reach predisturbance levels and about 50 to 60 years before pole-sized trees of useful native species appeared in the understory of secondary forests.

Some attributes of ecosystems may rehabilitate faster than others, but those that take the most time are also the most difficult for humans to replace. For example, diverse and suitable genetic material, soil organic matter, and soil fertility usually take the most time to rehabilitate. A short supply of any of these components prevents complete restoration. Supplying seeds, soil, or fertilizers for large areas is extremely expensive and often impractical. Examples of situations that tax the limits of practicality are the rehabilitation of mangroves in Vietnam (because of limitations on the quantity of mangrove seeds) and bulldozed pastures and landslide areas (because of limitations on the availability of soil and fertilizer).

Requirements and Strategies

A fundamental requirement for successful rehabilitation of forestlands is conservation and restoration of soil organic matter and soil fertility. An ample supply of genetic material and favorable land form are also critical elements. These requirements have been well established for temperate systems. But in the moist and wet tropics, these principles are put to the test by the high leaching caused by heavy rains.

Exotic tree plantations may be considered to be foster ecosystems for endangered species and for the rehabilitation of highly damaged sites. These plantations satisfy many criteria, and the feasibility of their establishment had already been proved. Plantations are normally established for wood or biomass energy. Some, however, are established for watershed protection and for other environmental reasons—namely, rehabilitation efforts. Experience in humid, wet, rainy, and dry climates in Puerto Rico shows that forest understory development is abundant under plantations of Caribbean pine (*Pincus caribaea*), mahogany (*Swietenia macrophylla* and *S. mahagoni*), and Almendrón, or West Indies laurelcherry (*Prunus occidentalis*). These understories are dominated by native tree species of mature forests. After the foster plantation has modified the microclimatic, biotic, and soil conditions, rapid establishment of native forests can be accomplished by thinning plantation species to favor growth of native tree cover. A usable wood yield is another benefit of this strategy.

If the ultimate objective is to restore native forest to a site, the strategy of establishing foster ecosystems through planting exotic trees has limitations. The regeneration of native tree species may be limited by the availability of seeds if natural stands are not available within a reasonable distance from the exotic tree plantation. Under these conditions it may be necessary to transport seeds or seedlings to the site. Similarly, afforestation with exotic tree species, as is now occurring in the Venezuelan savannas, may induce changes in site conditions so that tree growth becomes possible where there was none before. Again, seed sources may limit any scheme designed to favor native tree species. Finally, extreme care is needed when experimenting with exotic species because there is always the danger of introducing species that create problems rather than solve them. Such introductions should always be preceded by careful research.

The biotic component of an ecosystem responds to and influences soil and climate. Damage, by people or natural events, to any of these three components of an ecosystem alters the system's response. The potential recovery (rehabilitation) of any site depends on the intensity and location of the human or natural impact upon the ecosystem. Events that have removed only biotic structure (for example, wood, litter, or animals) are less severe and easier to rehabilitate than those that have removed substrate, nutrients, or other core factors (such as seed sources) of the ecosystem. Therefore, if the fundamental conditions of the ecosystem have been significantly altered, the rehabilitation strategy must take into consideration the establishment of an ecosystem that is different from the original one. A new ecosystem will be required to cope with a new environment if the rehabilitation is to be economically and ecologically feasible. Exotic species are generally successful in human-created environments because these environments usually include new conditions to which native species are poorly adapted.

Lessons

Rehabilitation projects must be preceded by assessments of substrate, climatic, and biotic conditions. Such assessments should compare existing conditions with those in target ecosystems to determine how much change is necessary and which ecosystem components need to be changed to achieve the goal of rehabilitation. The feasibility of bridging the differences in conditions should be considered carefully to avoid hidden costs. The possibility that stressful environmental factors are cyclic or chronic in their action should also be considered in any rehabilitation plan. Thus, removal of chronic stressors such as fire, grazing, or flooding may be sufficient to set in motion rehabilitation mechanisms in chronically stressed systems.

In short, rehabilitation requires managers to "roll with the punches," to accept the opportunities that nature provides as insurance for success. Success or failure can be measured according to five criteria—sustainability of the system, vulnerability to invasions, productivity, nutrient retention, and biotic interactions—which provide ecological measures of success. It may be possible that, from a human perspective, some of these criteria can be ignored (at a cost) in order to attain a useful yield from a rehabilitation. Sustaining high yields usually requires continuous human inputs, a situation that conditions sustainability to the presence of human intervention.

Each tropical climate offers special challenges and opportunities for rehabilitation efforts. Growth conditions are optimal in the lowland humid, wet, and rain forest climates. In these environments, however, problems emerge because of the high leaching potential. Rapid establishment of a diverse vegetation cover through multiple seeding is a solution for this problem.

In the dry tropics the problem is low water availability, which slows down succession by putting stress on plants and animals. This makes the "time payment" of land-use mistakes more costly. In most cases it is not feasible to irrigate with surface water, construct wells, or induce rains artificially. These solutions work best in small-scale projects. The best alternatives for the rehabilitation of large areas of dry forest ecosystems are planting, transplanting genetic material from natural or exotic pools, optimizing land forms, removing human stressors (such as grazing, excessive harvesting, or fire), and conserving soil organic matter so that water is the only limiting factor to recover. Similar strategies apply to altitudinal gradients in the tropics where low temperatures and low atmospheric saturation deficits slow down biotic responses.

The most important lesson of rehabilitation work so far is that tropical ecosystems *can* recover from intensive and sometimes catastrophic human impacts. However, the recovery of forest cover does not imply a return to original conditions. Recovery usually implies the restoration of forest cover on a sustainable basis. It is particularly important to assess the resiliency of tropical ecosystems and the functional attributes of rehabilitated vegetation more precisely.

KUNA INDIANS: BUILDING A BRIGHT FUTURE[4]

Standing atop the San Blas Mountains of Panama, I tried to reconcile sight and sound. I was gazing eastward across the rain forest, my eyes sweeping a lush green carpet that rolled unbroken to the shore of the Caribbean Sea. At my back, however, on the Pacific slope of the Continental Divide, chain saws whined. It was the sound of hell nipping at the heels of paradise.

Starting up that hellish slope, I had passed cattle pastures with eroding soil on all sides. Higher up, I came upon freshly felled forest, where tree trunks and branches had only recently stopped smoldering. Nearest the top, trees were still falling. The chain saws were wielded by *campesinos*, who had undertaken the labor of slash-and-burn for ranchers. In 30 years of roaming the tropics, I had seldom seen worse deforestation. Nor had I seen any jungle more luxuriant than the one that fell away to the sea from the ridge.

"It's going to stay like that." So I was assured by Guillermo Archibold, technical director of this unique tropical park, and by Balbino Gonzales, a local forest ranger. Both men are Kuna Indians, the astute and well-organized native people of northeastern Panama.

As guardians of one of the last tracts of virgin forest in Central America, the Kuna have demonstrated that native people can both safeguard and use their natural resources for long-term human well-being. The crux of their management has been to head off forest clearing on erosion-prone lands at high altitudes in order to protect farming in the lowlands. This simple concept is based as much on their own experience interacting with nature as on scientific tenents of modern ecology, but making the idea succeed has hardly been easy. In fact, the story of the Kuna is a remarkable tale of political acumen, industriousness, follow-through, flexibility, environmental savvy, enlightened self-government, international help and sometimes just plain muscle—all at a time when outside population pressure in Panama has begun closing in.

[4]Article by Norman Myers, a scientist and environmental consultant. *International Wildlife*. 17:18+. J1.–Ag. '87. Copyright 1987 by the National Wildlife Federation. All rights reserved. Reprinted by permission.

As part of their plan, the Kuna have managed to establish a 230-square-mile forest park and botanical reserve on the border of their 1,180-spare-mile reservation. Scientists believe this key land is biologically unique, and the Kuna have benefited by attracting bird-watchers and other paying "scientific tourists." Most important, the Indians have moved to control their own destiny, protecting their culture as well as their resources.

That the Kuna would develop so effective a solution to the threat of deforestation comes as little surprise. "They have a tremendous sense of self-identity and a very sophisticated culture," says R. Michael Wright, a vice president of the World Wildlife Fund–U.S. Wright tells of returning from a trip to San Blas and looking at the photographs he had shot. Only then, he says, did he become truly aware of the small stature of the Indians he had met with. In person, the Kuna invariably project the kind of "presence" that makes one forget that they are among the world's shortest people.

Some 30,000 Kuna Indians live in villages on the tiny coral islands just off Panama's Caribbean Coast. Each morning, Kuna men travel by dugout canoes to their mainland farm plots at the base of the thick jungle that has kept Kuna land virtually inaccessible for centuries.

When Columbus landed in the New World, these Indians occupied a much larger slice of Central America. Their villages extended for almost 500 miles along the Caribbean, and Kuna also inhabited parts of the Pacific Coast. Over the centuries, pressed by Spanish colonists, they concentrated themselves into what the Indians call Kuna Yala—Kuna Earth—a narrow strip of jungle that stretches more than 100 miles along Panama's Coast. About two centuries back, they moved their villages to the palm-ringed islands offshore, while keeping their communal farm plots on the mainland coastal plain. There the Kuna grow bananas, sweet manioc, yams, corn and other crops.

Never conquered by the Spanish or the Panamanians (a 1925 war between the Kuna and Panama resulted in official recognition of the Indians' autonomy), the keepers of the rain forest have managed to enter modern times with their culture and political ways intact. Each Kuna village chief presides over nightly gatherings in the village congress house and represents his community at the Kuna General Congress. Three regional *caciques* (higher-ranking chiefs) preside over the congress, and represent the Kuna nation in dealings with Panama.

Panamanian law holds that no non-Kuna may own land in San Blas. Tourists who come to visit the islands and to buy molas, the colorful needlework blouses made by Kuna women, spend the night in hotels owned and run by the Indians. So far at least, the Kuna remain masters of their territory.

Until recently, Kuna Yala could be reached only by boat or small plane. But during the 1970s, a feeder road from the Pan-American Highway began snaking toward San Blas, to serve a proposed hotel on the Caribbean. The El Llano–Cartí road provided the Kuna with easier access to the modern world. But it also left their reservation vulnerable to cattle ranchers and peasant colonists. Panama's government has encouraged colonization of "unused" rain forest. Much of the land on the Pacific side of the Continental Divide (the ridge marks the legal boundary of Kuna Yala) has already been devastated. And more and more land-starved outsiders, pouring forth from Panama's crowded interior, stand poised to cross the divide.

In response, the Kuna have embarked on their own "development" plans, starting at that portion of the divide where the feeder road enters their territory, and where Kuna land is thus immediately vulnerable.

It all began in 1975, when Guillermo Archibold and some other Kuna youths attempted to establish a small agricultural colony on the divide. In large part, they were launching a preemptive strike against the deforesters. They hoped to establish a Kuna presence that would show this portion of the forest was most definitely in use. Within a few years, however, it became clear that the fragile forest soils and the climate were unsuitable for farming. The Kuna colonists sought advice from forestry experts at the Tropical Agronomic Center for Research and Training (CATIE) in Costa Rica. The experts proposed that the best use for the forest would be to preserve it as a park, and to build facilities for scientists and tourists.

By 1983, the Kuna had established a planning committee and had lined up technical and financial help from a variety of international institutions. "The Kuna want to manage their own resources," says Brian Houseal, an American landscape architect who, through CATIE, has worked with the Kuna for more than two years.

One way the Indians hope to ensure that they, and only they, determine the future of Kuna Yala is by attempting to have the reservation decalred a Biosphere Reserve and a World Heritage Site. These are United Nations classifications that, explains Houseal, would grant the Kuna "international recognition as an autonomous indigenous people."

Closer to home, the Indians have been cutting a trail along the ridge of the San Blas Mountains in order to define the border of Kuna Yala (thanks to the densely forested terrain, the precise boundary of Kuna land had never been marked). "Kuna guards and cartographers have been working up there for the better part of three years marking the 120-kilometer trail," says Houseal. Volunteers from the island villages help with the labor.

One day, while I walked the border trail through the rain forest, I came across a Kuna man gazing at the jungle. Asked to share his thoughts, the man told me he was enjoying the spectacle of the forest apparently doing nothing while in fact it was doing so much.

The Kuna are keenly aware of the environmental benefits provided by the rain forest. The healthy watershed yields the pure drinking water carried in gourds to island villages. The forest's vegetation holds the soil (on Kuna farm plots) that would otherwise be washed to sea. Deforestation means more than denuded slopes. In a region with up to 140 inches of annual rainfall, soil erosion would quickly smother the offshore coral reefs, thus destroying the fishery that is the Kuna's principal source of protein.

The Kuna also look to the forest for "green medicine." They refuse to cultivate portions of the jungle, even though the alluvial soils offer unusual potential for agriculture. These undisturbed areas are sanctuaries for forest spirits who, if disrupted, says the Kuna, may bring retribution upon Kuna communities. Gathering medicinal plants, however, is permitted in the sanctuaries.

Thus, when experts from CATIE suggested establishing a botanical preserve, the Indians considered it a splendid notion. The idea mirrored a preservation strategy they had practiced for generations.

The Kuna tell the story of an occasion in 1980, when Panama's former strongman, Gen. Omar Torrijos, visited a number of Indian leaders at an island village. Torrijos, having flown in by helicopter over the rain forest, asked, "Why do you Kuna need so much land? You don't do anything with it. You don't use it. And if anyone else cuts down so much as a single tree, you shout and scream."

To which Kuna leader Rafael Harris responded, "Suppose I go to Panama City and stand in front of a pharmacy, and because I need medicine but have none of your money, I pick up a rock and break the window. You will take me away and put me in your jail. For me, the forest is my pharmacy. If I have sores on my legs, I go to the forest and get the medicine I need to cure them. We Kuna need the forest, and we use it and take much from it. But we take only what we need, without having to destroy everything as your people do."

The rain forest that so impressed Torrijos is part of the land bridge connecting the distinct biological realms of Central and South America. Botanists have already identified 35 new species of plants in the Kuna jungle; the forest's wildlife includes giant anteaters, Baird's tapirs, harpy eagles and many species of over-wintering migrating birds.

Those are riches from which the Kuna hope to profit by playing host to jet-set birders and other tourists in pursuit of nature. The tourists, meanwhile, gain access to one of Central America's last tracts of original forest, which is just a two-hour drive from Panama's capital and airport.

The Kuna have constructed a 30-bed dormitory at Nusagandi, a small clearing on the Continental Divide. While the Indians have not even begun "actively advertising" the site, says Brian Houseal, about 200 foreign bird-watchers on nature tours have already visited Nusagandi. Panamanian Boy Scouts, as well as scientists from the Smithsonian Tropical Research Institute, which is located in Panama, have also stayed there.

Money to help construct the Nusagandi dormitory and to cut the trail along the divide has come from the Inter-American Foundation, the World Wildlife Fund–U.S. (WWF) and other institutions. The U.S. Agency for International Development provided funds to train Kuna in park management at CATIE. (U.S. AID also financed construction of the El Llano road that threatens Kuna Yala.)

The Indians themselves have come up with $100,000 to help finance park plans, and, says WWF's R. Michael Wright, "The main thing about the project is the incredible initiative that has come from the Kuna."

"This was a Kuna project," says Wright. "They led us, we didn't lead them. Conservationists come and go, but the Kuna are going to stay."

If the Kuna do stay—which means keeping the rest of Panama out of Kuna Yala—their success may stand as a guide for similar ventures elsewhere. Just next door, in Panama's Darien Province, a vast rain forest is inhabited by indigenous people who object to encroachment by outsiders advancing along the Pan-American Highway. Like the Kuna, they are contestants in a struggle for control of natural resources. Can these Indians duplicate the success of the inhabitants of Kuna Yala?

"When there's a clear coming-together of interests—the Kuna want to protect their land and we want to protect the forest—you get something really powerful," says Wright. But to date, the Kuna are the only Indians in Latin America, and perhaps the only group in all the world's developing tropics, who are systematically managing their own natural resources on a comprehensive scale.

"The Kuna know where they stand in the world," says Brian Houseal, "and they want to preserve and enhance what is intrinsically valuable in their culture." Yet that is no easy task, even for so savvy a group of people as the natives of San Blas.

So far, the Indians have accepted few intrusions from the world beyond Kuna Yala. Some of their boats sport outboard motors. Some villages have voted to accept electricity, while others still reject it (in fact, islands have even split into two villages over the electricity question). Some Kuna enjoy listening to transistor radios, a form of evening entertainment, says *cacique* Leonidas Valdez, that is undermining the Kuna song tradition.

A well-educated people, the Kuna frequently send their children away from San Blas to study for professional careers. Many Kuna men are lured by wage-earning opportunities in Panama City or Colón. Women, also, are increasingly cash earners, making molas for tourists. Some Kuna women now earn more than their husbands—an unusual situation for these tradition-minded people.

Obviously, the dangers to the Kuna way of life include more than cattle barons or *campesinos* with chain saws. But the Kuna seem uniquely alive to the challenges thrown down by the last part of the twentieth century. By protecting the rain forest, they have launched their nation on a brave experiment, one that represents more than conservation in the usual sense.

Or perhaps it is conservation as it always should be, protecting not just nature but also man's role within it.

PEOPLE WHO MAKE A DIFFERENCE[5]

SHIRLEE CAVALIERE: Getting the Word Out

Gettysburg seems like an odd place to mount an educational effort to help clean up the Chesapeake Bay. The south-central Pennsylvania town is, after all, located almost 100 miles inland from the huge freshwater estuary that feeds into the Atlantic Ocean. But to Shirlee Gavaliere, small rural farming communities like Gettysburg are the sources of many of the bay's pollution problems, and people who live in such places need to understand why. With the aid of some local high school students, she is getting the word out.

For the past five years, the Gettysburg High School biology teacher has been the motivating force behind a program called "The Chesapeake Bay Kids," which uses the power of young people to spread a conservation message throughout the region.

"Almost every creek that flows through Adams County [where Gettysburg is located] eventually winds up in the Chesapeake Bay," says Cavaliere. She has taught her students to collect and test water samples from local streams and use this data to inform groups and individuals about how fertilizer, cow manure and other types of agricultural runoff go into local waterways, contributing to the explosive algae blooms that are choking off life in the bay. The students' main message: "We all live downstream" and we all can do our part to prevent pollution.

Cavaliere feels that teenagers need to feel responsible for their community. And moving them to action is a way to accomplish this goal. Her work with the Bay Kids has been so effective that, earlier this year, she received a National Wildlife Federation Conservation Achievement Award for Education.

"Her exemplary educational skills and enthusiasm have been contagious," observes Federation President Jay D. Hair. "About a third of her students have gone on to further environmental education."

[5]Article by National Wildlife Federation staff. *National Wildlife*. 27:4+. Ag.–S. '89. Copyright 1989 by the National Wildlife Federation. All rights reserved. Reprinted by permission.

Through workshops presented to other students, teachers and local clubs, the Chesapeake Bay Kids have worked to get their message across in an entertaining fashion. The workshops include an overview of the pollution problems in the bay, followed by a play, written and performed by the students.

The students also spend time with area farmers, learning how conservation practices and manure storages prevent runoff and decrease fertilizer bills. And they work with homeowners, discussing the dangers of overfertilizing lawns, the need to recycle motor oil and read labels for toxic contents in products, and how to properly dispose of all household wastes.

Cavaliere finds that students are very effective in conveying to audiences the notion that individuals must take responsibility for their own actions. "One of the joys of teaching this way," she says, "is that the students are participants in helping to improve the environment."

MARION STODDART: Rescuing a River

Marion Stoddart moved with her family to the northern Massachusetts town of Groton in the early 1960s, she knew that the adjacent Nashua River was considered one of the nation's filthiest waterways. But she had no idea how bad it was.

For decades, the industries and communities that line the 57-mile-long river had used it as a dump. The Nashua was clogged with chemical wastes and sewage. Dead fish floated on the surface. Huge piles of sludge backed up behind dams. And stained by paper mill pigments, the river at times ran green, red or blue.

"Because the Nashua looked so awful, people continued to throw junk in it," recalls the 60-year-old Stoddart, who previously had spearheaded an effort to protect wetlands near her former New England home. "I made a commitment to myself that I would restore the Nashua River and establish a greenway along its banks."

Today, more than two decades later, it's clear that Stoddart is one person who keeps her commitments. The Nashua, kept clean by several new water treatment facilities and the vigilance of a 1,000-member group founded by Stoddart, is considered a model for other states. Its waters now support recreation and wildlife, and some 6,000 acres of woodlands and park along its banks are open to the public. Such change didn't come easily.

When Stoddart first approached state officials with plans to clean up the river in 1962, she was laughed at. The task was seemingly impossible, but Stoddart refused to give up. "I identified people who had the most power in the communities along the river," she says. "Then I began educating them and winning them over."

"Marion Stoddart has a disarming style," says William Flynn, former mayor of Fitchburg, the riverside paper mill town that was responsible for much of the pollution entering the Nashua. "One of her talents is getting people to work together. She is so committed that she makes believers out of non-believers."

After Stoddart was instrumental in getting the state to change the Nashua's official classification to protect it from open dumping, officials of one industry threatened to shut down their factory rather than help finance clean-up facilities. But with Flynn's help, Stoddart persuaded paper mills in Fitchburg to cooperate with authorities to build a treatment plant. Then, after matching federal funds for such construction failed to arrive, she organized a petition drive that netted 13,000 signatures, which she sent to President Nixon. The funds arrived shortly thereafter.

Next, Stoddart was instrumental in securing a federal grant to groom the river, hiring high school dropouts to clear tons of debris. And she worked with each river community to establish a wildlife and recreation greenway along both banks.

Two years ago, the United Nations Environment Programme cited Stoddart as one of 90 exemplary workers for the environment worldwide. But her most lasting award is the Nashua itself, which now flows cleaner and teems with wildlife.

JOHN OSBORN: Wearing Many Hats

From 8:00 A.M. to 4:30 P.M. every work day, Dr. John Osborn runs the AIDS clinic of the Veterans Administration Hospital in Spokane, Washington, where he sees patients, trains residents and supervises nurses. It is, he says, "a madhouse, an utterly crazy juggling act." It is also, by any definition, a job that should satisfy whatever human requirement there is to do good in this world. But Osborn has just begun when he steps out of the hospital at the end of the day and heads home to what he calls "my other office."

That office is the living room of his apartment, which also serves as the headquarters for the Inland Empire Public Lands

Council (IEPLC), a coalition of some 30 groups of sportsmen and other environmentalists, Indian tribes and homeowners that was organized by Osborn to act as a watchdog on public forest development in parts of the Northwest.

"There is a massive transition underway in this area," says Osborn. "We have to stop thinking we're on the frontier and that there will always be another stand of white pine just over the hill." The 32-year-old medical doctor has devoted hundreds of hours of his free time to help make sure that the U.S. Forest Service acts in a responsible manner.

For 13 years, the Forest Service has been under a Congressional mandate to come up with the first comprehensive, long-range plans for the country's 190 million acres of national forests. included in the 1976 Forest Management Act were provisions for public participation in the planning of how those acres should be used. And conservationists like Osborn have taken those provisions seriously.

Thus far, the five-year-old IEPLC has taken part in appeals—along with such groups as the Idaho Wildlife Federation—of four major management plans of forests in the region. AS IEPLC coordinator, Osborn has waded through thousands of pages of federal documents, attended every forest hearing in the area, drafted two of the appeals and published a bimonthly newsletter at his own expense to keep other members of the coalition informed. "It's the same thing I do with patients at the hospital," he notes. "I say, 'This is the data. These are the risks and benefits. Now you make the decisions.'"

In doing so, however, Osborn also has frequently found himself at odds with both the timber industry and some federal authorities. One local newspaper called him a "small David standing up to a giant bureaucratic Goliath."

"Through his dedication, John has been an inspiration to all of us who would emulate his efforts to protect some of our most valuable scenic treasures," says Kent Henderson, president of the Idaho Wildlife Federation. Last year, the NWF affiliate honored Osborn with its annual President's Conservation Award.

ELANOR STOPPS: Seabird's Best Friend

Protection Island rises fortresslike from the waters off the north coast of Wahington State. Two sandspits, steep cliffs and loose glacial soil make the windswept island an ideal nesting site for an amazing variety of seabirds that includes tufted puffins, pelagic cormorants, Pacific oystercatchers and the world's fourth largest colony of rhinoceros auklets. In all, nearly 75 percent of the seabirds found in Puget Sound nest on the island.

"There's hardly a square foot of land that isn't used by some bird during breeding season," says Elanor Stopps, a 69-year-old homemaker from the Olympic Peninsula community of Port Townsend who led a 14-year effort to keep the island out of the hands of developers.

That effort culminated last summer, when the Protection Island National Wildlife Refuge was officially dedicated by the U.S. Fish and Wildlife Service. It was the first such refuge established during the years of the Reagan Administration. "Nothing was more important [in the creation of the refuge] than the tireless devotion and dedication of one person—Elanor Stopps," observes former Washington Representative Don Bonker, who had introduced the refuge bill into Congress.

Stopps began visiting Protection Island in the mid-1960s with her friend Zella Schultz, an ornithologist who was studying the birds there. "I'd help her band gulls for the Fish and Wildlife Service and we would talk about what we could do to help protect the island for the birds," says Stopps. Soon, it was evident that the birds did indeed need help.

In 1974, after Schultz passed away, Stopps decided that it was up to her to do something about getting the island under public control. A developer had purchased the entire 400-acre land mass and was slicing it into 900 tiny lots under guise of a retirement community, even though there was virtually no good water source on the island.

"The plan was simply unbelieveable," says Stopps. "Can you imagine the impact of 900 septic systems alone? I wasn't an activist in any sense of the word. I was a housewife and a Girl Scout leader. But I had to learn."

Stopps soon realized that she had to build a base of support if she was ever going to interest the federal government in gaining control of the island. She wrote hundreds of letters and made thousands of phone calls to conservation groups around the country. She also created an "Adopt a Seabird" campaign that in time raised more than $50,000 for the effort to buy back the island.

Eventually, she enlisted the aid of Bonker, who brought the measure before Congress. "When the Reagan Administration took power, all the professional lobbyists told me the refuge was dead," says Stopps. "But I just couln't give up." She didn't.

In 1982, President Reagan signed the refuge into law. It took another six years, however, to secure enough funds to buy back the entire island. "Now I can relax a little," says Stopps, adding: "You know, there's nothing all that special about me. I just think I am an example of what ordinary people can accomplish if they truly believe in what they are doing."

ROLF BENIRSCHKE: Cans for Critters

When Rolf Benirschke was selected earlier this year as the new daytime host of the popular "Wheel of Fortune" television game show, few people in San Diego were surprised. After all, for ten years now, the affable, 34-year-old former professional football player has been one of the California seaside city's most popular—and accessible—local celebrities.

His popularity, however, is not pegged so much to his athletic achievements as it is to his ceaseless efforts to gain greater support for the San Diego Zoo's endangered species breeding and education programs. In recent years, Benirschke has devoted hundreds of hours to talking with school children and community groups about the plight of wildlife, and getting those groups to help raise funds—literally millions of dollars—for the zoo's Center for the Reproduction of Endangered Species (CRES). And despite his recent entry into the world of show business, Benirschke is more active than ever in promoting conservation programs in Southern California.

"The zoo is blessed to have Rolf's help," says Betty Joe Williams, president of the San Diego Zoological Society.

Benirschke's interest in wildlife was fostered in part by his father, Kurt, a scientist who for 12 years was research director at the San Diego Zoo. A talented placekicker, the younger Benirschke turned down several scholarship offers from major football powers to attend the University of California at Davis, where he earned a degree in zoology.

Later, after joining the San Diego Chargers in the National Football League, he initiated a program called "Kicks for Critters," in which supporters agreed to donate funds to CRES for each field goal Benirschke kicked successfully. "My goal," says Benirschke, "was not only to raise money but also to raise awareness of the problems associated with endangered animals."

By the early 1980s, the placekicker knew he had made headway into achieving that awareness after a tough game in which he missed four field goal attempts. "The next day," says Benirschke, "the headline in the local newspaper read: 'There Were No Kicks for Critters.'"

Fortunately for wildlife and the Chargers, Benirschke did not have many days like that one. When he retired from football two years ago, he left as the Chargers' all-time leading scorer with a total of 766 points. And during the seven years of "Kicks for Critters," he raised more than $1.3 million for CRES.

Almost immediately upon retiring, Benirschke initiated a new program called "Cans for Critters," in which he began seeking the aid of San Diego school children. Now, every spring, students at more than 100 area schools collect aluminum cans for recycling, with the money raised from those collections going to zoo efforts. To get students interested, Benirschke makes appearances at schools.

Says zoo spokesperson Gabriella Green: "He makes children realize that they can do something that will help make a difference in this world."

GUDY GASKILL: Keeping a Dream Alive

Chances are, Gudy Gaskill was out hiking on the day in 1973 when the first Colorado Mountain Trail Foundation was established. There were offices, an executive director, endless meetings and feasibility studies—all created around the idea of building a hiking trail across hundreds of miles of the Rocky Mountains, from Denver to Durango, in honor of Colorado's Centennial celebration in 1976.

Out in the mountains, however, there was no action. That much was evident to Gaskill, a volunteer with the Colorado Mountain Club who was supervising maintenance of existing trails in the state's national forests. When the foundation fizzled out in the late 1970s, the big trail idea seemed doomed. "It was as if nothing had ever happened," says Norwegian-born, 62-year-old Gaskill.

Without any fanfare, Gaskill decided on her own not to let the dream die. At first, working vountarily, she and her crew spent a week or two each summer breaking new ground for the trail. It was slow-going; they averaged about one mile per week. "At that time, I never thought we could get the entire trail done," she recalls.

By the early 1980s, though, word of the trail had spread and other volunteers began to show up. By 1984, Gaskill had an army of hundreds of summer helpers. Most of them were 50 years old or more. To help defray the costs of the project, they each paid $25 a week for the privilege of cutting underbrush and lugging rocks.

Gaskill was determined that the trail wind through as many diverse settings as possible, and that it be accessible to a wide range of people. It was constructed on no more than a 10 percent grade through seven national forests, six wilderness areas and across five river systems.

Finally, last July, one of the most remarkable outdoor volunteer achievements in recent decades was completed when the 470-mile Colorado Trail was officially opened to the public. Gaskill turned up at the ceremonies at the trail's western end, after leading a group on a five-week hike over the entire length at breakneck pace. "She held things together when times were tough," observes a U.S. Forest Service official. "She's the soul and spirit behind the trail."

Work on the Colorado Trail is far from finished. Gaskill has marshaled volunteers to create side loops, and she has persuaded groups such as the Boy Scouts to adopt sections of the route to maintain. And if the past is any measure of her success, it's doubtful she will have trouble keeping people interested in the project. As one volunteer put it: "No one can say 'no' to Gudy."

PAUL KERZNER: Street Tree Champion

New Yorker Paul Kerzner began giving serious thought to street trees as a kid, growing up in the borough of Queens. "It just bugged me," he recalls, "that I could never find a shade tree to sit under after a game of stickball." On the block where he spent his youth, only a handful of trees survived.

By the time he was a senior in college in 1971, Kerzner decided to stop thinking about foliage and do something about it. He went to the municipal park commissioner and learned that the city would plant a $200 tree for every $20 contribution from a homeowner. The catch: each application required a minimum of ten trees per block.

Undaunted, Kerzner canvassed the area and within months, he was enjoying the shade of 137 new trees in his old neighborhood. But that was only the beginning. With help from other volunteers, he went on to raise more than $70,000 in the years that followed, and the result was some 3,500 new street trees were planted during that period in Queens.

New York City's fiscal crisis in the late 1970s put a halt to its tree-planting program. However, it didn't stop Kerzner, who by then had earned a degree from a local law school.

"I had noticed that after new trees were planted on a block, all of a sudden there was scaffolding going up, new cement work, people fixing up their houses," he says. "There were no block associations, no organized efforts. The only common component seemed to be tree planting." Kerzner surmised that for every $1 that went into the planting of new trees, there was a $10 investment in homeowner improvements.

Soon, he helped secure federal grant funds to improve neighborhoods with tree plantings. At local budget hearings, he promoted the ability of street trees to filter city air and help keep summer air-conditioning bills down by providing shade. He also spoke of their significance to real estate values and their aesthetic appeal. And, as an attorney working for Consolidated Edison, he became director of a company program designed to bring back failing neighborhoods by helping restore buildings and making affordable units available—a program that included street tree planting.

In all, the 39-year-old Kerzner has been instrumental in the planting of more than 9,000 new trees throughout Queens. Today, he owns a home on the same block where he grew up; the street has more than twice as many trees as it did when he was young, including a recently planted maple that rises up from the sidewalk in front of his house. You might say, commented Queens Borough President Claire Shulman last year, that "he's our own Johnny Appleseed."

THE DEATH OF DUCKTOWN[6]

Twisting through the Cherokee National Forest in southeastern Tennessee, Route 64 circles around the green, cool shore of Parksville Lake. The traffic crawls as campers, vans, and tour buses negotiate the turns. Vacationers flock to visit this lushness that the locals take almost for granted, and business is brisk. Little roadside shacks hawk supplies for hunting and fishing; signs point the way toward river rafting, picnic areas, campgrounds, and nature trails.

But Route 64 doesn't *just* wind through heaven. It can also lead to hell. To the east, toward the spot where Tennessee meets Georgia and North Carolina, the greenery starts to thin, the landscape opens up, and suddenly there is a vast, raw plain, cooking in the summer sun. No trees, no plants, no sign of life, just a great expanse of dry red-clay hills cut deep with massive gullies.

It's like a mirage, stark and quite beautiful in its way, but so strange, so sudden, so out of place. How did this swatch of Arizona end up in the middle of the verdant Blue Ridge Mountains?

At a gas-station café called the Copper Station, an old picture postcard offers some answers. "The Copper Basin," it says, "is an area that looks like the desert regions of our West. The trees and vegetation were killed a number of years ago by fumes from the copper smelters, and due to erosion, reforestation has been prevented."

A woman standing by the counter confirms the postcard's accusation. "It was them smelters that did it," she says. "They put out all this sulfur gas, and then it killed everything."

But that's incredible, inconceivable. How could anyone have let that happen?

"Honey," she says patiently, clearly used to naive tourists, "it all happened long before anyone knew what they were doing— way back before this century. It's always been like this, as long as anyone can remember."

In fact, the Copper Basin is the only bona fide desert east of the Mississippi, the handiwork not of nature but of man. It is a

    [6]Article by freelance writer Wilton Barnhardt. *Discover.* 8:34+. O. '87. Copyright 1987 by Discover Publications. All rights reserved. Reprinted by permission.

paradigm of environmental disaster, a testament to the devastation that can result from neglect. It is a scar so vast that it is one of the few man-made landmarks visible from outer space.

But the Copper Basin is more than a patch of ecological ruin; it is also a place of economic and social destruction. Today, close to a century and a half after the first gouge was taken out of the Tennessee earth, the gritty folks who have adapted to life here—and who still count on the mines for the food on their tables—are being threatened anew. Even as reforestation science is slowly helping to heal the valley's wounds, the mining industry is inflicting new ones—this time not on the land but on the homes and livelihoods of the people. While government officials arrive in swarms, tenderly reseeding the dead land, mine officials may soon be *departing* in swarms, leaving the locals to make their own way for the first time in seven generations.

WELCOME TO COPPERHILL, says a sign at the entry to town. COPPER MADE US FAMOUS. OUR PEOPLE MADE US GREAT. Residents seem to make two main demands on outsiders: one, that they understand that the townfolk really *like* where they're living; and, two, that nobody say anything bad about the mines. Before long, both rules may change.

The story began in 1843, when a gold rush in the area brought prospectors to the valley. The "gold" they discovered turned out to be copper, and they left disillusioned. But seven years later mining began, and it quickly became clear that the fat lode of dark metal under the valley carpet was a gold mine in its own right.

By 1855 thirty companies were transporting tons of copper ore by mule over the mountains to a railhead 70 miles away; the valley became known as the Copper Basin, and the basin became the country's leading producer of copper.

All that ore had to be roasted at extremely high temperatures to separate the copper from the zinc, iron, and sulfur also present in the rock. The ovens were vast open pits, some as wide as 600 feet and as deep as a ten-story building. And fuel for these ravenous fires came from the cheapest, most convenient source around: the surrounding forest. Gradually every tree for more than 50 square miles was mowed down—even the stumps were dug out—and turned into charcoal.

As the fires burned and the ore melted, great clouds of noxious sulfur dioxide gas billowed into the air; the smoke was so thick that the mules had to wear bells to keep from colliding, and people were said to get lost in the sooty gas even at midday. The sulfur dioxide combined with water and oxygen to form sulfuric acid and fell to the earth as acid rain. It also descended in its original gaseous form, and as a fine acidic dust.

Deforestation and acid saturation made a deadly combination. Whatever wasn't chopped down was killed off by the sulfuric fallout, which also made the soil hostile to any new growth. With no vegetation, the animal habitat was destroyed, and all wildlife soon disappeared. Without root systems to hold the soil in place, massive erosion set in. Almost all the soil was stripped away, leaving behind a hard, mineralized, rocky covering.

The soil ended up in the Ocoee River, and it wiped out most of the aquatic population. Between 1912 and 1943 three hydroelectric dams were built along the Ocoee. The two lakes and a flume that formed behind them were also rendered virtually lifeless.

All this was exacerbated by the valley's naturally wet climate, which increased acid precipitation and hastened erosion. As if ecological matters weren't bad enough, Tennessee also permitted open-range grazing of cattle until 1946. The animals roamed freely, consuming whatever plants had managed to survive.

To be sure, this savaging of the land did not go completely unopposed. In 1907 the state of Georgia sued to stop the export of deadly fumes across its borders and, in what was one of the nation's first environmental-rights decisions, won. Said U.S. Supreme Court Justice Oliver Wendell Holmes, Georgia should have "the last word as to whether its mountains shall be stripped of their forests and its inhabitants shall breathe pure air."

The Tennessee Copper Company, which by that time ran all the mines, might have fought the Supreme Court decision, but in that same year company technicians came up with a way to capture the sulfur dioxide and turn it into sulfuric acid, which soon became the company's primary product. With that, Tennessee Copper was only too happy to bring open-air smelting to an end.

When the smoke cleared, a 56-square-mile area had been turned into desert. Plant life was gone; land animals were gone; aquatic life was gone. Whether the human population suffered as well is not clear. Sulfur emissions can affect the respiratory tract, skin, and eyes. But no medical study of the basin people has yet been conducted.

Today, at the northwestern end of the Copper Basin, hard against the Tennessee-Georgia border, sits the old and tiny community of Ducktown, populaiton 583. Ducktown is the granddad of the basin's mining communities, the first settlement to spring up around one of the first mines.

A walk around town makes it clear that the residents are proud of this distinction. There's the Ole Copper Inn, the Mine City Baptist Church, the Copper Basin High School, and the Kopper Kurl Beauty Salon. No matter who has owned the mines over the years—since 1982 it's been the Tennessee Chemical Company (TTC)—"the Company" has always been the town's leading employer; working in the mines has been like a family tradition, passed on from father to son. As late as the 1960s workers could charge everything from groceries to medicines to coffins at the company store.

But with the TCC stimulating the local economy, the Ducktowners' shopping options have expanded considerably. Today, reports the local *Polk County News*, Ducktown "boasts a drugstore, a Piggly Wiggly market, a barber shop, two hardware stores, a mini-market, an arcade, a Dollar General store, a legal office, and a Rotary Club." There's also a Best Western motel and two restaurants, "with a Hardee's on the drawing board." But Main Street still looks much as it did at the turn of the century. And mining has remained the economic and spiritual center of the community.

At least, until last summer.

On July 31 the mines were shut down. Company officials said that they couldn't compete with the low-cost, higher-grade imports from such Third World countries as Chile, Peru, and Zambia, where the industry is nationalized, labor is cheap, and there are no environmental constraints. The TCC will continue to produce sulfuric acid in its chemical plant, using imported sulfur. But it will need a staff of only 375 to do the job; at its peak the TCC employed more than 2,000 workers.

What will happen to the rest of the Ducktown work force is anyone's guess. "It's like death," said one local resident. "You know it's out there. You just can't realize what it's going to be like."

The company did inform workers of the closing two and a half years ago, and it has provided retraining and education programs, partially paid for by government funds. But the problem will be finding some place to put those skills to use. Though two much-publicized industrial parks have been built in the basin in recent years, not one substantial business has moved in, and there is little other industry.

Some stubborn residents, determined not to leave their homes, have found work 100 miles away in Atlanta or 60 miles away in Chattanooga and resolutely commute each day. But many will be forced to move unless current efforts to attract new industry to the area succeed. The communities that mining spawned have begun to fade into ghost towns.

At the same time, the landscape that mining fashioned is also rapidly fading—back to green.

Since the 1930s "the Company," as well as the Tennessee Valley Authority (TVA), the U.S. Soil Conservation Service, and various local agencies, has been busy planting trees, trying heroically to reclaim the land. In the past half century 14 million seedlings have been planted, mostly loblolly pines and some black locusts, as well as various forms of acid-tolerant ground cover, such as weeping love grass, Japanese knotwood, and, for a short time, the pestiferous kudzu vine, until it began growing so quickly that it smothered the young trees that were trying to get established.

For decades the efforts were only marginally successful. There was no topsoil. The ground was acidic, mineralized, and virtually sterile. It couldn't hold water. And the continued sulfur pollution helped maintain these hostile conditions. Though some patchy covering did take root, the valley was a long way from what it once had been.

But in the 1970s new reforestation techniques came into use. Land-reclamation specialists learned how to plant time-released fertilizer pellets with every seedling; they developed crawler-type tractors with rippers that could cut and churn turf to a depth of two feet; perhaps most significantly, they became adept at spreading grass seed, fertilizer, and other materials by helicopter, some in concentrations of five tons per acre.

"Often, all these trees need is a little fertilizer," says Arthur Wardner, a forester with the reclamation program. "Our helicopters do a pretty fair job of getting it to them."

Once the plantings started to take root, the ground became more and more able to hold water, which encouraged greater growth. Says Roger Bollinger, director of the TVA's reclamation group: "Over the years it's become easier and easier to establish vegetation." The change has been dramatic.

About two thirds of what used to be desert now sprouts some kind of vegetation. Entire pine stands have taken firm hold; they're even reseeding themselves, starting the life cycle anew. The leaves they drop provide the organic ingredients for topsoil, and the shade they create shelters creatures of the forest floor, which have been warily creeping back.

It is perhaps this cautious return of the animals that has gratified foresters most. "You can hear songbirds whistling and singing as you work in the area" says Bollinger, "and there are signs of rabbits and quail." Snakes have also been sighted, a sure sign that their favorite meals—mice and other rodents—can't be far.

This year the scatter of groups and agencies working on the reclamation project decided to pool their knowledge and resources to develop ways of completing the job more quickly and efficiently. The most expensive of the proposed plans would have not only reforested the land but completely reconfigured it, setting aside patches that could be used for agriculture, home building, or industry. But the $17 million price tag was simply too steep. Instead the groups have chosen a more modest $6 million plan designed simply to blanket the area with new growth anywhere and everywhere the seeds will take root. Even for this cutrate plan funds have not been guaranteed, but there is hope that the state of Tennessee will step in and provide some of the needed capital. If the project does proceed, the remaining desert could be covered in green within 10 to 20 years.

Don Sisson, superintendent of safety at the TCC and a candidate for the Georgia House of Representatives, thinks that would happen even if the agencies didn't plant another tree; natural reseeding, he believes, may have taken hold sufficiently to allow the forest to revitalize itself. "I think we'd be basically covered in ten to fifteen years, twenty at most," Sisson says. "When that happens, the erosion will gradually stop, and the river will start to revive."

Still, Sisson guesses that it could be at least another 100 years before the ecosystem gets back to what it was before man intervened.

Strangely, for some Ducktown traditionalists, a century may not be long enough. "It's sort of sad," says Lorraine Lee, former curator of the Ducktown Basin Museum. "I've grown up with the painted cliffs and the red hills, and in a curious way, they're quite lovely—and unique. Where else could you find something like this? It's our history, and we're proud of it."

The museum, located in the old Burra Burra mine, is the center of a movement dedicated to keeping the history of mining alive, and to keeping the landscape that mining created. Though local activists concede that much of the reclamation work is necessary—especially to combat the relentless erosion that is continually polluting the area's waterways—they are trying to get the reforesters to keep at least a small patch of land around the museum as burned and bare as it ever was.

"They ought to leave it to show what man can do to nature, as well as what man can undo," says Lee.

"The way I look at it," says museum vice president Sue Mitchell, "they ruined a much larger piece of land in Atlanta with concrete buildings and asphalt. This is such a teeny area, beautiful and special, and we're turning it into a dull, boring pine forest."

To many, there is something simple and persuasive about the arguments of the Ducktown preservationists. *They* live here after all, not the bureaucrats and botanists from the TVA. If the natives want a desert, they're *entitled* to a desert. But the reclamationists counter that there are bigger issues at stake—much bigger. The world, they warn, is full of potential Ducktowns, full of possible sites for synthetic deserts. The officials are here in Tennessee not simply to force their federal will on the local people but to learn just how the Copper Basin died and to practice and perfect the techniques needed to bring such sites back to life.

The urgency they feel is not without cause. In Sudbury, Ontario, an area more than three times larger than the Tennessee Copper Basin was also ravaged by mining, in 1886. Like Ducktown and its surroundings, Sudbury was turned from a forest into a desert in just a tick of the geologic clock. And, like Ducktown, it is slowly, painstakingly being revived and reforested. Indeed, many of the techniques the Tennessee botanists are using were first tried out north of the border.

More troubling, however, are not Copper Basins in the industrial world, where at least *some* pollution lessons have been learned and *some* cleanup technologies mastered. The real danger, many believe, lies in the Third World.

"There are plenty of Copper Basins actively operating in the Third World," says Ellis Cowling, associate dean of the School of Forest Resources at North Carolina State University, Raleigh.

"Vegetation is being depleted around industrial regions in Mexico, Brazil, and other nations where environmental concerns have not kept pace with industrialization. The problem is only now being recognized. There is not yet a single paper published on the injuries to vegetation in these areas."

Third World deforestation is likely to be slower but more widespread than the devastation that took place in Tennessee and Ontario. Old-style open-pit burning in the United States and Canada kept the sulfur and acids swirling about within a small radius. The destruction was therefore quick and utter but at least confined. Today's tall, pollutant-dispersing smokestacks keep the concentration of contaminants down but at the same time expand their reach. Depending on where the smoke travels, it can be a flip of the scientific coin as to which situation does more ecological damage.

"I sometimes think we ought to have a short-stack policy that would mean only the local people would 'enjoy' the fruits of their pollution," says Cowling. "But, of course, we can't impose these kinds of solutions on the Third World. If these people believe it's in their interest to have industry that makes you cough but makes you rich, that's their choice. There *is* hope for solving this worldwide problem, but it lies in responsible decision making by the local citizens."

There is hope in Ducktown, too, but hope on a smaller scale: the residents merely want to believe that, with or without the mine, their community will survive. Retirees from a number of neighboring states have begun to move into the area, attracted by its strange history and stranger geography. Tourism also continues to thrive, as visitors who have seen the landscape of the Cherokee National Forest come to see the moonscape of the Copper Basin. At the same time, local boosters continue to try to attract industry to the basin's silent pair of industrial parks.

If all these groups are to be wooed, however, at least a bit of the old Ducktown—the desert Ducktown—must be preserved. "Sometimes," jokes Sue Mitchell, "we talk about going out there and pulling out some of those trees."

But Mitchell and Lee and the other Ducktown preservationists have a more practical—and a more lyrical—philosophy about their work. Yes, progress must be made; yes, reforestation must continue. But during their public speeches and presentations they are also always careful to conclude with the same thought: "Let us help to heal," they say, "but let us also keep a beloved scar."

BIBLIOGRAPHY

An asterisk (*) preceding a reference indicates that the article or part of it has been reprinted in this book.

BOOKS AND PAMPHLETS

Abrahamson, Dean Edwin, ed. The challenge of global warming. Island Press. '89.

Allaby, Michael. Dictionary of the environment. New York Univ. Press. '89.

Anderson, J. M. Ecology for environmental sciences: biosphere, ecosystems and man. E. Arnold '81.

Anderson, Stanley H., Beiswenger, Ronald E., and Purdom, P. Walton. Environmental science. Merrill Pub. Co. '87.

Arnold, Ron. Ecology wars: environmentalism as if people mattered. Free Enterprise Press. '87.

Ayensu, Edward S. Our green and living world: the wisdom to save it. Smithsonian Institution Press. '84.

Banks, Martin. Endangered wildlife. Wayland Pubs. '87.

Bates, Marston. The forest and the sea: a look at the economy of nature and the ecology of man. Nick Lyons Bks. '88.

Botkin, Daniel B. and Keller, Edward A. Environmental studies: Earth as a living planet. Merrill. '87.

Bramwell, Anna. Ecology in the 20th century: a history. Yale Univ. Press. '89.

Brewer, Richard. The science of ecology. Saunders College Pub. '88.

Caldwell, Douglas E., Brierley, James A., and Brierley, Corale L., eds. Planetary ecology. Van Nostrand Reinhold. '85.

Caldwell, Lynton Keith. International environmental policy: emergence and dimensions. Duke Univ. Press. '84.

Canter, David, Krampen, Martin, and Stea, David, eds. Environmental policy, assessment, and communication. Avebury.'88.

Champ, Michael A. and Park, Paul Kilho, eds. Marine waste management: science and policy. Krieger. '89.

Clarke, Robin, ed. The handbook of ecological monitoring. Clarendon Press. '86.

Cogan, Douglas. Stones in a glass house: CFCs and ozone depletion. Investor Responsibility Res. Center. '88.

Committee on Selected Biological Problems in the Humid Tropics, Division of Biological Sciences, Assembly of Life Sciences, National Research Council. Ecological aspects of development in the humid tropics. National Acad. Press. '82.

Committee on the Applications of Ecological Theory to Environmental Problems, Commission on Life Sciences, National Research Council. Ecological knowledge and environmental problem-solving. National Acad. Press. '86.

Cook, Earleen H. Desertification and deforestation: a selected bibliography of English language sources. Vance Bibls. '85.

Cooley, June H. and Golley, Frank B., eds. Trends in ecological research for the 1980s. Plenum Press. '84.

Cranbrook, Earl of, ed. Malaysia. Pergamon Press; published in collaboration with the International Union for Conservation of Nature and Natural Resources. '88.

Dasmann, Raymond Fredric. Environmental conservation. Wiley. '84.

Denny, Patrick, ed. The ecology and management of African wetland vegetation: a botanical account of African swamps and shallow waterbodies. Junk: The Hauge. '85.

Deshmukh, Ian. Ecology and tropical biology. Blackwell Scientific Publs. '86.

Devall, Bill. Simple in means, rich in ends: practicing deep ecology. Peregrine Smith Bks. '88.

DiSilvestro, Roger L. The endangered kingdom: the struggle to save America's wildlife. Wiley. '89.

Dryzek, John S. Rational ecology: environment and political economy. Blackwell. '87.

Eckenfelder, William Wesley. Industrial water pollution control. McGraw-Hill. '89.

Ehrlich, Paul R. The machinery of nature. Grafton Bks. '88.

Environment abstracts annual, 1988. Bowker A&I Pub. '89.

Environment Development Action (ENDA) for the United Nations Environment Programme. Environment and development in Africa. Pergamon Press. '81.

Fantechi, Roberto and Ghazi, Anver, eds. Carbon dioxide and other greenhouse gases. Kluwer Acad. Pubs. Group. '89.

Friday, Laurie and Laskey, Ronald, eds. The fragile environment. Cambridge Univ. Press. '89.

Frsund, Finn R. and Strm, Steinar. Environmental economics and management: pollution and natural resources. Croom Helm. '88.

Galtung, John. Environment, development and military activity: towards alternative security doctrines. Universitetsforlaget. '82.

Gibbs, Jeffrey N., Cooper, Iver P., and Mackler, Bruce F. Biotechnology & the environment: international regulation. Stockton Press. '87.

Goldsmith, Edward and Hildyard, Nicholas, eds. The Earth report: the essential guide to global ecological issues. Price/Stern/Sloan. '88.

Gomez-Campo, C., ed. Plant conservation in the Mediterranean area. Junk: The Hague. '85.

Gradwohl, Judith and Greenberg, Russell. Saving the tropical forests. Island Press. '88.

Greene, Owen, Percival, Ian, and Ridge, Irene. Nuclear winter: the evidence and the risks. Polity Press. '85.

Harte, John. Consider a spherical cow: a course in environmental problem solving. Kaufmann. '85.

Harwell, Mark A. and Berry, Joseph. Nuclear winter: the human and environmental consequences of nuclear war. Springer-Verlag. '84.

Hillary, Sir Edmund, ed. Ecology 2000: the changing face of Earth. Beaufort Bks. '84.

Holzner, W., Werger, M. J. A., and Ikushima, Isao. Man's impact on vegetation. Junk: The Hague. '83.

Hutchinson, Thomas C. and Meema, K. M., eds. Effects of atmospheric pollutants on forests, wetlands, and agricultural ecosystems. Springer-Verlag. '87.

Irvine, Sandy and Ponton, Alec. A Green manifesto: policies for a green future. Macdonald & Co. '88.

Jeffers, John Norman Richard. Practitioner's handbook on the modelling of dynamic change in ecosystems. Wiley. '88.

Jordan, Carl F., ed. Tropical ecology. Hutchinson Ross. '81.

Jordan, William R. III, Gilpin, Michael E., and Aber, John D., eds. Restoration ecology: a synthetic approach to ecological research. Cambridge Univ. Press. '87.

Jrgensen, Sven Erik and Mitsch, William J., eds. Application of ecological modelling in environmental management. Elsevier Scientific. '83.

Kaufman, Les and Mallory, Ken, eds. The last extinction (based on a public lecture series, Extinction: saving the sinking ark). MIT Press. '88.

Kennedy, John G. and Edgerton, Robert B., eds. Culture and ecology: eclectic perspectives. American Anthropological Assn. '82.

Kindt, John Warren. Marine pollution and the law of the sea. W.S. Hein. '86.

Krebs, Charles J. Ecological methodology. Harper & Row. '89.

Krebs, Charles J. The message of ecology. Harper & Row. '88.

Kristensen, Thorkil and Paludan, Johan Peter, eds. The Earth's fragile systems: perspectives on global change. Westview Press. '88.

Kupchella, Charles E. and Hyland, Margaret C. Environmental science: living within the system of nature. Allyn & Bacon. '89.

Lahde, James A. Planning for change: a course of study in ecological planning. Teachers College Press. '82.

Leopold, A. Starker and Dasmann, Raymond Fredric. Wild California: vanishing lands, vanishing wildlife. University of Calif. Press. '85.

Likens, Gene E., ed. Long-term studies in ecology: approaches and alternatives. Springer-Verlag. '89.

Malone, Thomas F. and Roederer, Juan G. Global change. Cambridge Univ. Press. '85.

Marsh, Clive W. and Mittermeier, Russell A., eds. Primate conservation in the tropical rain forest. Liss. '87.

Maxwell, Kenneth E., Mansfield-Jones, Greayer, and Mansfield-Jones, Dorothy. Environment of life. Brooks/Cole. '85.

Mellanby, Kenneth, ed. Air pollution, acid rain, and the environment. Elsevier Applied Science. '88.

Miller, George Tyler. Environmental science. Wadsworth Pub. Co. '88.

Mooney, Harold A. and Godron, Michel, eds. Disturbance and ecosystems: components of response. Springer-Verlag. '83.

Munro, R. D. and Lammers, J. G. Environmental protection and sustainable development: legal principles and recommendations. Graham & Trotman. '87.

Nagchaudhuri, B. D. and Bhatt, S. The global environment movement: a new hope for mankind. Sterling Pubs. Pvt. '87.

Nanda, Ved P., ed. World climate change: the role of international law and institutions. Westview Press. '83.

Nebel, Bernard J. Environmental science: the way the world works. Prentice-Hall. '87.

Nemerow, Nelson Leonard. Stream, lake, estuary, and ocean pollution. Van Nostrand Reinhold. '85.

North, Richard. The real cost. Chatto & Windus. '86.

Norton, Bryan G. Why preserve natural variety? Princeton Univ. Press. '87.

Odum, Eugene P. Ecology and our endangered life-support systems. Sinauer Assocs. '89.

Omenn, Gilbert S., ed. Environmental biotechnology: reducing risks from environmental chemicals through biotechnology. Plenum Press. '88.

Owen, Oliver S. Natural resource conservation: an ecological approach. Macmillan. '85.

Parratt, Mark W. and Parratt, Margaret E. A spaceship called Earth: our living environment. Kendall/Hunt. '85.

Peccei, Aurelio and Ikeda, Daisaku. Before it is too late. Kodansha Int. '84.

Pepper, David M., Perkins, John W., and Youngs, Martyn J. The roots of modern environmentalism. Croom Helm. '84.

Pomeroy, D. E. and Service, M. W. Tropical ecology. Longman Scientific & Tech. '88.

Prance, Ghillean T., ed. Tropical rain forests and the world atmosphere. Westview Press. '86.

Pross, Catherine A. and Dwyer-Rigby, Mary, comps. Sustaining Earth: a bibliography of the holdings of the Ecology Action Resource Centre, Halifax, Canada. Dalhousie Univ. School of Library & Information Studies. '88.

Purdom, P. Walton and Anderson, Stanley H. Environmental science: managing the environment. Merrill. '83.

Ramade, François. Ecology of natural resources. Wiley. '84.

Rambler, Mitchell B., Margulis, Lynn, and Fester, Rene, eds. Global ecology: towards a science of the biosphere. Academic Press. '89.

Richards, J. F. and Tucker, Richard P., eds. World deforestation in the twentieth century. Duke Univ. Press. '88.

Roberts, R. D. and Roberts, T. M., eds. Planning and ecology. Chapman & Hall. '84.

Rolston, Holmes. Philosophy gone wild: essays in environmental ethics. Prometheus Bks. '86.

Rowan-Robinson, Michael. Fire & ice: the nuclear winter. Longman. '85.

Ryle, Martin. Ecology and socialism. Hutchinson Radius. '88.

Sale, Kirkpatrick. Dwellers in the land: the bioregional vision. Sierra Club Bks. '85.

Sands, Philippe, ed. Chernobyl, law and communication: transboundary nuclear air pollution, the legal materials. Grotius Publs. '88.

Schneider, Stephen Henry. Global warming: are we entering the greenhouse century? Sierra Club Bks. '89.

Sederberg, Peter C., ed. Nuclear winter, deterrence, and the prevention of nuclear war. Praeger Pubs. '86.

Selman, Paul H. Ecology and planning: an introductory study. Godwin. '81.

Shane, Douglas R. Hoofprints on the forest: cattle ranching and the destruction of Latin America's tropical forests. Institute for the Study of Human Issues. '86.

Shukla, J. B., Hallam, T. G., and Capasso, V., eds. Mathematical modelling of environmental and ecological systems. Elsevier. '87.

Simon, Anne W. Neptune's revenge: the ocean of tomorrow. Watts. '84.

Singer, S. Fred, ed. Global climate change: human and natural influences. Paragon House. '89.

Smith, Brian Dale. State responsibility and the marine environment: the rules of decision. Clarendon Press. '88.

Soderqvist, Thomas. The ecologists—from merry naturalists to saviours of the nation: a sociologically informed narrative survey of the ecologization of Sweden, 1895–1975. Almqvist & Wiksell. '86.

Southwick, Charles H., ed. Global ecology. Sinauer Assocs. '85.

Springer, Allen L. The international law of pollution: protecting the global environment in a world of sovereign states. Quorum Bks. '83.

Synge, Hugh, ed. The biological aspects of rare plant conservation. Wiley. '81.

Templeton, Virginia Evans and Taubenfeld, Howard Jack. World environment law bibliography: non-periodical literature in law and the social sciences published since 1970 in various languages with selected reviews and annotations from periodicals. Rothman. '87.

Tickell, Crispin. Climatic change and world affairs. Harvard Univ. Center for Int. Affairs. '86.

Tober, James A. Wildlife and the public interest: nonprofit organizations and federal wildlife policy. Praeger Pubs. '89.

Turk, Jonathan and Turk, Amos. Environmental science. Saunders College Pub. '88.

Udall, Stewart L. The quiet crisis and the next generation. G. M. Smith. '88.

Vink, A. P. A. Landscape ecology and land use. Longman. '83.

Vittachi, Anuradha. Earth Conference one: sharing a vision for our planet. New Science Lib. '89.

Warren, Andrew and Goldsmith, Frank Barrie, eds. Conservation in perspective. Wiley. '83.

Westman, Walter E. Ecology, impact assessment, and environmental planning. Wiley. '85.

Wilcox, Bruce A. 1988 IUCN red list of threatened animals. International Union for Conservation of Nature & Natural Resources. '88.

World Commission on Environment and Development. Our common future. Oxford Univ. Press. '87.

Worster, Donald E., ed. The ends of the Earth: perspectives on modern environmental history. Cambridge Univ. Press. '88.

Yaffee, Steven Lewis. Prohibitive policy: implementing the Federal Endangered Species Act. MIT Press. '82.

For those who wish to read more widely on the subject of preserving the world ecology, this section contains abstracts of additional articles that bear on the topic. Readers who require a comprehensive list of materials are advised to consult the *Readers' Guide to Periodical Literature* and other Wilson indexes.

A WORLD AT RISK

Who's polluting Antarctica? Laura Tangley *BioScience* 38:590–4 O '88

The fragile environment of Antarctica may be threatened by both tourists and scientists. The National Science Foundation (NSF) recently held a public hearing on tourism on the continent, at which NSF officials and scientists raised such concerns as the disruption of research projects, possible harassment of wildlife, disposal of wastes from cruise ships, and the potential liability of the NSF in the event of accidents involving tourists. The scientists' arguments were countered by representatives of several companies that sponsor expeditions to Antarctica, who asserted that their clients are sensitive to environmental issues, are closely supervised, and can become proponents of Antarctic conservation. A recent report from the Environmental Defense Fund in Washington, D.C., argues that science has had a more devastating impact on Antarctic ecosystems than has tourism and charges that the NSF's pollution practices violate national and international laws.

Pollution unlimited. France Bequette *The Courier (Unesco)* 42:24–30 Mr '89

Despite widespread concern about pollution, humans continue to inflict irreversible damage on the natural environment. Emissions of carbon dioxide, the most widespread pollutant, are contributing to the greenhouse effect or the heating of the Earth's atmosphere. The deforestation of mountain areas is reducing the number of trees, which are needed to absorb carbon dioxide, and is causing flooding. Deposits of the acid produced by burning coal are destroying lakes and adversely affecting forests and buildings. Heavy metals are polluting the atmosphere, the soil, and the water table. National and international efforts are under way to fight pollution, but they are hampered by powerful economic and social interests.

The Earth as transformed by human action (report of international symposium held at Clark University). Timothy O'Riordan *Environment* 30:25–8 Ja/F '88

In October 1987, Clark University hosted an international symposium examining the impact of human activity on the Earth's ecosystems over the past 300 years. The meeting, which took three years to organize, included 41 scholarly presentations and 80 expert commentaries, many of which involved intensive research and international cooperation. The symposium covered topics such as population growth, the mining of groundwater reserves, tropical forest depletion, and fossil-fuel burning. The symposium's editors and contributors must now shape the information into a coherent historical perspective that can be used to guide future policy decisions concerning the environment.

Don't blame me. George Reiger *Field & Stream* 92:14+ Ag '87

Most people refuse to acknowledge that mankind is its own worst enemy. History is full of examples of civilizations that collapsed because increasing human populations destroyed the local environment. Today the population explosion, with its resultant plague of garbage and waste, threatens to produce the same conditions on a worldwide scale.

New pollution problems. *The Futurist* 20:58 My/Je '86

The Organisation for Economic Co-operation and Development has identified a new set of pollution concerns that may be harder to address than conventional types. Sophisticated instruments have detected previously unsuspected pollutants in the water, soil, and air. The changes in the varieties of pollutants discovered reflect changes in industrial processes. Although pollution from chimneys and sewage outlets has decreased, there have been increases in pollution from sources such as agriculture, urban run-off, and abandoned waste sites. It is difficult to assess the hazards to people exposed to several different contaminants. It is becoming clear that attempts to solve pollution problems one at a time may only transfer the pollution to a different medium.

Our threatened planet (cover story; special section; with editorial comment by Kevin Doyle). *Maclean's* 101:2, 38–43+ S 5 '88

A cover story on worldwide environmental destruction includes discussions of a PCB fire at Saint-Basile-le-Grand, overpopulation in developing countries, waste disposal, marine pollution, and Biosphere II. Environmentalists have long warned that the Earth cannot sustain an infinite amount of damage, and recent trends indicate that large-scale global change is under way. Industrialized societies are wreaking havoc on the atmosphere through the burning of fossil fuels, while developing countries are plundering resources in a desperate fight for survival. Some scientists blame the greenhouse effect, a global warming caused by the buildup of heat-trapping gases in the atmosphere, for this summer's drought and high temperatures. Many experts believe that the only solution to environmental destruction is for human habits of consumption and waste to change.

Stretched to the limit. Jerry Adler *Newsweek* 112:23–4 Jl 11 '88

Part of a special section on the greenhouse effect. Acid rain, desertification, and deforestation are effects of overpopulation. The industrialized nations can be held responsible for acid rain, a by-product of fossil fuel combustion that pollutes lakes and decimates forests. The low technology of more primitive nations is also taking its toll on the Earth. Jungles are being destroyed for conversion to farmland, and grasslands and forests are being stripped bare by overgrazing. The end result is the formation of about 14.8 million acres of new desert per year. Unfortunately, the immediate economic woes of crowded, developing countries make it difficult for them to respond to calls for environmental prudence.

The ultimate wildlife threat (human population expansion). Lonnie Williamson *Outdoor Life* 180:28+ D '87

Human population expansion is the ultimate threat to the world's wildlife. As people demand more land and water for food production and living space, wildlife habitat is sacrificed. Before long, the waves of population and development emanating from urban centers will begin overlapping, eliminating the huntable wildlife in between. Some legislators and activists have been calling for a national policy on population control, and Congress finally appears to be listening. Republican senator Mark Hatfield of Oregon and Democratic representative Buddy MacKay of Florida have introduced the Global Resources, Environment and Population Act of 1987 to establish population stabilization as a national goal. Several conservation groups have thrown their support behind the bill, but the issue of population control remains controversial.

Warning: planet in peril (cover story; special issue). *Scholastic Update (Teachers' edition)* 121:2–8+ Ap 21 '89

An issue on the environment discusses the greenhouse effect and other threats to the environment; the pollution of the world's oceans; the destruction of rain forests; the progress that has been made toward cleaning up America's land, air, and water; President George Bush's stance on the environment; the dispute between rich and poor nations on how to save the environment; and ways individuals can help in the effort to protect the environment. Some of the worst environmental problems of the past year are pinpointed on a world map.

First world estimate of metal pollution. Stefi Weisburd *Science News* 133:309 My 14 '88

It appears that the toxicity of the trace metals released each year now exceeds that of all radioactive and organic pollutants combined. Jerome O. Nriagu, an environmental geochemist at Canada's National Water Research Institute in Burlington, Ontario, compiled the figures for 1984 emissions with atmospheric chemist Jozef M. Pacyna of the Norwegian Institute for Air Pollution Research in Lillestrom to produce the first quantitative worldwide estimate of the annual industrial input of 16 trace metals into the air, soil, and water. According to Nriagu, the accumulation of toxic metals in the human food chain is accelerating, but atmospheric levels of lead, zinc, cadmium, and copper dropped between 1975 and 1984. The results of the research were reported in the May 12 issue of *Nature*.

International cooperation to study climate change (statement, March 10, 1988). Richard J. Smith *Department of State Bulletin* 88:52-3 Je '88

In a statement before the House Foreign Affairs Committee, the acting assistant secretary of state for oceans and international environmental and scientific affairs discusses global climate change. He stresses that international cooperation is necessary to increase knowledge of climate change and to develop and evaluate possible response strategies. He describes the activities of the world climate program, which was set up in 1979 to strengthen international cooperation on potential climate change.

Our fragile Earth. Jonathan Schell *Discover* 10:44-7+ O '89

Part of a special issue on the greatest scientific achievements of the 1980s. Scientists have discovered several potentially disastrous changes in our environment during the past decade that have raised questions about the future of the planet. Mainstream scientific opinion predicts that the greenhouse effect could lead to a global warming of at least 3 to 9 degrees, which could result in a melting of the polar ice caps. New research indicates a thinning of the ozone layer, bringing threats of skin cancer and cataracts to humans and unknown dangers to insects, plants, and aquatic microorganisms. A host of variables makes it impossible to predict with certainty which potential dangers will develop, but scientists need to be able to understand as much as they can about the Earth, and the rest of us must take action to mitigate the predicted disasters.

The environmental consequences of nuclear war (cover story; special issue; with editorial comment by Alan McGowan). *Environment* 38:inside cover, 2-20+ Je '88

A special issue examines the effects that nuclear war could have on the Earth's environment. Some of the information generated by the environmental consequences of nuclear war study undertaken by the Scientific Committee on Problems of the Environment has yet to enter the policy debate over nuclear weapons. The new information, which concerns effects on crop production and other sensitive environmental questions, in-

dicates that the long-term environmental damage from a nuclear war may
be even greater than the immediate physical damage. Articles examine
the global, biological, radiological, climatic, and health consequences of
nuclear war and review the lessons that have been learned from the
Chernobyl accident.

Turning down the heat. Claudine Schneider *National Parks*
63:16–17+ Jl/Ag '89

Action is necessary to stop the global warming, or greenhouse effect, and
the ozone-layer depletion that human development has produced
through the release of massive amounts of chemicals into the atmosphere.
According to Dr. Stephen Schneider of the National Center for Atmospheric Research, humans are causing the Earth's atmosphere to change
10 to 40 times more swiftly than natural climate changes have occurred
in the past. In the past year, people have witnessed the kinds of events that
scientists believe will be more common as greenhouse gases increase,
including drought, forest fires, increased tropical storm activity, a record
heat wave, and flooding. A proposed bill called the Global Warming Prevention Act would help limit global warming and its effects through such
measures as protecting the Tongass National Forest in Alaska, reforest-
ing urban communities, and promoting a least-cost national energy plan.

Human activities, greenhouse effect and climate change.
Physics Today 42:28–9 My '89

Human industrial activities have significantly altered the chemical composition of the Earth's atmosphere, causing perturbations to the planetary radiative heating that rival or exceed those due to natural changes.
These activities involve the release of several radiatively active gases that
contribute to the so-called greenhouse effect. Although it seems reasonably certain that these gases are heating the planet, the magnitudes of
global warming and accompanying regional changes are difficult to determine. Global warming is influenced by numerous feedbacks, of which two
that are essential—cloud-radiative and ocean-atmosphere interactions—
are not well understood. It may take decades to produce a model that accounts for these complex feedbacks, but at present it is necessary to judge
the seriousness of the greenhouse effect with limited comprehension of
the climate system.

Global climatic change. Richard A. Houghton and George M.
Woodwell *Scientific American* 260:36–44 Ap '89

There is strong evidence that the global climate is becoming warmer as
human activities put increasing amounts of carbon dioxide, methane, and
other greenhouse gases into the atmosphere. Analyses of temperature records dating back to 1860 indicate that the average global temperature
has increased since that time by an amount between 0.5 and 0.7 C. The
greatest increases have occurred during the past decade. The burning of

fossil fuels releases approximately 5.6 billion tons of carbon into the atmosphere each year, and deforestation probably adds between 0.4 and 2.5 billion tons annually. Warming will continue indefinitely unless these practices are halted. No single remedy is likely to stabilize atmospheric carbon dioxide and methane levels, but industrial innovation and international cooperation can lead to effective action.

Crow's nest. Christopher G. Harrison *Sea Frontiers* 35:195 Jl/Ag '89

Much has been written lately on the greenhouse effect and global warming, but very little has been said about how these conditions might affect the oceans. Most scientists agree that substantial changes in the Earth's climate will occur someday because of the release of gases into the atmosphere by human activity, but they are hard-pressed to predict the response of the oceans to this trend. To better understand global climate change and its consequences, we must learn more about the oceans and their interaction with the atmosphere.

Preparing for the worst. Philip Elmer-Dewitt *Time* 133:70-1 Ja 2 '89

Part of a cover story on the global ecological crisis. The writer discusses the ways in which people might cope with climatic changes such as rising sea levels, deforestation, desertification, drought, and the depletion of the ozone layer.

Rediscovering planet Earth (cover story; special section). *U. S. News & World Report* 105:56-61+ O 31 '88

A cover story examines scientific discoveries about how Earth functions and how it may respond to changes precipitated by human activity. Human life became possible through an ecological disaster in which bacteria polluted their environment with oxygen. The organisms' ability to remake the atmosphere underscores the view that Earth is a complex, interdependent system in which oceans, atmosphere, and all life affect one another and help shape the planet. Scientists have made new discoveries about the planet's workings, driven by an imperative to understand environmental problems like deforestation, global warming, and the depletion of the ozone layer.

The nuclear twilight. *UN Chronicle* 25:16-17 S '88

Part of a special section on the United Nations' third Special Session on Disarmament. In a report prepared for the UN, a group of experts on nuclear winter stated that they have conclusive evidence that a large-scale nuclear war may have a disastrous and lasting impact on the world's climate. Among the effects would be lower temperatures, less sunlight, and fewer rains, which would combine to threaten world food production and natural ecosytems. Details of the 70-page report on the environmental effects of nuclear war are discussed.

THE POLITICS OF ECOLOGY

Political science. Peter A. A. Berle *Audubon* 91:8 Jl '89

Several recent incidents point to the manipulation of research data by government officials to support previously determined environmental policy positions. National Aeronautics and Space Administration scientist James Hansen has accused the Office of Management and Budget of rewriting his conclusions about global warming, and the General Accounting Office has charged that officials of the U.S. Fish and Wildlife Service have altered evidence that had been gathered to determine whether the spotted owl should be listed as an endangered species. Data on the violation of environmental regulations by oil drillers in Alaska's Prudhoe Bay region has been suppressed, and the U.S. Fish and Wildlife Service has refused to issue a jeopardy opinion on the risks to endangered species posed by a proposed dam on the South Platte River. The president should insist that policymakers avoid manipulating scientific findings.

The environment: a North-South conflict. Milton Copulos *Current (Washington, D.C.)* 317:35–9 N '89

A reprint of "The Coming North-South Conflict," which appeared in the June 1989 issue of *World & I*. Tensions between underdeveloped and developed nations over economic growth and environmental protection are likely to get worse before they get better. The international environmental community has warned that the destruction of the Amazon Basin's rain forests in Brazil threatens the Earth's ecology. The Brazilian government has responded with a plan to manage the Amazon Basin's development, but Brazilians resent international interference in determining the future of the region, which they view as the key to their economic development. One Brazilian official argues that environmental concerns are a luxury that developing countries can ill afford.

Ecopolitics in the global greenhouse. William B. Wood, George J. Demko, and Phyllis Mofson *Environment* 31:12–17+ S '89

The growing public fear that the Earth's ecology is in danger has prompted increased national and international efforts to manage global environmental change. A protocol aimed at curbing chlorofluorocarbon use has been signed by 80 nations, and several international forums concerning the global environment have taken place. The actors in environmental politics now include forces such as nongovernmental organizations, political parties, supranational organizations, and the media. International demands for environmental action present sovereignty issues, and some nations have condemned foreign meddling in their affairs. There is also debate over who will pay for the desired changes.

The politics of planetary management. William C. Clark
Environment 31:inside cover S '89

The increasing desire to manage global environmental change has resulted in an expanding range of players participating in environmental politics, including nongovernmental and supranational organizations, political parties, and the media. The greater participation is probably benefiting the cause of conservation, but problems can develop when environmentalist actions cause countries to perceive that constraints are being imposed on their national sovereignty.

Sovereignty and the environment. Kenneth Piddington
Environment 31:18–20+ S '89

International actions to improve the global environment must take the sovereignty of nations into account. Many people in the Third World suspect that the environmental debate is an excuse for advanced countries to impede progress in their countries. To implement environmental policy on a global level, common interests must be made clear to all parties. Leaders of developed nations must also realize that the environmental crisis does not demand a halt in development but rather an increase in properly targeted development aid. A United Nations green-keeping force is needed to help disparate parties negotiate environmental policy.

The industrial nations make a start (Paris economic summit).
Jay D. Hair *International Wildlife* 19:26 N/D '89

The leaders of the seven major industrial nations have produced a historic document that gives environmentalists hope that global ecological problems will finally be addressed. At the 15th annual economic summit in Paris, the leaders of the United States, Japan, West Germany, France, Britain, Italy, and Canada placed the environment at the top of their common agenda for the first time. The Bush administration deserves credit for its role in the document.

Political update. Tom Turner *The Mother Earth News* 119:24
S/O '89

Recent actions of the federal government suggest that the environmental movement will continue to meet with high-level opposition. Most Bush administration nominees for environmentally important posts are known anti-environmentalists, although a single exception is Michael Deland, who is headed for the chairmanship of the Council on Environmental Quality. The arrest of Earth First founder Dave Foreman on charges of conspiring to sabotage two nuclear power plants and a weapons plant near Denver raises the question of whether Foreman has been framed by the government. It also adds to indications that the federal government is in-filtrating environmental organizations as it once did civil rights and anti-war groups. A report from the General Accounting Office (GAO) shows that the government is making only meager progress in its effort to pro-tect threatened and endangered species. An address from which the GAO report can be obtained is provided.

It's not nice to mess with Mother Nature. Lindsy Van Gelder *Ms.* 17:60-3 Ja/F '89

Ecofeminism, a relatively small but growing movement, consists of wom-en who are working for ecological concerns specifically as feminists. Al-though the term ecofeminism was first coined by French writer Françoise d'Eaubonne in 1974, it wasn't until 1980 that the first ecofeminist confer-ence was organized at the University of Massachusetts at Amherst. The conference was followed by a West Coast ecofeminist gathering in 1981. Shortly thereafter the WomanEarth Institute, the first national ecofemin-ist organization, was formed. Ecofeminism argues not only against the domination of the Earth by polluters but also against domination in all forms. Its adherents believe that traditionally female values of caretaking are now humankind's best shot at saving the environment.

The ecology of survival. Albert Gore, Jr. *The New Republic* 201:26+ N 6 '89

Part of a special 75th anniversary issue. The survival of humankind de-pends on its ability to quickly understand that the ecological system that sustains life is threatened by the current pattern of world civilization. Faced with the prospect of ecological and civil collapse, we must be open to drastic global action. The idea of mutual security must now be defined to include concern for the global environment. The time has come for a Strategic Environment Initiative that would promote environmentally sustainable development by making new technologies available to devel-oping countries and encouraging the modernization of technologies and practices in every economic sector of the United States. In addition, we must learn to see ourselves as part of our ecological system and begin to make sacrifices for the future.

E pluribus, plures (states set environmental agenda). Sharon Begley *Newsweek* 114:70-2 N 13 '89

Lack of leadership from Washington has prompted states to set their own environmental standards. States and cities are passing stringent controls to protect groundwater and recycle garbage, mandate the use of clean fuels, and reduce acid rain. New Jersey's Global Climate Initiative and a California environmental proposition, both designed to reduce CO_2 emis-sions, reveal that states are willing to take a more global view of pollution than the White House. Individual states are finding it easier to act than Congress, which is hindered by the conflict between nationwide environmental standards and states' local industrial interests. Because the states' environmental reforms have proven technically feasible and economically sound, the federal government and industry may be inspired to follow suit.

Culture and conservation. Jeffrey P. Cohn *BioScience* 38:450-3 Jl/Ag '88

Culture: The Missing Element in Conservation and Development, sponsored by the National Zoological Park, was the latest in a series of zoo symposia on human understanding and protection of animals. Speakers and participants at the two-day event analyzed how local culture can be integrated into development and conservation plans. A golden lion tamarin program in Brazil, which has instilled a sense of national pride in the conservation of these animals, was described by Lou Ann Dietz, a World Wildlife Fund coordinator. Speakers emphasized the need for conservationists to understand the cultures of indigenous peoples. They pointed out that more consideration of the interests of local inhabitants could improve the outcome of world wildlife and wildland conservation efforts.

Planning for our common future. Martin W. Holdgate *Environment* 31:14-17+ O '89

Global policies must be instituted as soon as possible to meet the threat of rising global temperatures, shifting precipitation patterns, rising sea levels, and increased ultraviolet radiation penetration. Such measures must begin by building personal, national, and international awareness of environmental problems. A global policy must include strategies for ceasing actions that contribute to environmental destruction and for shifting investment and development onto a sustainable course. In addition, the causes of global change must be attacked, beginning with the elimination of the production and use of chlorofluorocarbons and halons. Financial and technical assistance must be made available to implement these policies in poorer nations.

Can man save this fragile Earth? (cover story; special issue; with editorial comment by Wilbur E. Garrett). *National Geographic* 174:765-945 D '88

A special issue on environmental stewardship discusses ecological changes in the Brazilian rain forest, the effect of encroachment on native peoples in the Amazon, the efforts of the Nature Conservancy to protect endangered and threatened species, the battle over oil exploration in Alaska's Arctic National Wildlife Refuge, advances in research on whales, and overpopulation in Kenya, China, Hungary, India, Brazil, and the United States. A photo essay chronicles the migration of caribou across the Alaskan tundra, and a supplementary map presents a new, more realistic view of the world.

Mission to planet Earth. Burton I. Edelson *Science* 227:367 Ja 25 '85

Little is known about the general mechanisms that govern changes in the Earth's environment. Many changes are evidently occurring now as a result of escalating human exploitation of global resources. In 1982, the United States proposed the Global Habitability research program to the United Nations Conference on Peaceful Uses of Outer Space. This program calls for an international multidisciplinary effort using modern technology to better understand the environment. Since Global Habitability was proposed, considerable work has been devoted to oulining specific experiments. The National Academy of Sciences is considering how the program may be coordinated with the International Geosphere Biosphere Program of the International Council of Scientific Unions. The scientific community should immediately proceed with this effort.

Managing planet Earth. William C. Clark *Scientific American* 261:46–54 S '89

Part of a special section on environmental protection and development. The goal of sustainable development is to encourage forms of social, economic, and political progress that meet the needs of the present without compromising future generations' chances of meeting their own needs. Such development will require the gathering and dissemination of scientific information about human-made ecological changes, the invention and implementation of nonpolluting technology, and the creation of national and international mechanisms for planetary management.

Back from the abyss (excert from Earth). Anne H. Ehrlich and Paul R. Ehrlich *Sierra* 72:54–60 Mr/Ap '87

Excerpted from the book *Earth*. Because none of the 5 billion people on Earth desire the planet's demise, they have a responsibility to work together to prevent it. There are several steps that must be taken to achieve this goal: The growth of the human population must be halted, and a slow decline toward a sustainable size must be initiated. The emission of pollutants into the air must be slowed, if not stopped. No development of the remaining virgin lands on the planet should be permitted; instead, new development should be restricted to already developed areas that no longer suit their original use. The pointless military competition between naitons must be converted into a competition to aid the poor. There are no insurmountable barriers to a peaceful, self-sustaining planet. People already have the power to change their future; they simply need the will.